# Graveyard for Dreamers

# Graveyard for Dreamers

## *One Woman's Odyssey in Africa*

## Joan Baxter

Pottersfield Press
Lawrencetown Beach,
R.R. 2 Porters Lake, Nova Scotia
Canada

# Dedicated to the dreams and memory of Thomas Sankara

## Canadian Catlaoguing in Publication Data

Baxter, Joan
Graveyard for Dreamers
ISBN: 0-919001-88-2
1. Baxter, Joan. 2. Women journalists — Canada — Biography.
3. Africa, West — Politics and government — 1960– 4. Africa, West — Social conditions — 1960– I. Title

PN4913.B39A3 1994        071'.1'092        C94-950176-X

Pottersfield Press gratefully acknowledges the ongoing support of the Nova Scotia Department of Tourism and Culture and the Canada Council.

Photographs by Joan Baxter (inside and front cover)
Back cover photograph by Susan Murray

Pottersfield Press
Lawrencetown Beach
R.R. 2 Porters Lake
Nova Scotia B0J 2S0

Printed in Canada

# Contents

# Acknowledgements

The ideas, images and interpretations in this book are my own and I take full responsibility for them. Thanks go to everyone who helped to shape the book, either knowingly or unknowingly. Without them, there would have been no story to tell and I would have remained trapped by my dark ignorance about a continent full of vitality, strength and brightness.

Many names of people and places have been altered, but the events described here are real. I especially wish to thank the many Africans — Halidou, Asseàta, Mary, Iliasu, Awudu, Lela, Eunice, Bernice, Mildred, Rose, Immanuel, Mariam, Iddrissu, Lawrence, Ben, John, Mohammed, Mumuni, Ibrahim, Rabiatu, Carolyn D. and many many more — who spent their time and energy showing me the bright side of their continent, helping me understand or just helping my family and me. Thanks too, to the many children of Ouagadougou and Tamale who befriended us and made my children's lives richer. I also wish to thank the non-Africans — Kate, Brigitte, Marco, Andreas, Vera, Paul, Felix, Maggie, Renate, Karen, Ted, Jean-Paul — who shared and re-inforced my love for West Africa. And to Susan Murray, Sharon Blakeney, and Linda Fedigan who came to visit and see what was keeping me so long in Africa, lots more thanks.

I also wish to thank my publisher, Lesley Choyce, who took on this project. Thanks, too, to Joanne Reilly, David Baxter and Debby Plestid who waded through the manuscript again and again and offered so much advice and invaluable criticism. And, to my parents who encouraged me and had the great idea of sending the manuscript out to a publisher, my never-ending gratitude for everything over the years. This book is for them.

And last but never least, thanks to Karl for bringing me to Africa, and for his patience and support through it all.

*Girl carrying her baby brother on her back in Tamale, Ghana, August 1992.*

## *Prologue*

# All days are not equal

*The traveller may tell all he has seen on his journey, but he cannot explain all. — an Akan proverb*

I am driving home from the market in Tamale, northern Ghana. The power in town is off (again), meaning the telex machine at the post office is also off (again), meaning I cannot send my report to BBC in London, meaning two days of work have been wasted. The water is off too, meaning just about every young female in town is on the road, with a bucket. Government and development project vehicles are requisitioned away from pressing tasks laid out in the official development plans, and are carting water to the homes of their directors and senior personnel.

I am reminded, as I often am in Africa, of the nonsense rhyme in one of my daughter's books, which has an empire falling for want of a nail for the horse's shoe.

My daughter is sick with fever, vomiting and headache — the symptoms of malaria and a dozen other potentially fatal diseases. Our trusted friend and doctor, who can arrange for blood tests for us at the Veterinary or the Guinea Worm Laboratory, is out of town. I am breaking all the rules by diagnosing and treating her myself, with chloroquin which is considered almost useless against new resistant malaria parasites. I wonder which of the other new medicines I should try when that fails — no two doctors I have consulted on that question have ever offered me the same answer.

I swerve to avoid a rush of flames. A bush fire has swept its way, apparently unnoticed, through a patch of grass on the roadside, licking at a stalwart telephone pole that has been here since colonial days. It encircles a new power line. On a whim, I pull into the fire station that is just across the road. I come to a dusty stop in front of the two shining red fire engines, recently donated by a European benefactor, and wake up the fireman on duty in a metal chair between the fire trucks. He leaps to his feet, smiling like a winner of the weekly lottery, and comes to the window of my car, asking what he can do for me. My eyes flicker from his open smile to the badge pinned on his khaki shirt, on his left breast pocket. It says "Smokey's Helper." I wonder which benevolent foreign donor contributed that trinket in the name of development.

"I want to report a fire," I say. He asks me with a furrowed brow where exactly that fire is, the one I wish to report. I point across the road at the blazing grass and trees and the smoke that funnels upwards like a tunnel to heaven. He looks very concerned and promises to get at it "right away." As I drive away, swerving to avoid the flames, I glance in my rear view mirror and see he is settling back onto his chair with his arms folded. I guess he was too polite to tell me there was no water in the tanks of the fire engines. He was certainly too polite to tell me — a foreigner — to mind my own business.

One hundred metres further down the road people from the Volta River Authority, the power company which has just brought electricity to the north from the Akosombo dam, are gleefully chopping down giant trees in the name of progress and valuable firewood. They are eliminating with a swipe of the chain-saw the only respite left in Tamale from the omnipotence of the April sun, the erosive winds, and the rains that should come in a few weeks.

The car is bottoming out on the potholes, which are now consuming the last remnants of post-independence pavement.

The heat is overwhelming. Sweat drips from my chin and nose onto my drenched t-shirt. I would like to close the car windows as I pass the Police Park, where these authorities dump their "nightsoil" or chamber buckets each morning — in spite of a sign they have erected themselves in the erstwhile playground, banning trespassing and defecation. Instead I hold my breath for the minute it takes to drive through the stench, because I would suffocate and melt if I closed the windows. I glance at the Police Park turned toilet. Some children in rags are climbing the rusty ladder on the bent and rusted slide, unbothered by the pervasive smell of human waste around them.

A seemingly endless parade of girls fills the road, as they trudge along in their seemingly endless search for water. They are dwarfed by the metal canisters on their heads, that I have on occasion tried to lift off the ground and been unable to budge. This elusive search for decent water goes on, in spite of a multi-million dollar project in the region that is supposed to solve water problems and get the pipes flowing regularly.

Driving home this morning, I am regretting many things. It is one of *those* moods, that strike every six months or so when minor and daily calamities that are part of one's life in this part of Africa, suddenly combine, swell and blot out my love for the place. This mood is triggered by any one of a hundred frustrations and cues, like an epileptic fit.

I feel my life is passing me by, eating me up, drying me out in this impoverished backwater. I have the feeling I am losing touch with my own country and people. I know the names of almost every political figure, aspirant, would-be president in Ghana and several other countries in West Africa, but I can't name the leaders of the Canadian political parties. I don't even know how many parties there are now. They seem irrelevant here and I've long since stopped trying to find Radio Canada International on my radio. Instead we live on a diet of BBC reports from Africa's latest trouble spots — such as Rwanda or Somalia or Angola.

My children don't know the joys of a snowy day. They think cold means 29° Centigrade. Most of my friends in Canada have long since stopped writing to me, and new ones, in Tamale for example, will probably be friends only as long as we stay. When we leave Tamale, they will quickly forget us. I wonder what on earth I like about the town and why we stay on.

Mostly I wonder, not for the first time, how it is that I have stayed ten years in West Africa. In 1982, I flew out to Niger to marry Karl, a German man I had met while working in Mexico. Africa had struck me as interesting and exciting, and anyway, Karl had written and asked me to come out and marry him, so why not? For a few months, it would be a nice change from the fog and drizzle and pre-fab development in Nova Scotia. After that? Well, anything could happen.

Anything — a lot of things — did happen. That first trip to Niger is already two children, a marriage, a decade, and four West African countries ago.

I step on the gas, passing over-loaded push carts, manned by small boys, struggling to convey tonnes of cement and sacks of corn through town. I dodge the usual herds of cows, goats, sheep and bicycles, anxious to get home to the relative sanctity of our house, anxious to check on my daughter's condition.

The truck in front of me, painted startling shades of green and blue and yellow and red, is belching out black fumes, through which the passengers, settled like produce on top of the sacks of corn in the back, stare down at me blankly, as though they too are asking themselves what that white woman in the green Volkswagen is doing there. I want to pass, but the pavement is only a few feet wide. Yawning ditches full of rubbish, rusted wrecks of harvesters and tractors prevent me from over-taking. I am tired of being stared at, called to, "Hey White Man," even though it is never meant derogatorily. At least I don't think it is. The "man" part doesn't bother me because it is just a generic term for person, but the "white" part does sometimes. It reminds me that I don't belong. That I am, in their words, a "stranger," no matter how much I try to understand their languages, their ways, their traditions, their beliefs, them. I can appreciate many things here — particularly the joy of being around people whose only poverty is physical — but I cannot explain much of anything around me. The guilt I feel at not being physically poor myself is useless and hypocritical, but it's still there.

At first I stubbornly refuse to acknowledge all the eyes focused on me in the back of that miserable truck ahead that would have been laid to rest years ago, if it were not here in Africa. My own eyes are watering from the black fumes that engulf the lorry each time it accelerates. Through the smoke, I try to make out the words neatly and elaborately printed across the wooden boards across the rear of the truck. At first I think it says "All Men Are Not Equal," which strikes me as rather obvious in this context, in spite of U.N. declarations to the contrary. Then I see the real words written there. With the profundity and conciseness of all folk wisdom, the message tells me *"All Days Are Not Equal."*

I begin to smile and then to laugh. All the people perched on the back of the truck notice me, and begin to laugh too.

And just as quickly as the black mood descended, it lifts. Instant laughter is the miraculous cure. I know, now, that the black moods have little to do with Ghana, or Africa. They come from deep within me; they are a symptom of my generation, my country, myself. They are my reaction to the turmoil, hardship, squalor, poverty and injustice, all so visible in Africa. They are my fault, not Africa's. It is because my dreams for a better Africa don't fit here and because the development assistance that our governments are offering fits even less than I do. Nor do I, or much of the development aid, have anything to do with the Africans' own dreams for this, their continent.

My dreams are global, shaped by many years of media coverage about the continental picture of doom, gloom and tragedy in Africa. The smaller pictures that form more slowly than the horrendous, heart-wrenching newsclips from Rwanda, or Somalia or southern Sudan, form in remote villages with inspiring African friends, and are the ones in which I find not just glimmers of hope, but blossoming dreams which no amount of reality can blot out. The question is not whether there is hope for Africa, but whether there is hope for the world. We are all in this together.

I feel foolish, smiling at the people on the back of the truck who continue to smile at me. A small boy wearing a ragged t-shirt bearing the name of a service station in America, starts to wave. I wave back. I turn off my thoughts — those rational, logical despairing thoughts about what chances he has for a long or healthy or fulfilling life. About what it must feel like to sit in the heat on that rickety truck, hour after hour, breathing the fumes from an ailing diesel engine, heading to a home in a village where there is no clean water to drink and probably only one meal a day, of corn porridge. Instead, I concentrate on his smile.

Like a wave of infatuation, my love for this place washes over me. I love these stalwart people, I love the diversity of their languages and cultures, I love their music, their legends, their proverbs, their dances. Most of all, I respect their ability to deal with the hardship of their lives, with the daily tragedies, and their ability to laugh and celebrate the passages of life. I marvel at the integrity of the friends I have made here, the Ghanaians who have chosen to stay or to return to their own country to join the uphill struggle for improvement in health, education and living standards. I also admire the intelligence, general knowledge and worldliness of a people who live in a country where a book costs a week's salary.

Instead of the squalor around me, I focus on the faces of the people cooking, walking, cycling on the roadside. I will bring my camera again tomorrow, try again and probably in vain to capture the essence of life here that seems to defy photographs and even words, apart from clichés and truisms. It has taken me a long time — ten years — to see and feel the intangible joys of life here, to wish that I were here to stay. First I had to bury my own dreams — foolish dreams of what I was going to do in Africa to make it a better place, dreams that in retrospect were arrogant and presumptuous. I know I will never really understand. But that doesn't mean I don't love trying. This book is about the burying of my dreams, about that long period of disillusionment which was, after all, more my problem than Africa's.

When I look back over the years I spent in West Africa it amazes and depresses me that it took me so long to learn that I had much more to learn from Africans than I had to offer them. I thank all of those who gave their patience and time to help me over that high barrier of western ignorance. Patience and time and small hopes are, after all, Africa's secret and greatest medicines.

## *Chapter 1*

# It pains you, why?

I might as well have been flying to the moon. The Air Canada ticket agent in Halifax repeated the destination "Miami" three times before I convinced her I did not want to fly to Florida, that I was headed for Niamey, capital of Niger, Africa. I didn't let on that I had never heard of the place before Karl wrote to me from Germany a year earlier to tell me he had a post there with the German volunteer service. I explained to her that it was north of Nigeria and south of Algeria, as if I knew these places well. On the edge of the Sahara was how I put it. It was about all I knew.

At check-in for my Air Afrique flight from Charles de Gaulle Airport in Paris I discovered that the ticket agent in Canada had not, in the end, booked me onto the Niamey-bound DC-10, and that it was full. The woman at the Air Afrique counter wanted to route me through a place called Abidjan. I looked up at the list of destinations on the departures monitor behind her head and wondered how it could be that so many new cities — Kinshasa, Bujumbura, Yaounde, Ouagadougou — could have sprung up overnight on the planet on which I had lived twenty-six years. I didn't want to go through Abidjan, I told her, tears pricking at my eyes. I couldn't possibly get on a plane and fly to a place I had never heard of. I stared hopelessly at the list of African capitals, wondering what had been wrong in my education that I could have somehow missed a whole continent full of bustling cities to which international jetliners flew almost daily.

She cocked her head at me, spotted the tears of youthful ignorance and innocence, smiled and said quietly, "Let me see what I can do. Maybe I can find a seat on the plane tomorrow, Bourdeaux, Niamey." And she did.

"Karl couldn't make it to the airport," said Felix, the blonde German development worker who stood at arrivals holding up a ragged piece of brown cardboard on which my name was spelled incorrectly. He wore a blue and white kerchief around his neck and jeans that were so dusty they looked like they might have been brown suede. "He's working until tomorrow but he said he'll try and get away the day after that."

Disappointment made me mute.

"It will take him two days to drive here from Zinder; if he gets away the day after tomorrow he should be here by Monday or Tuesday, Wednesday at the latest."

It was Friday evening. The sun was a blaze of red heat over the horizon as we drove towards town. Felix seemed to be in a terrible hurry, roaring the engine of the Land Cruiser. He had nothing much to say to me, perched across from him in the passenger seat.

"So *this* is Africa!" I said breathlessly, beginning to grin as we sped up the four-lane boulevard leading into Niamey. It was a misleading stretch of ultra-modern tarred road with street-lights arching overhead, flanked by mile after mile of makeshift hovels and lean-tos ingeniously constructed with tin scraps, auto bodies and mud.

"Yeah, so?" He had been in Niger for six months. He had no time for the effusive excitement of the newly-landed. "What did you expect?" Eventually he deposited me at the Hotel Rivoli, promising to come and take me swimming at one of the city's nicer hotels the next day.

He didn't show up. In the next four days I read all the books I had brought for a six month stay, devouring them as fast as I could to prevent my mind from wandering to the question of what could be keeping the man who had written and invited me to come over and marry him.

After a day and a night in the room I grew suicidally tired of the brown curtains and black walls of the room. Summoning my battered resolve I forced myself to go out there to see what it was all about. I believed this wouldn't take long.

I headed downstairs, through the noise of the bar and opened the door. Stepping out of the hotel, I took four steps and stopped, to avoid an oncoming camel with a giant stack of firewood on its back. The ragged man who was leading the camel shouted. It was difficult to tell whether his anger was directed at me or at his animal. The camel balked, stood still and refused to continue. When the camel-driver tried to pull it, the animal let loose a flood of urine. Backing away from the camel and its master, I was tripped by a beggar who was holding up his leprous stump by way of an appeal for alms. I had no CFA francs to give him, just a few French franc notes tucked inside a money belt which I was afraid to open.

Plagued by guilt, thirst and hunger, I moved back inside the restaurant of the hotel, a hang-out for shady desert crossers and car sellers from Europe and gravelly-voiced French men with Gauloises cigarettes drooping from their mouths. They seemed to spend most of their days sipping a deliciously cool-looking yellow drink from tall glasses. It looked like lemonade.

I slipped into a chair at a corner table, and attempted, using school French that came out as street Spanish, which surfaced more readily and uselessly, to order one of those glasses of lemonade. I had not had anything to drink for a day, and I gulped down half the glass before I realized it was a strong alcoholic concoction that burned all the way down to my feet. This Ouzo-flavoured drink was Pastis and it was favoured by French expatriates who regarded it as a tonic for intestinal plumbing problems and a remedy for the noon-day heat.

The Pastis made me gag, which brought me to the attention of a short, stocky and cocky French man with a handlebar moustache and gold chains to his belly button. He moved to my table, smiled, and began to talk. I managed to communicate to him that I didn't care for the yellow stuff I was drinking, and he promptly ordered me a beer. This he interpreted as the beginning of a long-term relationship, which I cut short by retreating at the first opportunity to my room. For the next two days I didn't answer his knocks and played hide and seek in the restaurant and in the communal water closets on my floor. When at last, on Tuesday, Karl finally made it to Niamey, and knocked on my door, he was greeted with a "go away. " This was not an auspicious beginning.

It seemed something had gone terribly wrong. Karl and I seemed to have nothing to talk about. Karl had been in Niger for almost a year, keeping track of emergency grain supplies in far-flung sandy corners of the country, and hanging out at Zinder's "Club Privé," a private club where cynicism and booze precluded idealism and dreams, where white males were king.

Visiting girlfriends — even fiancés — were tiresome. Especially when the girlfriend or fiancé put a sudden end to a sizzling affair with a Nigerien woman, or as it had in Karl's case, with an American Peace Corps volunteer, to whom the "houseboy" referred longingly as "Madame Number One."

This was not exactly what I had in mind when I decided to come to Africa. What did I have in mind? I wish I knew. Exotic cultures and landscapes, women carrying enormous pots of water on their heads, a pair of elephants or giraffes perhaps, poverty and hungry children? I saw all of these on the way from the airport to my hotel in the Niger's capital, except the elephants which now survived only in the country's national park. I had also seen a fleet of jet-fighters at the Niamey airport, grandiose hotels and palatial government buildings and residences, thousands of camels, and practically indescribable squalor and toiling villagers everywhere I looked. But what was I doing there? I had no sense of purpose. I simply did not belong.

It was the hardship in that cruel landscape and the loss of the cushioning effect of a society that could afford to, and appeared to, care not just for its people but also for its animals, that bothered me most. Trivial and fleeting images began to haunt me. There was the long drive, a thousand kilometres over parched scrubland from Niamey to Zinder, on a ribbon of rough grey pavement. A shining white Peugeot, windows up and air conditioning on, overtook us and sped ahead, its back end dancing in the squirming waves of heat over the pavement. The driver didn't apply his brakes and didn't swerve when the small white goat bounced onto the road; didn't slow for the collision or after it had occurred. We approached the bloodied remains of the goat as the young shepherd boy emerged from the scrub. He stood over the dead goat, staring at it. His legs and feet were bare, covered with the brown dust of the Sahel. His dress, brown and threadbare, left his bony knees exposed. He cradled his staff in his arms, as he might — I thought — have picked up and held the baby goat were it alive. His wide-brimmed straw hat shielded his head from the blazing sun, and from our view. As we drove slowly past, he glanced up for a second, and looked at us blankly, then returned his hopeless stare to the dead goat. We left him there in the blowing dust and wind howling across the dehydrated country, alone with his sheep and goats in his own world, which did not include roads or cars, shoes or white men, alphabets or clear drinking water.

"The driver did that deliberately," I said to Karl. "He could have avoided it."

"He couldn't. Why should he risk his life for a goat?" Karl, since our tenuous and awkward reunion in the dark hotel room, had seemed intent on showing me that sentimentality had no place in Niger.

"But he has brakes. He could have swerved."

"There are too many goats and sheep here. They destroy all the vegetation."

"That doesn't mean passing motorists have the right to kill them like flies."

"They shouldn't be on the road. Livestock are signs of wealth here; if people want to be rich and own large herds, then they should have to pay for fencing and for damages caused by over-grazing."

"Yes, but what about that poor shepherd? Didn't you see the look on his face?" Apparently he hadn't, or perhaps he did but it made no mark on him, and his new tough approach to a tough country. He glanced at me and said, impassively, "In Africa, you don't brake for chickens or goats."

I wondered if Karl was just trying to sound tough and hard-nosed, part of the expatriate image he had cultivated, or if he had actually become so in the months since he had come to Niger, in the year since I had last seen him.

The expatriates told me that kindness would not pay in Niger. "If you are kind, people will think that you're stupid," a French engineer told me. "Kindness is not respected here. It's seen as a weakness." I wished to argue, but had no evidence to support my case.

Except for a daily outing to the market, and a weekly outing to the animal market, I didn't go out or mingle much with anyone in my early months in Niger. I was struggling to improve my French, but most people in the street spoke only Hausa. In villages surrounding Zinder there were Fulani herders and Tuareg nomads, each with their own distinct culture and language.

I couldn't get used to the hooting and yelling for my attention at the market, and scuttled through it as fast as I could, paying outrageous prices for tomatoes and onions because I couldn't bring myself to haggle over a few francs with the market women. Sometimes I ventured out on a bicycle to do a bit of discovering on my own. The townspeople were unused to seeing foreigners on a bicycle — poor peoples' transport. I would have been no more conspicuous if I had hired a camel for my forays into the back alleys of Zinder. After braving the mobs of squealing children and the boisterous laughter of the women on the roadside, there would still be the clique of expatriate development workers to face. "We'll get you a donkey!" "In training for the Tour de France, n'est-ce pas?"

So, at the beginning, I tended to stay home, or I walked to market, picking up a copy of *Le Sahel*, Niger's national state-controlled newspaper, along the way.

Our house was on the outskirts of a town that had no real downtown and no real borders; Zinder seemed to fade away in the blowing dust. The house was considered modern, with three small bedrooms, one living room, thick mud walls, concrete floors and metal doors and shutters. The sandy road and the northern wall of our house provided a setting for a neighbourhood Koran school each morning. For hours two dozen ragged boys sat cross-legged on the roadside, leaning against our wall in the waning strip of shade it afforded, with pages of the Koran or wooden boards inscribed with holy passages in their small laps, reciting the Holy Book in Arabic. None of them understood a word of Arabic, but that did not appear to lessen their dedication to enthusiastic recitals of the passages they were learning by heart.

When we wished to slaughter a sheep for special occasions, the Marabout — the boys' teacher — came and did so in a manner which was acceptable to the Muslim neighbourhood. He received the head and organs as compensation.

I listened to Niger Radio when there were broadcasts in the official language — French, to international short wave stations for world and African news, which I tried to follow and comprehend. I made notes in my journal about stories I heard on the BBC African Service, trying to get the continent and its politics in some perspective. I was beginning to notice the level of corruption in the system, and wonder at the blatant abuse of state monies for ceremonies glorifying the men of status — be they traditional kings such as the Sultan in Zinder or the top-level government officials, who seemed able to operate with absolute impunity in a country of abject poverty. When we accompanied the German ambassador on a visit to the Sultan, a twenty-eight-year-old man with a harem of eight young wives who were not permitted out of their rooms in the labyrinth of his clay palace, he unabashedly asked for a new Mercedes to add to his fleet.

Radio Canada broadcast its news for Canadians at 5 A.M. and usually faded out when it got to the part I so inexplicably wanted to hear — the weather. I think the weather reports made the existence of Canada, and such unimaginable natural phenomena as snowstorms, comfortingly real for me.

I spent a lot of time writing lachrymose letters to friends and family, and started thousands of articles, that seldom progressed past an opening line that went something like, "Here on the doorstep to the Sahara the sky glistens with sand and cynicism prevails," or something equally melodramatic that led nowhere.

Unable to put my own impressions and thoughts into any coherent shape or words, I began to pour over *Le Sahel* and take notes on Nigerien thoughts as expressed in that daily government paper. If I couldn't decide how I felt about Niger or comprehend what I was seeing and hearing, then at least I could learn something of how Nigeriens viewed us.

In April 1982 a columnist called Arbi wrote: "The gossip that reaches us from certain developed and 'civilized' countries can't give us much comfort about our desire to seek to perfect our model society." He was worried about the way justice was being carried out in a "small city in a large North American country," his specific complaint being how a society that called itself civilized would have to force jury duty on its people and then sequester them. It appalled him that individuals were "isolated from their families, forbidden from using a telephone, from reading newspapers, from listening to the radio." "This demonstrates," he wrote, "that 'civilization' over there has reached a point where selfishness and individuality of men is so great that no one will go out of his way for anything, not to help a brother or to save a brother's head. Ah, if the same thing were to happen in our 'savage' country, what indignation, what scandal this would raise in the minds of the 'civilized' man."

Articles like this made their impact on me — I felt I had no right or legitimate reason to be in, to write about Africa. Would everything I wrote about Africa sound as ludicrous, so drastically out-of-context, as what Arbi had written about America? Yes, I told myself, in despair.

I had given up a job with Canadian Radio to fly to Niger and (a) get married and (b) to work as a freelance journalist.

As for Plan B, it would be several years before we moved to an African capital where communications facilities enabled me to work as a correspondent, and before I would feel I knew enough of the basics of African politics and life to write so much as a line for publication.

Plan A wasn't going so well either. Snags had appeared in our betrothal, which had a lot to do with the fact that Karl was behaving, at least with me, like one of those disillusioned Europeans who saw the whole development process and indeed Africa, as a negative experience. Romance was out of the question. And I, new and full of dreams and illusions about the continent, refused to bury them even in the face of their growing irrelevance. I felt I no longer knew him — the setting had changed and we were at logger-heads about everything from how beggars should be handled to the value of development assistance and human life.

During the early weeks in Niger I plied him with questions about everything I saw — from the villages perched on rocky outcrops that looked as fertile as the moon, to the political situation in the country. He said the Togolese and Nigerien tutors who schooled the incoming volunteers on the whys and wherefores of living in their countries had been adamant that the first six months on the continent should be spent learning how things and people work, through observation, the same way African children learned. Questions, poorly phrased or timed, would only make people clam up, he said. It did not pay to jump in and start asking stupid questions, trying to change things when you did not understand what those things were you were trying to change. There were many things to be learned from Africans — he had been told and proceeded to tell me — who may want change, but may not want to change in the ways well-intentioned Europeans deemed appropriate. I stopped asking so many questions and it was agreed that we would go ahead with our wedding plans — but not immediately.

I joined him on his working trips into Niger's outback, to visit grain warehouses that had been set up to stock emergency provisions should another drought occur — as it would two years later. The purpose of the project was to establish these warehouses throughout the country, and to stock them with local grains when the harvest had been sufficient, or with donated grains, in years of shortage. The warehouses were inevitably the largest and most imposing structures in the tiny settlements in which they were built. Life in the community tended to centre around these modern, concrete buildings that lent a defiant air of permanency to villages which might otherwise disappear after a single sandstorm, or be abandoned during years of drought. Women and girls were almost always present, purchasing small bowls of rice from the man in charge of the warehouse and they would gather in the shade provided by the tall building, to rest and exchange greetings and gossip. Everything appeared to happen very slowly — time seemed to stretch and warp under the oppressive heat of the Sahelian sun in that vast desert sky. If we stopped for two hours, while Karl checked on inventory and stock rotation, I could fall easily into a kind of trance, in which a moment could seem like an eternity, time I had borrowed from another life, a time-out from my own. I would wander around the warehouse, past the scattered compounds of mud huts with thatched roofs, wondering what would bring people to erect their dwellings in a place like this, and more confounding, keep them there. There were no schools, wells, clinics, and during the dry season, nothing that was not faded brown except the large white grain warehouse. Dust and sand covered everything, and during the long dry season when water might be found only many many miles away in a tiny swamp oasis, children's faces grew lighter and lighter as the powder caked on in semi-permanent layers of grey. Noses were always dry, stinging and filled with dust or blood.

Voices seemed muted under the immensity of that sand-brushed sky, shadows on the ground more clearly defined, images etched in my mind during those trips stayed there, indelible as tattoos. Wandering back towards the warehouse, desperate for a drink of water, I happened upon five boys. They did not seem to be part of the tiny village of Damagaram Takaya — in their bright t-shirts, each a different colour: blue, green, red, white and black. When they saw me coming towards them, they stopped what they were doing — I couldn't see what it was — and waved, smiled and shouted greetings. I smiled back. As I got closer I realized there was something attached to a rope, which was tied to a stick in the ground, and which they were beating with more sticks. I thought perhaps they were threshing grain, without taking it out of the sack. Closer still, I realized it was some kind of animal; then I saw it was a dog. They leaned on their sticks as I passed, offering me another round of bright smiles and greetings. I avoided examining the state of the dog. I waited until I heard the thumping sounds and the squeals of delight, and turned around, to be sure that they had resumed their diligent beating of the brown mutt. In front of the warehouse it was business as usual. No one appeared to see the boys at play, and I looked again to assure myself that I was not suffering desert hallucinations.

Karl was laughing with the store-keeper, and women were still measuring out small bowls of millet and rice. Some men were wrestling camels to their knees, one by one, to load them with provisions for the trek back to some sandy village in the middle of a place that to me was nowhere, and to them home. As we got into the car to drive away, another four hours to the next warehouse, I looked behind to see that the boy in the red shirt had untied the dog's rope from the stick and was pulling the pathetic remains through a dried millet field that appeared to stretch forever. When I mentioned the incident to Karl, he said he had seen people beaten in the same way, when they had been accused of petty theft. "It's village justice," he said finally.

In the next community, Kelle, we stopped again at a warehouse. Immediately we were invited to someone's home to eat. I didn't know who was inviting us — there were several men milling about the warehouse and there was no way of knowing who was really in charge of things. The wind was blowing hot air and flies into my mouth, and all I craved was some cold water. The water in our plastic jerry can was hot. I didn't want to complain — the water I saw people around me drinking from bowls was not just hot, it was green.

As we walked towards our host's compound, we attracted a crowd of followers, dozens of exuberant children pointing and laughing at us. A few neem trees shaded the sandy path through the labyrinth of mud walls that constituted family homes in Kelle. We eventually found ourselves sitting on stools in the shade of one of these trees, confronting two giant enamelled bowls, one filled with brown lumps of millet porridge, or "tuo," another with an oily stew. As the only woman present, the only woman to share this meal with the men, I was supposed to begin. I didn't know how — had never tried to eat with my hand and didn't wish to begin before this audience. A bowl and a spoon appeared, passed from one hand to another until it reached the young man in clean and well-pressed shirt and trousers who, I decided, was the host. He examined the spoon, wiped it on his shirt, and dished up a heaping mound of tuo and stew that would have fed, I thought, a camel or at least a family of twelve. It was placed in front of me on the ground, and might have been delicious if I had not been in dire need of water, had I not felt a thousand pairs of eyes were envying each bite I took, and had the stew not been filled with lengths of intestines, gritty with sand and bone chips. I handed the bowl over to Karl, and our host commented on me being a "good wife." It bothered me that I did not feel grateful for the food and hospitality.

Back in Zinder I was struggling with persistent guilt, that would not go away. I felt it was wrong to have a "houseboy," hating even the term which was in Zinder, and most of West Africa, ubiquitous. Hassan, the man Karl employed in the house before I had arrived on the scene, was a good organizer. He excelled when it came to monitoring the slaughtering of sheep by the neighbourhood Marabout, and then disembowelling them — something he liked to do on Sunday mornings while we ate breakfast a few feet away on a small concrete patio. Karl often received livestock as gifts from colleagues at work, and since we had no place to graze them, their arrival usually meant a feast for Hassan and neighbours.

Hassan was a mechanic by trade. His favourite task was washing the car, a miniature and open-topped Suzuki jeep which may have been an ideal vehicle for playing on miniature sand dunes in, say, California but which was hell on the long desert stretches which it had to traverse once a week. This was ir-relevant to Hassan; he loved that vehicle. If not denied the pleasure, he would wash it three or four times a day, allowing the water to run from the hose for hours as he polished bumpers and chrome trim. Perhaps as a result of this obsession with clean cars, which reached epidemic proportions in Zinder shortly after various foreign development agencies installed a water tower and a town water system — the water table in the area was dropping at an alarming rate. Taps all over town ran the entire day. It became perilous to shower late in the afternoon, especially to work up good lathers of soap and shampoo, for that was invariably when the water would peter out. Car washing, a man's job, took precedence over water fetching, which was still woman's work, whether the water came from a fetid swamp or a communal faucet.

Water engineers from still more development agencies were brought in to deepen the holes which were supplying the water tower, and they came with more vehicles, which their drivers and "houseboys" lovingly washed four or five times a day, and well, the more things changed, the more they stayed the same.

Zinder, described by explorers as tropical forest a hundred years earlier, was now on the edge of the Sahara that was moving south at a rate of ten to thirty kilometres a year. The desert, with its sand dunes and rocky outcrops, was separated from Zinder by a sixty-kilometre buffer zone of dying trees, which rapidly turned bone white and littered the sand and laterite soil like ancient skeletons of extinct beasts. The sight of these newly fallen trees was chilling, even in the suffocating heat.

The only tree that survived and flourished in the town was the hardy neem, native to India, which withstood the arid climate and annual bush fires, and bore leaves too bitter for wandering livestock to devour from its seedlings.

The tough and tanned experts who worked "en brosse" during the week seemed to like sharing their tales of doom and gloom with everyone. One man who said he had been flying over West Africa for twenty years, told us that Lake Chad, that great patch of blue on the brown African map, was drying up. He speculated grimly that within a couple of generations the whole Sahel would be completely uninhabitable — except perhaps by the nomadic Tuaregs who had mastered the skills of surviving in the sandy wasteland aeons earlier.

Hassan was blissfully unaware of such predictions. He went about his chores merrily, and continued to wash the car with a dedication and affection that I suspected, based on what I saw of them, that neither his wife nor his children received from him.

Being a mechanic, he also tinkered with the engine and changed the oil from time to time. One Saturday I saw him heading off at the end of the day with a beer bottle full of the blackened crud that had been lubricating the car engine for a few dusty weeks and a few thousand sandy kilometres in the great expanse of desert north of Zinder.

"Hassan, where are you going to dump that?" I called. I was afraid that he would just pour it out somewhere along the road, which was the accepted form of waste disposal in town.

"I'm taking it home," he said.

"You're taking it home?"

"Yes, Madame. It's for salad. I will strain it and give it to my wife for salad."

I tried to explain why this was not a good idea, and Hassan, who never had much patience with me — reminding me often that I had been preceeded in Karl's house by a "first wife" who had left for the United States, shrugged and left. He had once told me that he had been in the house longer than I had, and that he worked for Monsieur Karl, not for me.

Meanwhile there were occasional invitations from seasoned development experts, who seemed determined not to let the world outside their walls infringe on their dogged attempts to reproduce the good life they had left behind in Europe. The first of these invitations was for a soirée at the lavish home of a lavish Italian, a United Nations water man. This man was known for his love of authentic pasta, and he had over a tonne of it shipped in from Italy, in the container which brought his personal belongings to Zinder for his posting. Over plates of this imported pasta and gallons of red wine, the talk was loud and boisterous. After dinner, the "boy" cleared off the table, and comments were made about the life span of a crystal glass in the hands of an African "houseboy." Crystal wine glasses made way for crystal champagne glasses.

Mine sat untouched beside me, partly because I suspected all the wine had impaired my eye-hand coordination and I was afraid if I reached for it I would knock it over and break it. I didn't want to be compared with one of the notoriously clumsy houseboys who were said to break glasses like a soufflé chef breaks eggs. Our Italian host noticed my untouched glass of no-longer-so-bubbly champagne, scooped it up with a great hullabaloo of Italian exclamations, and examined the yellow liquid which did look a little like urine in the light of the green and red patio lights. With considerable fanfare, he tossed the glass into the spotlit bushes. The sound of shattering crystal was drowned out by the tinkling laughter of the women around me. I was given a new glass, which was filled with more French champagne, and ordered to drink.

It was very difficult to keep things in perspective, very difficult to find someone to blame for all the ills that seemed to close in on me from all sides.

A short walk to the post office meant passing hundreds of beggars — men and women whose eyes had been destroyed (sometimes deliberately) so that they might spend their lives seeking alms, being pulled along by a stick and an unfortunate child. There was the woman who crawled on her hands and knees, a rusted enamel bowl for donations on her head, a small child tied onto her back in her "pagne" or cloth, who was also pregnant. The logistics of this pregnancy, how it came about and how it would end, kept my mind churning for weeks. The child would eventually replace the one on her back as she crawled through town, and the one on her back would begin to carry the bowl for alms.

Even the children of some of the town's well-to-do looked, to me, as though they were in need of a square meal, clothing and assistance. Children were not given names until the seventh year of life — indicative perhaps of the chances they were given — statistically and by their parents — to survive to that age.

Boys roamed in small gangs, finding their amusement in garbage piles, pushing old tires with sticks, and chasing after them, or fabricating their own ingenious playthings — trucks, model bicycles and motorcycles with bits of tin, shreds of flip flops and wire. Girls were put to work, fetching water, carrying firewood, carrying younger siblings, peddling. When the children who attended Koran school outside our window finished their lessons, they took to the streets with tin cans dangling on wire like billy-cans, begging in the name of Allah.

Although high walls at home separated us from the people next door, there were no secrets from neighbours. Ours was an Alhaji, a corpulent man whose millions were made in trading. The great history of the Hausa civilization was made by trading; it was on the trans-Sahara route which linked North Africa and the Arab countries with ancient market cities like Kano and the African coast. It was not just goods that had been traded up and down this caravan trail, but also slaves.

Our neighbour drove a new Mercedes, and the television set in his compound was colour. We often listened to Niger's evening news broadcast — *TéléSahel Actualités*, over the wall. On the eve of the feast following Ramadan, the holy Muslim month of fasting and prayer, Alhaji purchased six cases of French champagne from the town's French store, filling the trunk of his lime-green Mercedes.

His wives were, day by day, chopping down the one tree on our lane. This made me furious. I knew, but did not care that I was being unfair — they needed firewood for cooking, and my need for the tree was purely aesthetic. It provided shade and was the only spot of green on the path.

Sometimes I went out and delivered lectures, explaining pedantically the word "desertification" — and the value of the tree. The women, who spoke no French, smiled and nodded and clapped their hands. I never dared broach this subject with the imposing Alhaji, who could have spared the tree by buying gas cookers for his wives. In fact Alhaji never once acknowledged my existence, although he thought the world of Karl and loaned him a colour television when World Cup Soccer time rolled around.

There was another contentious issue that made me alternate between feeling pity and respect for, as well as exasperation with, these wives — I tried to find out how many there were but could never get past six without getting confused over who was a daughter or grand-daughter and who was a wife. Counting heads, mouths to feed, was something which was done in broad terms — there were a "few" or "plenty." The issue between myself and the women next door was the tiny obnoxious stream trickling snake-like out into the sand directly in front of our gate, from a hole clawed into the base of their wall. Not only was this an unpleasant septic surprise about which I frequently forgot and stepped in when leaving my house, but it infused our entire compound with the strong stench of faecal matter. When the first rains came, the road flooded and all that effluent was washed in torrents back into our neighbour's (and our) compound. Then the wives emerged and using small plastic bowls, began frantically trying to block up the hole with the mud and effluent. This then became a playground for black swarms of blue-tailed flies, which then migrated over the wall into our compound, and wiped their tiny but dirty feet on whatever I was at that moment in the process of eating.

When I was down with stomach problems and vomiting, as I often was, I rehearsed petulant lectures about hygiene which I planned to march over and deliver to the family next door. But then, I would recover and emerge from the house, and meet those indefatigable smiles and greetings from my neighbours and be filled with warmth and affection for them, and my anger and resolve to "do something" would evaporate in the African sun.

I used to wonder how many of the children from such a large family such as the one next door with no indoor plumbing or toilet facility, were free of intestinal parasites. They did not distinguish between safe and clean water from a borehole or a faucet, or that which was not fit for drinking or wading, which was used to flush out human and other wastes. The children in Zinder frolicked in sumps that collected in small valleys during the rainy season. With exuberant joy they scooped up the sewerage into their mouths and over their heads, squealing with delight.

It was not surprising that dysentery was still the biggest immediate killer of children in Zinder. Everywhere there were children crippled with polio. Dutch health workers stationed out in the villages moaned about the spoilage and disappearance of vaccines, because government health workers absconded with them and with the special refrigeration units that constituted the cold chain, or they used the government vehicles as taxis and family cars.

A Dutch health worker finally quit in exasperation after she demanded that men who came for weekly antibiotic injections against raging cases of syphilis bring their wives for similar treatment, and was told by the health authorities that she had no right to make any such demands.

I took note of everything I was told, wrote it all down, and tried very hard to suppress a youthful rage and indignation that Niger evoked. Anyway, all these unpleasant realities could be forgotten — at least temporarily at the Private Club.

## *Chapter 2*

# The private club

More than a decade later I still have a t-shirt to remind me of my initiation into the private club in Zinder. It shows a woozy orange camel sucking through a straw on a bottle of beer, on a white background. I can't bring myself to throw it out, anymore than I can at this late date, make excuses to myself for beginning my stay in Africa in the Club Privé. If I had wanted to observe expatriates at work and play in francophone Africa — it was probably as good a place as any to start.

The Club Privé was a hangover from the French colonial period, a refuge perched beside the high-walled prison on a windswept rocky hill overlooking mud houses, mosques and markets. Beyond that there was the Sahara desert. Up until independence, it would have been an oasis for the French préfet or mayor, and his staff of colonial administrators; a place to escape, temporarily, from Africa.

In 1982, it served the same purpose, except that the French administrators had officially handed Niger over to its rightful owners twenty-two years earlier. Members now were primarily expatriate development workers, foreigners who, for their own diverse reasons, had chosen to make their homes, most only temporarily, in this desert outpost. At the Club one could play "boules," the French version of lawn (in this case, sand) bowling, swim, engage in tennis tournaments, play table tennis, attend Saturday evening soirées, watch young French co-operants swap spouses, and last but not least, one could drink. The bar was open twenty-four hours a day. While the taped accolades to Allah serenaded the town throughout the night, the bar men at the Club served up drinks to the non-Muslim foreigners.

Apart from the bar men, I only recall seeing one Nigerien in the Club, and he was said to be a spy for the president. I was warned to keep away from him. I ignored the warning once, and found myself being quizzed about my reason for being in Niger, and then lectured about white crimes in Africa. I remember feeling guilty for months about the disappearance of the elephants, something he said white hunters had caused. He didn't bother speaking to me again, although he socialized quite freely with many of the expatriate men in the club who did go big-game hunting in the national reserve.

Edwin, a Lebanese textile merchant, was one of the Club's most eminent members, probably because he was its oldest. He had been there twenty-two years earlier, sharing the bar with the colonists. He swilled back whisky in quantities I associated with camels at oases. His face was yellow and I wondered if he had hepatitis. Everyone in the Club Privé seemed to have recently recovered from hepatitis, or malaria. An alcoholic French man with thirty years in Niger behind him had just passed away at the hospital with hepatitis B, they said.

I had had no idea that there was a difference between hepatitis A and B; I certainly didn't know there was a hepatitis C. While doctors may have been in short supply, there was never a shortage of expatriates willing to help me with the ABC's of tropical medicine. Tropical diseases were a favourite topic in the Club, and everyone seemed to have a good idea of how each of these many maladies could be prevented, or cured; each person with their own — different — idea of what cured what. Much the same as the various doctors I had consulted before coming to Niger.

Meanwhile, most Club members succumbed to perhaps the most common disease of all among expatriates in such places — alcoholism.

Edwin represented the old school of expatriate. Fleeing his native Lebanon forty years earlier he landed in Conakry, Guinea, where he spent a few years before moving to Zinder, halfway between Timbuctou and Lake Chad. The Lebanese families in West Africa had their own system for divvying up the spoils and the territory. I never did understand how Edwin wound up in Zinder with his wife and three children — who were grown up and running their own shops all over the country and in neighbouring West African lands. Officially, his family sold dusty textiles — seconds sold as firsts, in a dusty shop in town. I was told I was being naive when I asked how he could be so rich — for he was rich — on the earnings from a little textile shop. There were other ways of making money in Niger, almost all of them illegal — smuggling, exchanging currency, hoarding grain, dealing gold, gouging contracts.

"Zinder may not be the end of the world," Edwin would say from time to time when I asked him why he stayed. "But you can see the end of the world from here." This was a favourite in the Club Privé. It never failed to evoke laughter. I used to write it in letters to friends back home.

"But Conakry is on the coast," I persisted. "It must have been much more pleasant than Zinder, wasn't it? It must have been a big change, coming to such a hot and dry place like Zinder?"

"Before independence, I was a king in Conakry," he said. "You understand? A king. But when Guinea became independent young men came into my office, boys really, who had been shining my shoes the year before, and instead of shining my shoes, they put their boots up on my desk and interrogated me, saying they were security agents."

Edwin alone seemed happy to see a new face in the Club, and from the beginning singled me out for his attentions. The trouble was that I didn't speak any French worth listening to and he didn't speak English. He had a joke that he used to overcome our linguistic barrier and break the ice.

"Il y a une belle femme. Ooh la la, très très belle. I ask her do you speak Eengleesh? If she say yes, I say, I loff you. If she say no, I say, I f___ you." I had grown up in provincial Nova Scotia, with a moderately liberal background which stressed good manners and respect for my elders. I laughed.

Newcomers in the Club, in Africa for the first time, tended to be regarded by older members with mistrust or as neophytes with whom it was not worth trying to discuss anything. I thought Edwin was flattering me by selecting me to hear his joke. I never really did get the joke, nor, I expect, did he.

Perched on the lofty bar stool, he was still shorter than I was when I was standing slouched over the bar. He became more loquacious after each telling of the joke and after a few glasses of whisky. Something about the combination of whisky and a tongue-tied newcomer to listen to him made Edwin turn maudlin, and he would launch into his stories of Lebanon, and a paradise on this earth called Beirut, which contrasted sharply with my sketchy image of the place, painted by dishevelled reporters doing courageous stand-ups on hotel balconies while mortar fire exploded around them.

According to Edwin, there was no country in the world more beautiful than Lebanon, no food more delectable than that one could purchase from roadside cafes in the mountainous country he had left a lifetime ago.

I listened for many hours to his recitals, which he punctuated every now and then with his joke — when he ran momentarily out of virtues of his homeland to extol.

There were about fifty French co-operants living in Zinder. This was France's way of alleviating the surfeit of teachers at home, while improving its aid profile. There were also a dozen United Nations people working primarily on wells, some Dutch health workers, the odd Belgian teaching flying and spraying one half of the country with crop protecting agents, a half dozen Peace Corps teaching everything from sports to baby-care, another half dozen German volunteers, a few Danes (another water project), and a few hangers-on from the French colonial period. And something that was easy to forget in the Club Privé, there were also about 80,000 Nigeriens. This number doubled on market days. Most of the people were herders, or subsistence farmers — or sub-subsistence farmers, and small-time traders. They traded everything and anything they could get their hands on: foreign currencies, grain, Spanish sardines, cans of Nestlé milk powder or instant coffee, Nigerian bubble gum, camels.

At the Club, alcohol and bitter comments about "Africans" flowed freely. I had nothing to say, and I drank more beer than I ever have in my life. That may also account for the blurriness and haziness I felt when I tried to decide what I was doing there.

Occasionally one of Edwin's daughters, a fleshy young woman who had just married into French Society and loved to exchange recipes with the French women from Marseilles, would invite me to one of the tables reserved for the women. They were experts' wives, who did their tanning (topless) and swimming (in G-strings) at pools at home. They had brought their culture with them; they were rigid on the matters of Camembert and cuts of beef and disciplining housestaff.

In the Club I tried to mingle and forget what was outside, but the guilt was always there. I was desperately afraid of becoming "one of them" and spent a lot of time casting judgement on them — much the way I had, at the age of fifteen, doggedly obeyed the prophets of my generation who had warned us not trust anyone over thirty. On the other hand, I was desperate to feel I belonged somewhere. I could not communicate with the Nigeriens, and could not come up with a good reason to inflict myself on them, except that I wanted to get to know them. I just didn't know how to begin.

At least I could pay my fees and call myself a member of the Club.

Perhaps it was because none of us knew how to cope with the enormity of the problems outside, that discussions among the expatriates, who saw each other day after day in the Club, often went astray, concentrating on things far removed from the here and now. Or maybe people just ran out of banter and tired of each others' development stories and wound up going off on tangents.

I would tune into the discussions in the middle, when I realized that talk had deviated from the usual reports on corruption or failures in the development project. Then I would hear a normally sober and retiring Dutch man bellowing at a German water engineer. "What did you bloody Germans do with all our bicycles you made off with during the war? You took thousands of them. We never got them back."

Sometimes I might be included in the conversation, if I had made an inadvertent comment about my country or the world in general that did not jive with the consensus around the bar. A Belgian man was particularly belligerent when he had too much to drink, and he had come to blows with French men several times over issues of European politics.

"You Americans!" he spat, one night, when I had said something in French, in an accent which did not please him.

"Je ne suis pas americaine," I said, slowly and clearly, "Je suis canadienne."

"Same thing."

A French teacher, who was standing beside me started to berate Canada, and the anglophone world in general. He was a great fan of the late Charles de Gaulle, and his famous words which were to fan the flames of Quebec separatism in the early seventies.

"Vive le Québec Libre!" he shouted, to enliven a lecture that criticized English speakers all over the world.

I pointed out that Canada had done a lot to help France in the Second World War.

"It's not true," he said. "The Americans defeated Germany. Canada didn't even fight."

"We did so," I snapped.

"You didn't. You better read your history books again."

This was not the first time I ran up head-first against that special intransigence of the Frenchman abroad nor was it the last. It surfaced easily in francophone Africa, where the over-riding impression I had was that the French had never really given up their empire and were free, even freer than they would be at home, to indulge themselves in the excesses of their unbridled personalities. The old boys in the Club reminded me more than once of the boys turned savage in William Golding's *Lord of the Flies*.

Late at night while the town slept a man atop the central mosque manned an automated muezzin that crooned to the black desert sky. The only activity in town was around the bar in the Club where talk frequently turned to World War II. Maybe it was because so many Europeans were closeted together for so long in self-imposed exile. The present was lost in dreams of that future return to their homelands, or it was submerged in rosy and distorted memories of a perfect homeland. And always there was an uneasy knowledge of what was out there, beyond the walls and greenery and lights of the Club.

When the muezzin sounded, I would imagine how much comfort faith would afford the beggars and the over-burdened in their struggle for their daily bread; faith that someone was listening to the prayers and that one day in the next world, those prayers would be answered. I would also feel deep secret anger at some of the prominent and wealthy men — many prominent citizens, who had grown enormously rich from ill-got gains, often at the expense of those around them with their hoarding of precious grains during times of hunger, or their selling of the grains abroad for exorbitant prices when hunger stared their people in the face. I wondered what was wrong with the system, the government that prattled on about the "Society of Development," to allow such flagrant disregard of laws, and morals, to occur and at such a great cost to so many people, for whom survival was difficult at the very best of times. I made the mistake too, of thinking military dictatorship would and should be as concerned with and constrained by the peoples' welfare as would a democratically elected parliament.

Generalizations flowed like champagne in the Club. Criticizing the workmanship, lethargy and reliability of an African worker was considered quite acceptable among Club members and Nigeriens I met who had been abroad to live, study or work. What was absolutely not to be tolerated was any criticism of the African powers that be in those independent nations. One had to be very careful not to insult any man of means in the new political and old traditional hierarchies; the overlap there was considerable. Volunteers had been clearly instructed never to mention the name of the president no matter what language they were speaking. Thus the terms "big Norwegian" or "big green man" which could be heard passing like codes around the bar late at night. These were the Club's pseudonyms for the president. And I used them.

I began, very tentatively, to look for information on what kinds of development projects everyone in the Club was involved in, and began to pester people to tell me more about their work. The development people did not seem to like outsiders examining their work, and expressed reluctance to talk to journalists who, they said, tended to take everything out of context and present distorted half-truths to readers back home. "They wouldn't understand," I was told. "They don't know the problems we face."

Occasionally though, a story would more or less come to me out of the blue, as it did one Sunday morning as I was drinking tea on the patio when a small airplane buzzed overhead. Several members of the Club were taking flying lessons from an expatriate pilot, when he wasn't engaged in his official job of aerial spraying. I assumed this was another of his teaching sessions, and wondered idly if he had sobered up from the night before — whether in fact I should be worried that the plane sounded as if it were stalling a few hundred feet overhead. Then white powder began to fall, like sifted snowflakes from the sky. In a few moments the compound and street were dusted with the white powder that was meant to kill grasshoppers and other pests on farmers' precious grain fields. Confronted with this at the Club later, the pilot apologized profusely for having poisoned half of Zinder — explaining that the winds had fooled him, and that his actual target, millet fields on the outskirts of town, had been missed.

I recognized the smell of the white powder that descended on Zinder that day. It was a sharp, pungent odour that permeated the entire market. This was not one of the usual smells in town — the unpleasant, but organic smells of faeces and urine heating in the sun. This was a toxic smell, something that froze my facial muscles. A man involved in crop protection services told me that it was a chemical called HCH, closely related to lindane, most commonly used, with cautions about its toxicity, as a tick-wash. Canada had begun supplying the Sahel countries with this insecticide back in the early 70s. Over the years, as attitudes towards such chemicals changed in North America, Canada no longer produced or shipped the stuff over, but provided the Nigerien government with the funds to purchase the chemicals of their choice in West African markets, such as Abidjan. The HCH, paid for by Canada, purchased in the Côte d'Ivoire, tended to come in nondescript sacks, without any sort of labelling — not that most of its users could have read the word 'poison' had it appeared on the bags.

"So many farmers die each year," said a German woman working in crop protection, who had nothing positive to say about this form of Canadian assistance. "They don't know the quantities to apply, don't know how to apply it, don't know that its toxins accumulate in tissues, and they just die. But no one is able to count these deaths. There are no autopsies performed and people don't often like to look for the reasons for deaths anyway."

"Will you tell me that in an interview?"

"No."

In 1982, HCH was sold in the Zinder markets from huge mounds in which children played, and market sellers doled it out in small handfuls to purchasers. HCH is a contact poison.

With the help of a translator, I questioned some of the HCH sellers about the pale brown powder they were dishing out like sugar.

"It's berry powder," said one old man, with a grin that exposed teeth and gums stained red from cola nuts. He offered me a spoonful to taste. "You put it on the tomatoes just before you harvest them, see, you sprinkle it like this, and the tomatoes will taste good." A child, perhaps his grandson, was shoving the powder into little mounds with his hands, as he made the "brmm brmm" sounds of an imaginary bulldozer.

I telephoned a development official in Ottawa when I returned to Canada, after leaving Niger a year later. At first she was delighted to share her travel stories with me, about the two-week trip she had made across Niger, and said she was sorry we hadn't met in Zinder. Then I questioned her on the advisability of the crop protection programme in Niger, particularly the aerial spraying on fields which are in the middle of villages, and of the advisability of paying for poisons like HCH. She said crops had to be protected, this was a matter of survival for the people, and that these chemicals were what the Nigerien government had demanded. She had nothing more to add on the subject.

Shortly after the aerial spraying incident, water and sanitation workers in Niamey, the nation's capital, dumped HCH into the water supply, mistaking it for chlorine. Foreigners were advised, by notices posted in their offices, to drink only imported bottled water for the next few weeks, until the situation cleared up.

What was I to do with my growing suspicion that something was terribly amiss in some of the aid packages?

In the Club, stories like these were a dime a dozen — a little like unemployed wives of the development workers. They always evoked laughter, but there was no mirth there. When the laughter died, people tended to shake their heads and shrug. There were often long periods of silence, as if it had all been said before, and the fun had gone out of the stories, and of life itself. Given the success rate of most development projects, it was not surprising that cynicism ran so high.

My own mental blocks began to shift, not without causing headaches and periods of confusion and depression during which I didn't leave the house. I had flown half way around the world, given up my job, my car, my cat and my apartment to take refuge inside a mud house, in a country that to my eye looked doomed to disappear under the Saharan sands sooner rather than later; the foreigners in the business of developing the country were jaded and cynical, and Nigerien President Kountche was busy broadcasting to the nation that "All Nigeriens are mobilized for the Development Society." Nigeriens could not mobilize for development; they were too busy trying to survive. To survive, they needed their extended family, and that family was part of the larger family, their tribe, to which they were deeply and almost without exception, eternally faithful.

For a time everything I saw looked bleak and hopeless and confusing. This was probably the closest I have ever come to empathizing completely with a person who is deaf and untrained in sign language or lip-reading. You can see, but you cannot understand what everyone is talking about. Even if I had understood all the languages, everyone was speaking about things I knew nothing about or found too incredible to acknowledge. It was like having walked into an advanced course in physics without having finished kindergarten.

One evening at the Club Privé, after Edwin had gone home suffering from a mysterious pain in the right side of his abdomen which was conceivably the beginnings of cirrhosis, I was sitting with my head in my hands nursing a headache which might have been the end of a hangover. The January wind was whipping up a terrible chill, covering us with sand and dry frigid air. I was bundled up inside three blouses, a sweater and a light jacket, which exhausted my wardrobe. I had packed for Africa, which was supposed to be hot and steamy. Another misconception. January on the edge of the desert was downright cold. Even in the afternoon when the temperature reached 30 or over, I was cold. The sun could be hot, and a few timid droplets of sweat might form on exposed skin before the wind kicked in and dried them off, the result being like a bath in alcohol.

For the thousandth time a large German engineer, whose folk heroes and favourite topics of conversation were a renowned Italian racing car driver and an up-and-coming German tennis star (and occasionally Jayne Mansfield), was telling us about the hopelessness of his African engineers. He had been working for four years on a sanitation project in Zinder, a series of drainage canals that, during the rainy season, would channel a year's worth of filth accumulated in gutters and ditches, into a large pond outside of town. There were many problems with his project. Those canals that had been finished were so filled with rubbish and waste, that when the rains came they would simply overflow onto the paths and into house compounds as before. There seemed to be no way the local authorities could get anyone to clean them out. And he himself had been spooked by what had been found in the canals — remains of discarded infants. In the digging of new canals he and his crew also unearthed a child's grave. Death, like life, seemed to close in on us in Zinder.

But he didn't talk much about those things. He was more vociferously concerned about how many precious German marks, taxpayers' money, were being thrown away in the name of development in this town he called the "asshole of the world." West German Chancellor Helmut Kohl had not yet made his famous speech to the German parliament defending the government's development assistance budget, by proclaiming that for every German mark spent, one and a half marks came back to the Federal Republic.

I could understand his frustration, but could not fathom why the problems of the project couldn't be solved, or why people who knew their projects were a waste of time and money stayed.

"Look," I said, teeth clattering, arms snuggled around my midriff for additional protection against the cold, "If it's such a waste, why don't you just go home and forget it? If you guys didn't come to work here, then there would be no way to throw the money away. Would there? If it's not helping and you hate it so much, why do you stay?" His eyebrows leapt a few centimetres up his forehead, trying to catch up with a receding hairline. He stared at me for a moment, then turned to discuss the upcoming World Cup Soccer Championships with some of the men.

Either he didn't want to answer me, perhaps because it would have meant admitting that he made more money and had more authority and freedom than he ever would as an engineer in Germany — or he couldn't. It would have meant explaining the mystique of those black Sahelian nights and the wonder of the continent that continues to bewitch strangers who wander onto it, for whatever reason — something that is inexplicable.

## *Chapter 3*

# Tying the knot

There were eminent members of the expatriate community in Zinder who did not frequent the Club Privé. One of these was Maxim. He was about two hundred pounds over the ideal weight for a man of his height — about 5'5", and his legs were blackened, swollen and bandaged. They looked remarkably like baobab trunks. The only time I had seen him was as his driver heaved him into the front seat of his tiny Renault in front of the tiny shop in Zinder which stocked French cheese and wine.

He was an old-timer, a relic from an earlier age when colonies were convenient havens for escaped convicts and exiled crooks from Europe, places for them to put down roots and pursue their careers with indemnity.

Maxim was a safe-cracker. But his skills and his expertise were much much broader than that. I would never have run into him if we hadn't needed someone who knew the ins and outs of Nigerien laws, to help us arrange our marriage.

I had not forgotten for a moment that I had come to Africa to get married. Karl hemmed and hawed when I brought up the subject in the first few months, suggesting we wait and see whether we might "grow back together" in the new setting. I thought if we didn't get married soon I would probably leave for good. Karl was thirty-seven, and he had enjoyed his single life, moving about the planet unfettered. The deciding factor, I believe, was the trouble he had renewing my visa every few weeks. Someone pointed out to him that if we were married, I would automatically get the official resident's visa to which I would be entitled as the wife of a German development worker.

He began making small noises that sounded promising, and finally announced that he had talked to some people about marriage procedures in Niger.

To start, we would need the help of Maxim, about whom we had heard many things, none of them believable.

Maxim was a good friend of the president; he was also an indispensable aid to the Préfet of Zinder on legal matters and on occasions when numbers and keys to important safes got mislaid. The Mayor of Zinder said Maxim was the man to draw up our marital papers. First though, he would need to interview us.

It was a hot day; the Harmattan was long gone; July and August rains had come and gone and the mini-hot season had begun. Temperatures ran above forty.

Following instructions, we arrived at his house at three in the afternoon. Through gaping holes in the wall around the compound I could see the pink and green bungalow, a few women in the shade of a large mango tree engaged in the relaxing and interminable process of tressing each other's hair, two enormous tortoises in the process of mating (at least that was my interpretation of their antics and loud grunting sounds) and a few car wrecks.

Two small boys, stark naked and different shades of brown, came running towards the wall and peered back at us through the holes in the wall.

"Ja, this is the place," said my husband to be.

"How do you know?"

"Look, see?" He was pointing.

"What do you mean? Those are just kids. All right, some of them look a little like they might have a white father, but still, I don't see..."

"Not the kids," he said. "The monkey, can't you see the monkey?"

There it was. Maxim's monkey, sitting like a sculpture on top of a large opened safe perched on a boulder in a far corner of the compound.

"I see it, but I don't see..."

"He's a safe cracker, isn't he? That's a safe, isn't it?"

After a good deal of pushing and lifting of the gate, we managed to gain entry to the compound. After we were inside, and had closed the heavy gate with a grinding screech that would have woken the dead in the hospital morgue fifty metres from the house, we noticed that the children were coming and going freely, not through the gate, but through the holes in the wall.

The women under the tree waved to us, showing no eagerness to stop what they were doing to each other's hair, which was being teased, pulled and twisted into tiny, erect braids, and to their fingernails, which were being lacquered various shades of green and purple, and get up and wake Maxim. The children, who ranged from deep black to pale shades of brown, squealed but did not come close to us. The tortoises were still otherwise occupied and didn't spare us a glance. The monkey blinked his glassy eyes a few times.

It was up to us to announce our visit. Trouble was, there was no door hanging from the hinges. We could, I suppose, have knocked on some of the tin cans and broken metal scraps laid on the doorstep, but that seemed discourteous. So we stood there for a couple of minutes discussing whether to come back at another time. I had heard Maxim had a Tuareg wife, who was said to be enormously fat, but there was no one who answered to that description in the makeshift beauty salon under the tree. The multitudes of small children of all shades were rumoured in town to be the progeny of Maxim's couplings with his own splendid daughters. Rumours in West Africa were as reliable as, and far more imaginative than, state-run newspapers, and the seasoned expatriate was wary of them. In Zinder I seem to have believed every rumour I heard.

Finally a startlingly pretty young woman, wearing a bright green pagne and new flip-flops to match, accented by apple red varnish on her toenails, came to the door and welcomed us with a dazzling smile. It wasn't until she turned to lead us inside that I saw her left foot and ankle were moulded into a solid lump of bone, on which she limped.

"*Come in. Come in.*" The voice coming from inside the house, a den of gloom and dust and assorted rubbish, caught us off guard. I pushed Karl in front, and followed.

He was seated on a rickety chair in front of a kitchen table covered with more papers and bric-a-brac — and dust — than I had ever seen collected in one place in my life. Most of it was radio equipment, or entire control panels from one form of military vehicle or another, vintage World War II, or maybe World War I.

In the relative darkness, his face loomed large and pale, almost greenish. He was wearing no shirt and sweat trickled in dark grey streams from underneath mottled and grey rolls of fat about his middle. Dirt was caked in the creases. His feet were bare, and blackened, poking like yams out from the greying bandages around his swollen legs. The woman in green left, slipping neatly past us with a musical "Excusez-moi."

"Come in. Or are you afraid? Come in, I think you want to tie the *knot*?" He made a gruesome choking noise in the back of his throat and twisted two hands about his sturdy neck, as though to remove his own head, with its neat crew cut. His tongue hung out of his mouth and his pale blue eyes bulged in their watery pink sockets. He laughed loudly at his joke.

We smiled nervously.

He proceeded to lecture us on the seriousness of the step we were about to take — into wedlock. Then he began to fill out a series of pink forms (I still have them) with surprising accuracy and neatness. A clock ticked very loudly. He printed very slowly.

"Where's Madame from?" he asked, licking the end of his red pen as he got down to work on the forms that required every bit of information I possessed on my own origins and family.

"Halifax, that's Canada," said Karl, who was doing most of the talking while I tried to take inventory of what all was in that room. Files were stored on top of bins of mouldy potatoes. "Halifax," I thought. "Bright blue summer skies, ice cream parlours and icy river swims."

"I know Halifax," he said in slow but clear English. "Ah, Halifax. I sailed all over the world. I was in Halifax in, ah, 1941." He mentioned a couple of locales he had known and liked in the city, but I had not heard of them, and imagine that over the years they had been removed, for aesthetic and moral reasons.

"I spoke good English then. Before that I was in Germany for seven years. Ich habe auch Deutsche gesprochen. Mais maintenant..." He lifted his palms and grinned with his tongue working its way around a broad gap where some front teeth were missing.

It would take three weeks, he said, for our papers to go through and then they would have to be displayed for a month in front of the Hotel de Ville, which is the peculiar French term for City Hall.

"That's in case someone has some objections to you tying the knot." He made that sound again, and Karl laughed — far too loudly. "Maybe one of your girlfriends will object." They shared this joke too.

He instructed us to proceed to the hospital to see one of the Russian doctors for medical examinations and more filling of forms, which would ensure that we were biologically compatible and not carrying any sexually transmitted diseases. If I have neglected to mention the presence of the Russian doctors in Zinder, this is because the only time I ever actually spoke to one was that day we were sent for our medical examinations.

This was years before Perestroika, and the three Russians in the hospital kept very much to themselves, away from the harmful influences of westerners and the local people. They travelled everywhere together, in an aging green transport vehicle of East German origins, and on Friday nights they held their Party meeting. They were not Club material.

Their offices were at the very end of the long dilapidated building that was known as Zinder Hospital. We passed the morgue and a group of women wailing over a body that had just been delivered in a small pick-up. I could see the bare feet and legs sticking out of the back. Vultures circled overhead and cluttered the grounds like gargoyles. Dozens of women were cooking over fires for relatives who were unfortunate enough to be patients inside the hospital — which was without windows, and for the most part, beds.

We knocked on the door indicated to us by a friendly white-coated male nurse, and walked in. The Russian doctor hastily sat up and snapped shut a French mail order catalogue in which he had been studying women's shoes, and eyed us through thick glasses. He surrepticiously stuffed the catalogue into a desk drawer and leaned forward, hands clasped, at our service. He had handled the catalogue as though it were a piece of pornography.

We explained what we needed and handed him the forms, which he started to fill out expeditiously with tick marks in all the correct boxes, indicating that we were quite healthy and able to go ahead with our marriage. He decided we were both RH positive. When he had finished this, he rose and scuttled across the office towards his white lab coat which was hanging on the back of the door, a stethescope dangling from the pocket.

"Strange," I murmured to Karl. "He filled out the forms and now he's going to do the examination."

Karl looked as perplexed as I. We watched as the doctor dipped into the pocket of the lab coat and extracted a handful of postage stamps of undetermined origin. He sidled back over to us, as though about to perform a top secret transaction. His eyes were darting about as he whispered. "Excuse me, but I collect stamps. I have many, see?" He held out the crumpled stamps in a sweaty hand. His French was almost worse than mine and I had difficulty understanding him. I thought he was going to give us the stamps. I reached out a hand, and he closed his fist over them. "I need postal stamps," he said. "Western country. Germany. America. England. Western stamps. You understand? Western stamps."

Three weeks later, after Karl had delivered an envelope full of Canadian and German postage stamps to the Russian physician, Maxim sent word that we were to meet on Saturday morning at 8, in front of the Hotel de Ville for the official marriage ceremony — with two witnesses to sign the papers. We recruited the German engineer who was in mourning because he was about to lose Karl, his best drinking buddy, to a woman who did not have the same body measurements as Jayne Mansfield.

As my witness cum bridesman, I solicited the services of an Egyptian, who said he had fled his country after shooting down six Israeli planes during the Yom Kippur war and taken up residence in Canada. He was now working for an American non-governmental development agency. Besides being the only man in the Club Privé who spoke perfect English, he seemed to like me well enough. After he had quelled his liver pains with a few bottles of beer in the evening, he would invite us back to his house where he could get into some serious drinking. I always surmised that his alcoholism stemmed from his unpleasant memories of his role in a war he said he neither agreed with nor wanted to participate in. He was always indulgent with me, if somewhat sentimental and overemotional after a bottle of whisky. Under the circumstances I thought he would do admirably as my bridesmaid, and he did give us a wedding gift, a pair of sheets still in their package from an Edmonton department store which his Canadian girlfriend had probably given him when he left for Niger. The other wedding gift we received was from Edwin and his family — a gold fertility pendant.

The night before the wedding I stayed home to prepare some snacks for this party of four that would gather at our house after the ceremony on Saturday morning. Karl went out with the best man and the bridesman to celebrate his last night as a bachelor. This trio wound up doing the town, and the next day, when the ceremony was over and Maxim had patted us both on the head and wished us a happy married life, I learned that my bridesman had told Karl in the wee hours of the morning that he would advise him not to marry a woman like me — he himself thought that a "femme femme" was the only suitable marriage material. Both of our hand-picked witnesses, apparently, thought that I was too deficient in the mammillary region to make a good wife.

It was the Mayor of Zinder who presided over the small ceremony in his office. When he learned by looking at our papers before pronouncing us man and wife, that my first name was Margaret, he gave me a long and meaningful stare, and announced, "You had better not behave like Margaret Thatcher, the Femme de Fer, who is your namesake. According to our laws, under which you are married, you are to follow your husband to whatever home he chooses for you."

Everyone chuckled. Then he told me my task would be to bear children for my husband, as many as he wished to have. He had to ask Karl to repeat his "I do" which came out as a doubting whisper the first two times.

Maxim, wearing dark sunglasses, chortled and bounced in his chair; the men thought this was pretty funny, and it was shortly after that the professional Zinder photographer we had hired for the occasion snapped a black and white shot of the wedding party, in which he cut off all our heads.

## *Chapter 4*

# Travel and see

Karl had decided that while he was ready to leave Zinder, he liked development work in Africa. When his contract in Niger was finished, he said he would accept another one, somewhere else on the continent. As his wife, I would need to carve out a life for myself too. It was time I started to do something, move out from behind the walls of the house and the Club. He encouraged me to tackle that journalism career I had talked about when I first came out to Niger. But first I had to see something. "Travel and See" was a common phrase on the back of African taxis and mini-buses. I set out to "Travel and See."

I landed, first, on Mary-Anne's doorstep in the village of Guidimodi. Mary-Anne was an American volunteer working as a nutritionist. She helped keep records of infant growth rates and taught women how to make high-protein infant cereals to prevent kwashiorkor. She tried to curtail the use of the expensive Nestlé cereals that women sometimes bought, at the expense of their own budgets, diets and the health of their infants, largely because they believed these "white man's" foods were modern and superior to their own.

She spent a lot of time weighing babies in a scale suspended from a tree, still more time trying to persuade women in the village to bring their babies to that makeshift health-care post under the tree to keep health records up to date and for advice on infant nutrition.

She was frustrated, tired and disillusioned. Young mothers were eager to attend her sessions and do their best to keep their babies healthy. But after the second or the third baby, the women seemed less interested in keeping their newborns alive and well.

Mary-Anne was Catholic. She said it had been Catholic guilt that had brought her out to Africa, but even her faith in God did not help her here. She felt that she was failing at her job.

One eighteen-month-old baby had just died. Mary-Anne had pleaded with the mother since the infant's birth, to bring the baby for weighing, to check on her growth. The mother never actually refused to come. She even promised, each time Mary-Anne visited her, that she would come — next week. She never came. For eighteen months the mother carried the tiny baby girl on her back, keeping her small head and eyes completely covered with the wrapper. Mary-Anne warned her that she would stunt the baby's development, that the child needed to learn to crawl, play and hold things. The baby girl had lived only in darkness; and was still being nourished solely by the breast. When the baby died, Mary-Anne was furious, and blamed the mother.

The mother was unapologetic. She said Allah had taken the child from her, that Allah had already provided her with eight children. If He took one away, that was natural. She was thankful to Allah for all the children she had, and for relieving her of the last one, which was one too many. "Allah gives and when He gives too much, he takes some back," she said. Mary-Anne guessed the mother was about twenty-six; age was a guessing game for most rural people because births were seldom recorded and birth certificates almost unknown, and she had been married for about twelve years. She looked closer to fifty, and next to her, both Mary-Anne and I felt like children, who had never experienced the challenges of adult life.

Apart from the hopelessness of her duty to keep babies alive, Mary-Anne was also tired of the dust and isolation she felt as a white woman in a remote desert village. She was also fed up with fending off questions about birth control.

Family planning and birth control in Niger in 1983 were taboo. Mere mention of the words could be grounds for expulsion. Two European health workers who had secretly given birth control pills to women who came to their dispensary asking for them, had been quickly and quietly sent home a few months earlier. There were African leaders who made headlines with speeches condemning birth control as a western plot to keep Africa's population down. There were also people who pointed to the vast tracts of virtually empty land in Niger, forgetting about the carrying capacity of land that was just sand, stones and scrub.

The village women began to bear children around the same time they underwent puberty and then stopped at death or at menopause, whichever came first. They were very interested in the subject of family planning and would sneak around the back of Mary-Anne's mud house, whispering that they needed one of "those comprimés," or pills, which Mary-Anne used to prevent pregnancy. They knew she had a boyfriend in Zinder who frequently came to spend nights with her and yet she still didn't get pregnant. They wanted to have whatever she had to prevent pregnancy. She could not give them anything.

The men in Guidimodi were delegated all tasks political or intellectual or religious; women and girls were responsible for almost all the physical labour. They rose long before the sun to fetch water from a distant swamp or to collect and chop firewood. They cooked and pounded the millet tuo, a back-breaking task performed in monumental wooden mortars with pestles so heavy that two or even three women were needed to raise them.

I spent a week in Guidimodi. In my diary I wrote of the compassion I felt, watching Mary-Anne at work, the babies crying as they were laid in that swinging scale, while the mothers looked on, uncomprehending. Compassion, I wrote, didn't alter the fact that women had too many babies too fast, and too little energy and food to care for them. Compassion didn't alter the fact that life was hard in that village, and that only the strong would survive. Perhaps only the strong should survive. A weakling would have no chance, would be a burden on the rest of the family that only just barely survived as it was.

The only time I felt at peace in the village was at dawn, as I lay on a camp-bed in the middle of a sandy compound and watched the red sun rise over the mud walls, listening to the hollow regular thumping of wooden pestles in wooden mortars. Inside Mary-Anne's compound I could forget the swarms of children, so many ragged, dusty children with mucky eyes and noses, clogged with flies.

The village was a labyrinth of these high mud walls, that enclosed family compounds, and formed paths for drainage and pedestrians. Inside, the floors of the compounds were of fine white sand, which the women sieved to keep it free of the small burrs or "cram-cram." Within the walls of one compound a man's wives and children ate and slept in individual mud houses. The walls muted the sounds of voices and the life inside; morning mist over the green swampy oasis air-brushed my memories of those dawns.

In the early morning, with the air almost cool and the shadows still deep, life in the village seemed idyllic. But that was the romance of rustic living for me, someone who knew there was another life waiting — with running water, no shortages of food and indoor plumbing. I wondered how it felt and looked to the women who had already put in a day of hard labour before the sun even rose. They appeared cheerful, exchanging long and ritual greetings as they passed each other on the paths. My pathos seemed irrelevant and uncalled for.

I tried to decide how I felt about their strength and resilience, and decided I felt sorry for myself, utterly inadequate and useless. It was impossible for me to put myself in their minds, and would be for anyone who had not grown up in the village learning its rules, limitations and patterns.

Mary-Anne took me to visit a young bride, the first wife of a wealthy trader who spent most of his time in Zinder, or in the north of neighbouring Nigeria. Aisha had a square hut to herself. It was almost cool inside. The concrete floor was covered with layers of red Persian-style mats from Saudi Arabia, with sprightly scenes of white-tailed deer on mountainsides or the mosque in Mecca. Floor-to-ceiling shelving housed hundreds of enamelled pots and dishes, many bearing the visage of the then-president of Nigeria. Her four-poster bed took up half the room. She invited us to sit with her on the floor.She said she didn't get out much; maid servants performed the chores in her household. She was waiting to get pregnant and bear her first child. She was listless and her face splotchy from applications of bleaching cream. She wanted Mary-Anne and me to be her "best friends" and visit her every day. She said she had no friends in no friends in the village, that they were all "illiterate peasants." I made false promises to visit her again. The other women may have been peasants and poor and over-worked, but they were full of life.

We went then to see Mariama, a feisty village woman who worked with Mary-Anne on the project of keeping babies alive. Mariama was compact, strong and her earthy sense of humour lit up her broad face with contagious laughter and mischief.

Midday meals had just been served to the men under the large palaver tree outside the compound walls. What was left was passed on to the women and children.

Mariama and her two co-wives put out a large bowl of tuo for us. This was my first attempt at eating with my hand. I was amazed at how difficult it was. You had to curl your fingertips to resemble the scooper of a backhoe, and operate the hand from the wrist so that a lump of porridge was neatly lodged safely on the inside of the bucket formed by your knuckles. This then had to be dipped into a gooey gumbo sauce that was still at boiling point and quickly transported to the mouth for unloading. I was happy that for the first time since I had arrived in Niger, I seemed to be serving a purpose. The entire compound came to be amused by the spectacle created by the white woman trying to eat.

Anyone who thinks that eating with the hands is primitive or childish, or somehow less advanced than eating with cutlery, has never tried mastering the African technique.

The meal was accompanied by a bowl of water for washing hands before the ritual begins and after it has finished. I concentrated on eating and tried not to look at the flies clustered in the children's running noses, at the sores on their legs, at the fetid green water in the basin where I had washed my hands.

After lunch the three wives shooed the children away with sticks and shouts, and Mariama directed her attention to me and my life. The first question was whether I was married. Yes, to Karl. She knew Karl, he worked from time to time in Guidimodi. He was German, wasn't he? Germans were good, she had decided. Did I have children? No. There was loud discussion and argument among the women. I had trouble following the conversation, which interspersed the occasional French word with Hausa. Mary-Anne provided sketchy translations from Hausa, but the heat and the heavy food made me drowsy. They appeared to have lost interest in me and my life, which must have seemed empty to them — no children. I was almost asleep when Mary-Anne turned to me, laughing.

"Do you know what they said?"

I shook my head.

"They said their lot in life is this. They pound all day, you know, the tuo. And then they get pounded all night. By their husbands." The women were wiping tears of mirth from their eyes with corners of their wrappers. I knew I was supposed to laugh. They wanted me to share the joke. I felt, not like crying, but like striking something or someone. I couldn't decide whether it was the men lounging on their mats in the shade of the tree outside, or the women who accepted and laughed about their own tragedy. I felt like a child, who could not understand or endure the complex ways of the adult world. Their world. Finally, I laughed.

Travel and See. It Pains You Why. Don't Cry, Laugh. Everything By God. Strangers Are Like Children. No Hurry in Life So My Brother Take Time. They wrote these words of wisdom everywhere, on buses, taxis, in chalk on house walls, on bicycles. Africans had so much to teach anyone who was willing, and able to learn. It was just so exhausting, coming to grips with their stoicism which was not apathy, just acceptance. It was also virtually impossible for the traveller to fathom the intricate tribal webs, and hierarchies. Anthropological and historical literature were scarce, or tucked away in European libraries and archives. I spoke none of the local languages, and as a traveller, had little chance to get past more than greetings or market prices with Nigeriens I met.

As I travelled about Niger, I realized that few of the foreigners who ventured into that sandy outback were any better at learning from Africa than I was.

In the north of Niger, not far from the border with Algeria and just before the Sahel turns into full-fledged desert, lies the town of Agadez. It was a favourite resting place for young overland travellers who had just traversed the Sahara, back in those days before Algeria began to seethe with political and religious turmoil and before the Tuaregs throughout the Sahel began stealing vehicles as part of their struggle for ethnic independence and land rights.

The north of Niger was also a place where drought and famine struck often. Karl had official reasons to go there. I, like the overland tourists, was there merely as an observer, a tourist on the look-out for snapshots and stories and mental souvenirs.

There were few expatriates living in Agadez in 1983. This made life very difficult for Ladine.

"Agadez doesn't even have a club," she moaned to me over dinner in her villa. "Of course we can go to Arlit, but we feel so excluded from life there."

Ladine was twenty-eight. She had come out to Niger with her husband Maurice, a forty-eight-year-old engineer who was teaching in the mining school in Agadez. This school fed the uranium mines in Arlit, an hour's drive north, with skilled Nigerien mine workers.

Maurice and Ladine befriended us in the Agadez market and took us home to dinner. They were desperate for company.

Over dinner Ladine assaulted us with a list of complaints that was longer than the five-course menu. She had a swimming pool behind the house, but due to the drought and water shortage, she had been asked to allow people to come and collect water. She had decided instead to drain the pool, which she did into the sandy compound around her house.

"Do you know the ground is so dry the water just disappeared into the sand. Or else it evaporated."

Maurice said wells in the town were going dry. This was the beginnning of the drought which would a year later, strike the continent from the Horn of Africa to the western coast.

"It's so dry here," Ladine continued. "Look at all these wrinkles." She massaged the skin around her eyes. She was plump and attractive, in the ways specific to a French Madame. She had plucked out her eyebrows and painted them back on. Her bleached hair was swept up into a tangled knot on the back of her head.

I said I thought that white people aged rapidly in Africa, but said I didn't think it was affecting her. I mentioned to her that one of the best skin balms in the world came from the Sahel countries. The local women picked the nuts from the "karité" or sheanut tree, and processed them into sheanut butter which could be used for cooking, healing wounds, or protecting and moisturizing skin. I had met a French businessman who exported the sheanut butter to French cosmetic firms. Ladine said she didn't think there was any sheanut butter in the creams she used.

"Oh, I have very good lotions," she said. They did their shopping in the uranium town of Arlit. There was a flight, a jumbo, they said, from France. It came once a week with provisions for the supermarket there. Ladine's cosmetics came from France, by jumbo, via Arlit.

Karl expressed his surprise that there was an airport in Arlit large enough to handle a jumbo jet. We had heard of the uranium mine north of Agadez, but knew little else about it. Maurice and Ladine offered to take us there the next day.

In the morning we set out in Maurice's Peugeot on the "uranium highway" leading to Arlit. We had gone a few kilometres when a tire exploded. There was no spare. There was little traffic on the road, and Ladine and I moved to the shade of a neem tree while Karl and Maurice decided that sooner or later some desert-crossers — with extra tires to sell — would come along.

Ladine had a stack of magazines with her, which we browsed as we waited in the silent heat. "You know *Paris Match*?" she asked, handing me a copy. "It's like your *Time*. It comes out every week with the latest news."

I flipped through the glossy pages, losing myself in the glamorous world of Monaco's royal family, in what must have been another galaxy. It removed me from the unpleasant reality of being stranded out in the desert.

"It's horrid here," Ladine said eventually.

I looked up from the glossy photographs of princesses in silk gowns that exposed milky shoulders and necks encircled by gleaming gold chains.

I was thirsty, and it was difficult to appreciate the special beauty of the faded browns and greens of the Sahelian plain, with its rocky outcrops and sandy valleys, when I so desperately wanted a cold glass of water. Except for the magazines and a suitcase with evening clothes for the Arlit Club, Ladine and Maurice travelled light — no spare tires, no water. Our small water bottle had been emptied very quickly, a half hour earlier.

She looked close to tears and I wanted to distract her, and myself, from our plight. I didn't like to think about what would happen to us if a car didn't happen along soon. I wondered if any of us would survive on foot, if we attempted to walk back to Agadez.

"Have you ever travelled around Niger?" I asked.

"No, whatever for?"

"Well, to see some of the country."

"Of course not."

"Well, what about Niamey? Last time we drove there we passed a Fulani caravan. It was incredible. There were hundreds of camels and the women were singing as they travelled. They move by night. You've heard them singing? It's almost like, well, yodelling..."

"We don't drive to Niamey," she said. "Maurice only gets four weeks of holiday a year and we fly from Agadez to Niamey and connect to Paris."

"But you've been here for six years? You've never once driven..."

"No. It's hot and there's nothing to see. Just desert. Look." She motioned with a soft, white hand that made her seem so vulnerable I felt like crying, not just for her, but for all of us who had landed in that country where we understood nothing.

We sat in silence for a few moments, until the sound of a vehicle became audible. It was a Peugeot full of French car-sellers, young people who drove vehicles stacked with sellable odds and ends across the desert to auction off in West Africa. They had six spare tires on the roof. I looked skyward to give thanks. The pale blue dome of desert sky suddenly looked almost benevolent.

At the gates to Arlit, Maurice showed his security pass. He argued with the guards that we, as his invited guests, were permitted to visit the mining town. He was upset by their "insolence," and threatened to report them. They sullenly lifted the gate and we entered into the treed oasis of Arlit. The airport, I noticed, was beyond the trees, surrounded by French tanks, Nigerien soldiers and barbed wire.

In Arlit, two French mining firms had built two cities. Each had established its own residential area with smart and comfortable houses, paved winding roads with sidewalks and fire hydrants. Ladine told me how joint efforts had been made to set up a Recreation Centre, a cinema and an equestrian club.

"At first things went well. There were lots of parties and activities and riding competitions. But last year, it was terrible. I don't know who started it really, but I think it started in the equestrian club. Then at the Christmas party in the Club there was a horrible fight, and people from the two firms started throwing each other into the pool. There were some injuries. Now the two are completely split. People in the two firms don't speak to each other. We each have our own equestrian clubs and recreation centres."

Ladine and I were in a large parking lot in front of the supermarket. "The trouble is, they all share this same shopping centre. It's okay, though. There hasn't been any fighting. They shop together but they don't socialize with each other."

I followed her into the frigid interior of the supermarket where soft rock music mollifed shoppers as they wheeled their carts up and down the aisles, picking up Camembert and Cognac and other delicacies for which the French are famous. A small fat girl in red frills, red hair ribbons and red shoes was making a fuss about a life-sized doll her mother emphatically did not want to buy.

Ladine paid for some cans of pâté and bottles of shampoo, and we left. Behind us, the little girl in red was heading towards the check-out counter with the doll. Her mother looked defeated and very pale.

"The disco was another story," she said, as we drove back down the curving streets to the Somaïr Club, where the men had stayed to slake their thirst. "They used to have a disco here. It was nice. The firm paid for it because they know that life is hard out here. But then the Nigerien staff started coming. Membership was supposed to be limited to French staff. At first the Manager just threw the Nigeriens out. But then some of them started saying they wanted to be members, and the Nigerien government sent a letter saying they had to open the disco up to everyone. You know what they did?"

I shook my head.

"They closed it down. They decided if the Nigeriens wanted to have a disco they could build their own. We wouldn't ask to come to theirs, so why did they want to come to ours? They just wanted to make trouble, that was all."

"Now there's no disco at all?"

"That's it."

"What do people do for entertainment?"

"There's the cinema and there are dinners and parties and dances. It's just a shame that Maurice has to work in Agadez. It wouldn't be so bad if we lived here."

That evening, after the manager of the Somaïr Club had given us permission to eat there, we joined a large table of people for a buffet-style dinner beside the pool. The food, drink and ambience were French; the music coming from the sound system was British. *"Sweet dreams are made of this. Who am I to disagree?"*

A teenage boy asked me to translate the words to the Eurhythmics song. I struggled to find the translation for "sweet dreams."

After dinner we were to move to the Club's outdoor cinema, to watch a film called *Pour La Peau d'un Flic*, starring Alain Delon. I had read a little about him that morning in *Paris Match*, as we sat under a tree waiting to be rescued. Ladine said she adored Alain Delon's police films, "adored Alain."

We assembled in our seats at curtain time. A light breeze was blowing in from the north. It was the lovely cool evening air of the Sahara. I studied the stars in the blackness overhead — with refrains of the Eurythmics song still weaving pictures in my head, savoured the whispering breeze on my parched skin, and remained for a time, blissfully unaware that something was amiss.

The cinema was almost full. Mothers spread blankets over their children's legs, and tried to still their whining and squirming. A half hour had already passed, and the film had not yet begun. The French audience began to murmur, then to curse and shout, demanding the film start. It was a belligerent tone, one that often surfaced in expatriates when they felt their rights had been infringed on, and by, Africa.

The timid projectionist, a young French man, walked to the front of the cinema and cleared his throat. He explained that according to Niger censor laws, the film was restricted to those thirteen and over. The place was crawling with children who, he said, would have to leave.

He fled to the back to escape the insults being hurled his way. No one moved. We waited another fifteen minutes. Then a Nigerien policeman, slim and proud and neat in his uniform, strode to the small stage at the front.

Very politely and firmly, he repeated what the projectionist had just said, adding, "I am sure that in France you would not break your own censor laws, nor permit an African to do so. Therefore, I implore those of you with children to take them home, so the film may begin."

An older French man, a retired army captain and a veteran of Africa, stood up to back the Nigerien policeman. "We are in Niger and not France," he said. "We must obey Nigerien law. All those under the age of thirteen must leave."

As though on cue, the French around us got up and filed out muttering profanities. In the end it was the retired army captain, Ladine, Maurice, Karl and I who stayed to watch the film. Ladine and Maurice, as indignant as the rest of the departed audience, stayed purely out of politeness to us, their guests. They had, they said, promised us a bit of civilization by bringing us to Arlit.

Ladine and Maurice seemed relieved to deposit us at our hotel back in Agadez. The trip to Arlit had depressed them. We had perhaps, asked too many questions about where the uranium was going (to Libya for the most part, said Maurice reluctantly), about the effects of the radioactive yellow slag heaps from the mine which were exposed to the blowing winds, about the inexplicable rivalry between the French mining firms.

They left us at the Hotel Aïr. This was a landmark hotel across the road from one of the region's most famous and most photographed mosques. It was also the point of arrival for desert-crossers. Agadez was a wonderful town to welcome them. It was not unusual to come across traditional wrestlers, Fulani men in indigo tunics flanked by women with magnificent arrangements of earrings and coins worn like crowns in intricately braided hair, performing on sandy roads. Most of the traffic in the narrow paths formed by mud walls of houses was camel, not vehicular.

A walk through the town was like a trip into a world I had thought had already disappeared into the dusts of time or Hollywood studios. I was enchanted, and in such a mood returned to the Hotel in the evening to find it had been taken over by a truckload of overland tourists with filthy shorts and matted hair and decked out like Christmas trees in ornaments, trinkets and bits of "juju," or talismans they had collected in the course of their travels through Africa. A dozen fleshy young English women sat with their bared legs draped over the walls of the hotel balcony above us. Oblivious to the local taboos on bared knees and legs, they were working on their tans. I thought they had no right to be there, then asked myself why. Which of us belonged there, had a right to be there? Karl was there to offer money and technical assistance which may or may not have been of use, but the rest of us? We were there to take, we offered nothing in exchange for exotic memories. We spawned beggars and left them with their hands outstretched after we left.

A red Range Rover was parked in front of the hotel, and a British couple were busy auctioning off the contents to passers-by who seemed eager to buy everything but who were short of cash. We stopped to watch, and met George and Melissa. They were, they told us, about to set out from Agadez to cross the desert, to return to England after three years in Nigeria. George had been working for an Italian steel firm in Lagos.

Melissa was distraught, terrified of the trip through the Sahara. She had decided at the last minute that the Range Rover was too heavily weighted down with their personal belongings; hence the spontaneous roadside flea market. She needled me to buy her curling iron and electric rollers, a wide range of teas approved by Her Majesty and a vacuum cleaner that had been a wedding gift.

They were a sweet pair, still deeply and openly in love with each other, and I imagined they would never leave the comforts of home and British telly again. Over dinner in the Hotel Aïr, Melissa moaned about the effect of the dryness on her hair, the outbreak of spots on her face which she attributed to the stress of the trip home, and she periodically scented the evening air with a bottle of Opium she kept in her handbag and used to douse her neck and drown the smell of Africa, which she said "simply stinks."

She was busy imagining the horrors of traversing the desert; she had already decided they were going to get stuck and die there. Karl assured her that there was a steady stream of traffic on the 700-kilometre stretch of sand in Algeria, and that they would even find markers to indicate the buried road. George repeated each of these statements to her in gentle tones.

"You'll be home in two weeks," Karl said.

The use of the word "home" set her off. Tears poured down her cheeks.

"I'm so homesick. You must really come and visit us in England," she sobbed. "My father has a lovely farm, and George collects motorcycles. Every year we go to New Forest, it's gorgeous there. You know, cobblestones and such nice shops. There's one place I always went every time my mother took me to the dentist, called the Pooh Shop. It's just full of teddy bears. Thousands and thousands of teddies. You really must go to New Forest when you go to England."

She said they were going to buy a house, and I wondered how the poor woman had been persuaded by her husband to take on the Sahara crossing, or even the job in the city of Lagos, about which everyone seemed to have only bad things to say.

"How *was* Lagos?" I asked.

"Terrible," she said, shaking her head. "Simply awful. I once saw a thief killed with the necklace. You know, they put a tire over his head and then poured petrol on it and set him alight."

"I thought that was something they did more in South Africa."

"Oh no, it was invented in Nigeria," George said. "Everything that's horrible was invented in Nigeria."

"Remember Lottie?" Melissa asked George. She turned to us. "There was a beggar who lived across the street from us, under a tree. I called her Lottie Lulu. I used to watch her out my window. One day I gave her some bread to eat, and she didn't eat it. She took it and tried to feed this man, another beggar, stark naked, who was sitting under a tree nearby. The man wouldn't eat and Lottie kept trying to put the bread in his mouth and she was talking to him. And then we realized he was *dead*. He had been dead for hours!"

Melissa's hands shook as she tried to fork chips into her mouth.

As night settled over the balcony of the hotel, and the red sphere of the sun sank behind the spiked minaret of the Agadez mosque, George took Melissa off to bed and another couple joined our table. They too were British. Kenneth was a man in his mid-fifties and Dave was his slender young companion. They had been trying for a week to arrange a ten-day camel trek into the Aïr, a fantastic region of rocky outcrops and sand dunes north of Agadez.

"Unfortunately, there are all sorts of regulations," said Dave. "Foreigners must take a Tuareg guide and the guides want £1,000 for the trek. We can't afford that."

"It's probably a good idea to have a guide. It's easy to get lost in the Aïr," Karl said.

"But don't you see? That would spoil our whole experience. We want to be alone with the Sahara."

"And with each other," said Kenneth, casting Dave an affectionate glance.

Kenneth was a sailor who had placed second, he said, in a trans-Atlantic race. He also organized motocross races on the Isle of Man. This journey on camel into the Aïr, was to discover more about waves and wave motion from the shapes of the sand dunes. This, he said, would enable him to design a new sailboat. He was soft-spoken and thoughtful and he had his own clear reasons for being there.

Dave was effusive about his afternoon in a Fulani camp, where he was invited to drink tea with the men and given the large straw hat he was still wearing at the dinner table. He showed us the four leather talismans he had bought from the men, each harbouring a small leather packet of "gri-gri," or juju. He deplored the overland tourists, the "heavy young women with their fat legs and lack of sensitivity," who were sharing the hotel balcony restaurant with us. "They're obscene," he said. "I don't like to intrude on the people here. It's very difficult. I love to take photographs but I hate to be seen with a camera. Kenneth and I have such beautiful memories here, though. It will be so nice to be able to recall them."

I told him I wrote things down, to be able to remember them and he said he did that too. I wonder, now, what he wrote about the bizarre travellers he met in Niger, about the hospitable nomads who offered him tea and company, in exchange for...what?

Nothing at all, I thought; none of us had anything to offer those desert dwellers to whom we must have looked like so many passing ghosts.

## *Chapter 5*

# The evil that men do

The best-selling beer in Niger was brewed in Maradi, a town on the Niger–Nigeria border about 300 kilometres from Zinder. If he were passing, Karl would drop into the brewery to visit Günter, the German brew master, with whom he had struck an acquaintance before I arrived in Niger. After Günter heard Karl had married, he insisted we come for a visit.

He was a gregarious man, eager to show us his small kingdom. He had his own kind of private club on the compound, which housed a swimming pool and tennis court. The tennis court was being paved gratis by the German construction firm that had won the contract to build a new stretch of highway linking Maradi and Zinder. The German firm had given the Nigerien minister a new car when they tendered their bid for the road, then added a VCR and managed to outbid the French firm which had contributed only a car.

Each evening Günter hosted a large number of sun-burnt and dehydrated Germans who spent their days roaring about on the dusty road, raging at their Nigerien crew, being raged at by the merciless sun.

He took us through the brewery, inviting us to taste his brew at each stop. Karl took advantage of this opportunity to inquire about the strong and unpleasant taste the beer had had in recent weeks.

"It's a chemical taste," Karl complained. "In fact, you can smell it before you even taste it. Like pesticide."

The brew master chortled, but didn't offer us any explanation until later, after he had lured us into his villa and was drowning us with fresh beer which the "boys" from the brewery were bringing in by the case.

"This beer is good," Karl said. "But what about the beer we get in Zinder?" Günter laughed. "So you want me to tell you that story, do you?"

We nodded.

"About a month ago," Günter began, "we had a little mishap here at the brewery. It was a Friday night, and I had closed up my office over there and come home. Sometime during the evening one of the boys came over to tell me that there had been an accident. Someone opened the wrong valve. They had poured a whole tank of cleaning fluid, the one we use to clean out the pipes and tanks, into about 50,000 litres of beer. They had managed to poison the whole week's production. I called our office in Dakar, to tell them I would have to get rid of it. They told me I'd have to call head office in Paris. So I did. Paris told me to start diluting the bad stock with fresh beer. I told them to go to hell, and they told me to go to hell, and I said I'm already in hell. But in the end, I had to do what they said. They're the boss. The French." He shook his head and laughed some more.

"I've been drinking whisky for the past month," he said. "Not one drop of beer. The Africans don't even notice."

More people arrived then and Günter launched into more of his stories, a repertoire that spanned twenty years in Africa. He began with the swimming races he said he had had against Uganda's former Head of State, Idi Amin, seventeen years earlier. Amin laid down the rules: each contestant had to swim with a pistol raised in one hand. Günter said he had, of course, allowed Idi Amin to win. He said he himself had always rather liked Alhaji Amin, but still, he wasn't the sort of man whom you'd want to outdo in the swimming pool, especially when contestants were holding pistols as Amin had stipulated. He said he had known Amin in his early days before the slaughters began, and he speculated that perhaps Amin's brain had been addled later by the very beer his brewery was producing in Uganda.

He said that for years in Uganda consumers of one of his brands of beer had been complaining of headaches. He usually advised them to reduce the quantities they consumed, assuming that the headaches were simple hangovers.

Several years later, Günter decided to run some tests to see whether in fact there was something about the beer that was not quite right. "I tested everything. The water, the chemicals, the ingredients. You know what it was? The carbon dioxide we were importing from Zaire wasn't carbon dioxide at all, but carbon monoxide. For seventeen years the people of Uganda were drinking carbon monoxide in their beer."

That was the prelude to an evening of debauchery in which Günter and his guests blearily watched blurry porno videos made, I gathered from the accents and the outfits, in the southern USA.

Up to then, the only experience we'd had with the cinema in Africa was in Zinder. The favourite films there were Indian romances with discordant and overpowering string music and love stories between Hindu heroes and plump, doll-like women, or Kung-Fu and pre-Rambo war movies made in Hong Kong, I imagine, especially for the undiscerning and enthusiastic audiences in out-of-the-way spots like Zinder.

We usually had balcony seats in the back of the open-air theatres. It was more pleasant up there. The air was fresher than down below, where mainstream movie-goers urinated indiscriminately, and where in the heat of the Bruce Lee battle, some of the younger members of the audience were prone to identify too closely with the karate-choppers on the screen and often started their own brawls. It didn't seem to matter to the audiences that four or five films were spliced together, with mismatching soundtracks and the volume was always so high that it was impossible to tell the difference between karate grunts and screams, and actual words.

The projectionists were good-natured and responsive to the mood of the audience. They rolled film much like a disk jockey spins records, on request. If the young men down below began calling for a replay, they would oblige. In one Hindu film a lovely and very well-endowed temptress finally submitted to the pleas of her lover, who was kneeling on the floor beside her bed. Hindu films were never explicit. Such a romantic climax as this one was handled with the utmost discretion, unlike the explicit American pornography the brew master showed us. The woman was shown slowly undoing the buttons on her pink blouse, while the music sent the young men in the audience, and the hero, into a frenzy of lust. There was a split second of blurry pale flesh as she started to peel off the pink satin blouse, then the screen went blank, the music peaked, and then cut to the next scene — the morning after, completely clothed. The audience hooted, and roared for a replay. The scene was replayed. Once again, the screen went blank at the moment of truth. The crowd demanded to see it again and again. After four re-runs they were satisfied that there was no chance of seeing more than just that fleeting glimpse of womanly flesh, and the film continued.

With the arrival of home videos, and the new hero of the African screen — Sylvester Stallone — some of the charm has gone out of the world of cinema in Africa. The larger cinemas are giving way to the small, individual household video theatres, popping up everywhere in villages, where generators are kept going for such essentials as videos but not for, say, the local health clinic, and in towns where they vie with lottery stands for supremacy on each corner. Hi-brow film buffs, those who want a little art mixed in with action, must have their own home video. Those who might be seeking a film made in Africa, should make their way to Ouagadougou for the Pan-African Festival of Cinematography, or to Europe.

Pornography, in the strict sexual sense, was still virtually unknown in West Africa, at least not in places where expatriates such as the brew master in Maradi, had not laid their contaminating spoor.

Maradi had more than just the brewery. It also had two Lebanese restaurants. One was a respectable establishment which observed the rules of the restaurant trade — with deference to good taste in decor and staffing. For this it charged an arm and a leg for a meal.

The other could have served up those arms and legs. Karl said he liked this place; he said the food was good. The restaurant was nestled in a back alley, between high mud walls in the shade of leafy neem trees. From the outside, it looked okay.

The first room was populated with young, sallow members of the proprietress's family, each of whom would have tipped the scales over, at three or four hundred pounds. They were devouring meat as we entered, seated around a large table. In the centre of the table was a metal cash box, around which were scattered papers and cigarette packages and discarded chunks of gristle and bone.

This room was not for the public. We moved deeper into the dark, gloomy catacombs that made up the establishment. There were three of these. I followed Karl past furnace-like fireplaces that took up entire walls. The stone walls were black with soot, and orange embers licked at open-mouthed sheep heads and legs and flanks, which were sizzling — hair and all — over enormous braziers. The sheep looked as surprised as I felt to have wound up there.

A hairy leg of lamb was sizzling over flames, while a young and extremely thin boy, not Lebanese, rolled a piece of red hot iron over the leg. The hair on the haunch vaporized with a crackling sound.

"Boy it stinks," I mouthed to Karl. "Why don't they take the hair off before they cook it?"

"The hair burns off," he said in that terse way he had when he was hungry and I was asking a childish "why" question that defied response. In fact both of us were hungry and irritable when we arrived at the restaurant; by now I was merely irritable.

The obese proprietress was slouched on a solid chair beside one of her fires. She was wearing a thin flowered frock that stuck to her bulk. It was without sleeves, the kind my grandmothers always termed a "house dress." Juices poured from her body as liberally as they did from the grilling meat. She was tending slabs of mutton, picking them up with bare hands and turning them from time to time, using a paintbrush to lubricate them with oil from a bucket on the floor.

"Karl, what kind of place is this?"

He moved on as though he hadn't heard me and I trotted after him.

"This isn't a restaurant," I muttered. "This is a sideshow of horrors, *hell on earth*, or something. I'm not eating here."

"The food is good," he said. "Really it is." One of Karl's intentions, stated shortly after my arrival, was to show me his version of African "reality" so that I might dispense with my naive touristic inclinations as quickly as possible. By now, I realized he was fascinated by the darker corners of the world, not just in Niger but everywhere he travelled. This meant that many of my first impressions of Africa were skewed towards the bizarre and unadorned African underworld. He, I believe, actually enjoyed it. After all of that, almost everything else I would encounter in Africa would look wonderfully normal and right-side up.

I blinked when we arrived in a bright room, with tables and chairs and cheery plastic table cloths advertising Canada Dry.

It seemed we had passed clear through the cavernous underworld, and come out on the other side of the Hades. Here was an open-air patio, daylight and fresh — albeit hot — air.

We took a table and waited for service. The menu lying on the table offered omelette, petits pois, bistek and grillades.

Behind us a man in a ragged shirt untucked over loose flapping pants, was attacking the near-naked white women inside the pinball machine with the word "Playboy" written across the top. The women behind the glass pouted back at him with thick red lips. Vulture-shaped phantom jets were painted in black on the red sides of the machine, and the man ground his pelvis against the front while he man-handled the levers that sent balls shooting up at the female targets. The machine chimed and beeped and whooped as the score mounted and flashed in red digits at the top.

Outside, in a sort of backyard, a band was striking up discordant tunes, doing some much-needed practising. The drummer was wearing glasses without any lenses, and beating with gusto on a single base drum. Red electric guitars were twanging through the feedback.

The top half of the walls had been painted a deep sea blue, the bottom half was blood red and the floor was raw concrete. A local artist whose name I could not decipher, had painted murals over the blue paint: a village scene of African huts and palm trees. The perspective was off, but the effect was somehow soothing. A white-faced virgin Mary, her head covered by a blue shawl, was painted over the door. In one corner a bored woman manned the bar. Mobil insecticide and bottles of exotically coloured French liqueurs lined the shelf over her head.

A towering teenager appeared at the door. From his appearance I took him to be a son of the great mound of flesh who ran the restaurant. He stood there filling the door, blocking out the daylight for a few minutes, staring down the meek clientele inside. He didn't seem interested in taking our order. His

eyebrows grew together over slit-eyes, encased in their own pads
of flesh. His nose was twitching, as though he were smelling
something unpleasant and foreign to him. Fresh air, perhaps.

"Fee fi fo fum," I thought.

I was distracted by a waif of a girl who had been hiding
underneath the next table. She reminded me in some ways of the
children featured in save-the-children posters; she was ragged,
barefoot, and visibly malnourished. But such a face would never
be used to try to elicit sympathy. Her teeth grew straight out of
her head, pushing her lips into a grimace. She wore a thin pink
blouse printed with rosebuds, a black brassiere over tiny new
breasts underneath. Her eyes were half closed in an alcoholic
stupor. She gazed at us, then spread her mouth into a silly grin.

She was holding a brown change-purse, the kind with two
interlocking baubles which snap together each time it is opened
or closed. She snapped it open and shut, the way a baby might
play with a rattle. She made me uncomfortable and I wanted her
to leave.

I reached for my own bag, that lay at my feet on the floor,
intending to offer her a hundred francs, wondering if she would
just drink it. When I handed it to her she grinned at Karl and said,
in slurred and childish French, "Come, we will work now." She
wiggled her bony pelvis. Karl told her no, she should go and buy
some food to eat.

She stayed there weaving and grimacing at him. The boy who
had been darkening the entrance, standing underneath the
demure visage of the Virgin Mary, lunged forward with a roar.

My eyes widened, and I was only partly aware of the girl as
she darted under our table, across the floor of the dining room,
out onto the patio, and somehow, went over the ten-foot wall
which separated us from the rest of the world. Out of the corner
of my eye, it looked as though she flew.

The waiter then turned on us and Karl ordered a plate of peas
and steak for each of us. The vestiges of appetite I still had, had
taken wing with the girl. I suffered through the meal in sulky
silence.

People in border towns like Maradi and Zinder often scooted
across the border to Nigeria for a weekend of shopping in the
city of Kano. There were great bargains to be had at that time of
the roaring black market in Nigerian nairas. Kano had always

been a major trading centre for trans-Saharan caravans. It had once been a major slave-trading centre in the heart of the great Hausa Kingdom. In 1983, they were no longer trading slaves in Kano, but they were trading everything else.

The wife of another German development worker who had recently got married in Zinder, invited me to go to Kano with her on the back of her motorcycle. I wanted very much to go to an English-speaking country; in fact I wanted to go anywhere at all. Margret inspired confidence. She had travelled throughout West Africa alone on her motorcycle and did not share most of my fears and guilt about what she saw. Nor was she intent, as was Karl, on dragging me into squalid restaurants just to show me the terrifying sights.

I was happy to tag along, and watched with awe and a guilty conscience as she charmed her way through a dozen border controls, flirting with drunken border guards and customs officials, her panties full of currencies that were illegal, in amounts that were punishable. We passed almost every vehicle in sight on the super highway into Kano. I scribbled down the slogans written on the backs of trucks on the road: "Fear Woman" and "The Evil That Men Do."

In Kano we had to shield ourselves from the barrage of the roadside hawkers who bombarded us with their wares as we paused in the congestion on the streets. I made lists of what was for sale: clocks, toothpaste, lamps, televisions, dashboard decorations, sweaty white bread, chairs, ladders, cassettes, car stereos, standing fans, video cassettes, cameras, belts, plastic dishes, superglue, porcelain dishes, silverware, bouquets of plastic flowers, even a sink or two. And all of this in the traffic jams of Kano.

Traffic in Kano — a city estimated then to have eight million inhabitants because of vastly inflated census figures meant to offset the imbalance of south versus north in Nigeria — was the worst I had encountered in my life, and that included Mexico City. But superlatives were beginning to lose their meaning.

There were cars, cars, cars, plus cows, cows, cows, compounded by hawkers and beggars. There were traffic lights and street lights, but during my short visit in 1983, these were only functioning for about one hour a day. The power company in Nigeria (local people called it "The God of Darkness") turned on the power at around noon each day. Possibly because every light and air conditioner switch in the city was left permanently in the optimistic "on" position just in case of electricity, the power company could not keep up with the demand, and at about 1 P.M., the power would go off again.

Margret said Kano had a Lebanese Club with a generator and good food. We went there. The first thing that greeted us in the pleasant indoor-outdoor gardens was a Volkswagen beetle — a raffle prize. We made our way around it, and sat down. We had not even received our menus when we were joined by a mob of young Lebanese men who appeared to have gone through puberty some time that afternoon. One of them was old enough to have a few sparse hairs dangling sorrowfully from his chin. The rest were late teen wonders. They invited us for dinner.

We didn't refuse. They were enthusiastic and pleased to have secured themselves company for dinner, and it *was* their club. After dinner, they wanted to take us for a ride around Kano. They had whittled down their own numbers to make an even match. This should have been a hint of what was to come, but we ignored it.

Out in the parking lot, a discussion ensued about which of their cars we should use. There was a Mercedes, a BMW and a white Alpha Romeo to choose from. They agreed eventually on the white Alpha Romeo, which we learned was new that day. Maybe it was a part of their puberty rite.

The moment the engine was started, I knew we had made a mistake. We tore out of the parking lot, around a traffic circle scattering cows and donkeys, and straight down a boulevard. The Saudi Airlines billboard at the end of the road advertised twice weekly flights from Kano to Jeddah, next door to Mecca. It welcomed pilgrims to "The Holy Land."

The two boys in front recounted the mythological tale about one such Hajj flight to Mecca, a favourite among expatriates, which had the plane crashing when one of the peasant passengers began to cook his tea over an open fire in the washroom. The date, location and specifics of this legendary piece of African folly, were never specified.

They took us past a large dreary factory for "sweets," which the driver said belonged to his father. There was no light in the city, and we were screaming through blackened streets in the same way I picture Cruise missiles heading for their target.

Margret and I dropped low in the back seat, and struggled to retrieve seat belts from underneath the rear seat. Our Lebanese friends in front seemed pleased that they were impressing us.

"We're going 160 kilometres an hour," I said to Margret.

"I know," she said. "Scheiß."

Then the driver turned out the headlights, for fun.

"Hey, that's enough," I shouted. "Turn them back on. This is dangerous."

"Don't worry," he yelled from the front seat. "We do it all the time."

A few minutes later we pulled up in cloud of dust in front of a deserted villa. "This is our house," said the driver, leaping out and coming around to the back of the car, where we were still cowering and recovering our breath. "I mean, it's the house my father gave us. We're going to get some furniture. It's more or less empty now, but we've got a sound system."

They did indeed have a sound system, with flashing coloured lights that switched on and off in time to the thundering disco beat emanating from a pair of floor to ceiling speakers. There were no chairs, so we sat on the floor while Aretha Franklin shouted for us to "Jump To It." They wanted to dance with us.

"I have a terrible headache," I said, truthfully.

"Let's get out of here," Margret said, in German.

She made up some stories about her husband waiting for her in the Central Hotel in the "Cock Tail Lounge." They were very downcast as they drove us there, two lost boys living out their lives of wealth and luxury, wanting for nothing except perhaps friends and a feeling that they belonged.

Margret wanted to book a flight from Europe for her mother-in-law. The next day we made a tour of airline offices. With the unofficial exchange rate for the naira, flying in and out of Nigeria was extraordinarily cheap in those days. The unofficial rate could be had from young money-changers on any corner or border, at any time. It was hard work to change money at the official — and less attractive — rate, in a bank where one had to wait in long queues and heed regular banking hours. There was a difference of about seven to one between the rates.

In one office we had to wait while a very wealthy Nigerian in a splendid blue "bou-bou" robe booked his trip around the world. First class. There was still a lot of oil money floating around Nigeria in those days, and for some Nigerians, like this corpulent man booking his round-the-world trip, no luxury was beyond their means or expectations. When he was told by the agent that the leg of the trip from one European city to Barcelona could not be had first class, he put up an enormous fuss and had the young man phone airlines in Europe to ensure that such a miscarriage of justice be rectified. It turned out there was no first class on the flights between these two cities, as the agent had originally said. In the end, the Big Man simply changed his itinerary — adding a first class flight to London, from which he could board first class to Spain. He swept out of the office, head high, and waited while his driver rushed to open the back door of a spanking new Mercedes.

Karl's contract in Zinder would soon be finished. He had had, he said, enough of the town and the project. He wanted to travel, have a honeymoon, before he decided where to go next.

He was tired of the politics of food aid. Canada was sending wheat that was being stock-piled in areas of the country where people didn't eat wheat, had never seen it before. There were warehouses where the sound of the insects crunching on the wheat could be heard from outside, where the sacks of now-empty wheat kernels were stacked floor to rafter, and Karl had no authority to dispense with the stock. The donor countries provided the grains at no cost to the government, and the government was to sell them at fixed prices in times of shortages, to finance the grain agency. No one would give him permission to dispense with the useless and sometimes toxic grains that had gone mouldy. Local harvests that were being bought up from local farmers had to be stored outside the warehouses, where they were destroyed by unseasonal rains.

There were internal problems too. One of the men entrusted with keeping emergency grain stocks in order had been caught pilfering. When the sacks of grain arrived he opened each one, took out a few kilograms of rice or wheat, and replaced them with gravel. He then sewed the bags back up — he had been trained as a tailor — and stacked them neatly in the warehouse. There was much heated discussion about how he should be punished. Karl thought he should be charged with theft, and tried in a court. His Nigerien colleagues thought he should be suspended, the matter buried and forgotten.

Karl and I spent weeks discussing the paradox of Nigerien law and morality. On one hand, this man, whose foul play might contribute to deaths in the advent of a famine and would certainly contribute to malnutrition and poverty in a family where scarce francs were used to buy a sack of grain, was protected by his colleagues from possible imprisonment which they thought would be "too cruel." On the other hand, if a petty thief were caught stealing as much as a bit of bread in a village, he could be stoned to death by the villagers. This was, and still is, "village justice."

Stealing from the state that consisted of self-appointed leaders and run by officials they appointed, who themselves grew rich or survived by dipping into state coffers, seemed to be acceptable. More analysis of who was stealing from whom, who was guilty and who was the victim, made it all very blurry and impossible to judge. The man was merely suspended, and Karl didn't make any noise when, just two weeks before he was to leave Zinder, the same thief was re-instated.

Karl's boss threw a farewell party for us a week before our departure. He invited a few expatriates and the entire staff of the grain agency in Zinder.

We were seated around small tables in his compound, and each table was filled with slices of bread spread with pâté. He was a devout Muslim, but as a concession to his guests, had provided not only pork spreads but alcohol — lots of it, a table full of Johnny Walker bottles.

These had disappeared within a half hour and our host was extremely apologetic that he had not provided enough drink for the thirsty expatriates. "Not being a drinking man, myself, I had no idea how much you Christians can drink," he said, and laughed. He sent out some of his boys to buy more beer.

The first of two sheep, grilled and juicy, was carried in on an over-sized platter. That was down to bones within minutes. Mahama clapped his hands, summoning his daughters to bring the second sheep. Everyone waited, expectantly. No sheep.

There was a lot of shouting in Hausa, which I could not follow, and a mad rush through the entrance, onto the road. Karl and I followed eventually, when the commotion outside precluded conversation inside.

The crowd was wild, and our host explained to us what had happened. The tailor-cum-storekeeper had been caught trying to start his moped. However, he was very drunk, and had fallen down. The missing grilled sheep and several bottles of whisky had fallen from his robes into the sand. He will go to prison, we were told. At that moment the thief was being clubbed over the head with hefty sticks. I wondered if he would survive long enough to go to prison.

The sheep was irretrievable. It was covered with sand and the children of the neighbourhood were already tearing it to pieces to take home.

Karl's boss couldn't apologize enough for this shameful incident in his house. He thought it would mar our memories of Zinder and of him. Karl tried to convince him that rogues were rogues all over the world, and that such things happened everywhere. He would not believe it.

The last time we saw him, when we went to snap a photograph of his family on our last day in Zinder, he was still mourning about the "terrible people" in his own country as he plied us with gifts to take home to sweeten our memories of Niger.

I left Niger with some bad memories, but they had almost nothing to do with Nigeriens, of whom in the end, I had met precious few.

I left very jaded, aware that many of Africa's perennial problems could be blamed as much on the new African leadership as on the former colonial powers, which I had been led somehow to believe were entirely to blame for the poverty and social ills. Nothing seemed to fit any more. The New World Order which leaders in the developing countries justifiably spoke about at international conferences in padded conference halls was a nice theory, but it would never work without a New Neighbourhood Order in places like Zinder, Kano and almost every town and city where I travelled and lived in West Africa. The old village order, whereby the poor helped the poorer, was alas, untenable in urban areas where workers and traders struggled to make ends meet, and might have to forfeit their own child's schooling or health, to help out unemployed brothers, cousins and distant relatives that comprise the extended family. Some sort of social equality, and equal opportunity for all, were requisites for development. And these two ideals were still a very long way away in West Africa. They required basic changes which no volunteer or outsider dared even mention, let alone tackle.

*Chapter 6*

# Ready for revolution

The journey would take us, Karl said, through several West African countries. He had bought an aging Renault that cruised nicely at eighty kilometres an hour, more if the Harmattan was pushing on our tail.

If that wind stopped for a few minutes, the horizon of muted greens and browns became almost visible through the sandy haze and it was almost possible to tell where the sky ended and the edge of the world began.

The air blowing through the car was so dry it seared my skin. The Tuareg nomads of the desert wrapped themselves up in layers of cotton, which prevent instant dehydration and insulate the body against the cold at night. The only part of the body exposed was around the eyes, and even the eyes were generally protected by mirror sunglasses — called locally "I-see-you-you-don't-see-me."

The noblemen of the desert created an impressive and lasting image with their sunglasses, billowing robes and turbans, which comprised thirty metres of cloth, their daggers and short wave radios clutched to their ears. In 1983, many of them were listening to a pirate station broadcasting in their own language, Tamasheq, from Libya. It urged them to revolt against the governments of Chad, Niger and Mali, heavily under French domination a quarter of a century after independence, something they have done in the past few years.

The Tuaregs were once a great threat to Europeans exploring the Sahara, but I had arrived at a time when they were best known as tenacious and tiresome sellers of leather boxes and daggers to tourists, and as night watchmen, who appeared far more dangerous than they were, and who were used to a nocturnal existence.

Unlike the indigenous people, I was unwisely trying to counter the heat by wearing as little as possible. I wore a flimsy tank top and a light skirt which covered my knees. Knees, in Niger, were taboo. Female students at the lycées, or high schools, obeyed social, rather than school rules, and undertook sports events — even high jumping — with their legs bound together in printed African pagnes.

In Birni 'n Koni, where we stopped for fuel, we met up with a group of overland tourists from France. One of the young women was wearing hot pink hot pants and there were matching streaks of colour in her hair, that matched the long feather earrings dangling from her earlobes. Around her a group of Fulani women had gathered, to giggle and gawk. The Fulani, no less exotic in their fantastic headgear of plaits and strings of silver coins and with their facial paint, posed while the girl photographed them. Then one of the girl's companions, a dusty young man with yellow hair, no shirt and a purple earring dangling onto his left shoulder, took the camera and photographed the exotically dressed French woman embracing the Fulani women. Everyone looked very happy; there was no irony at all.

We had been on the road for several hours and I had finished our supply of cold water. I mentioned this to Karl.

"You shouldn't drink cold water while you're hot and sweating," Karl said, using his voice of reason. "It only makes you sweat more, and it's not good for your stomach."

The image of a Canadian river — ice cold and pure as the driven snow — was forming in my mind and pricking at my tongue. The villages flipped past, each looking much the same. There were brown mud huts clustered together and linked by mud brick walls, and women pounding grain in wooden mortars not much smaller than their houses, while wind whipped the wrappers to shreds. Herders, the young boys who spent their early years counting cattle and sheep in the ruthless heat and scrub, kept flashing us joyous smiles. They appeared not to need any water at all; they drank milk directly from the cow, like calves. What did they have to smile about? They *had* to be suffering.

Trouble was, it looked like I was the only one suffering. I felt twinges in my right side, and put them down to the initial stages of something fatal.

We spent the night in a roadside motel, furnished with colour television and lots of red plush furniture from Nigeria. Only the bedbugs were local. There was no electricity to power the television or the frilly lamps, and the bed was so soft we moved the mattress onto the floor to avoid smothering each other. I was not in a honeymoon mood.

In the morning, with the sun just a glimmer of red in the silver haze on the eastern horizon, we had breakfast at a roadside cafe. There were long wooden tables, covered with plastic oilcloths, set up at the edge of the pavement that was Niger's National Highway. The breakfast menu consisted of a chunk of baguette lathered with orange-tinged margarine from Holland which left a fishy aftertaste, or a king-sized bowl of rice and a leg of guinea fowl drenched in peppery red palm oil.

It was cold, and we sat huddled in our jackets waiting for a cup of the hot coffee that was boiling in a cauldron over a fire.

The proprietor dipped cups into the boiling liquid.

"It looks awfully weak," I said.

"That's not the coffee," Karl replied. "That's the water. They put a little charcoal in it, so they don't have to use so much Nescafé to make it dark."

The two cups of charcoal water were placed on the table and a few grains of Nescafé added. Then the man dropped five sugar cubes into each, and poured in sweetened condensed milk to top up the cup. In the frigid dryness of that desert morning, on the edge of a highway that led from one bleak destination to another, that cup of coffee tasted wonderful.

Karl ordered guinea fowl and rice, I chose bread without margarine. The sun was rising and nearly naked village boys had begun to collect around us, their skin dusted almost white from blowing sand, their skinny arms wrapped around their bony torsos for warmth.

Karl tucked into his guinea fowl, which was coated with fiery "pili pili" pepper that could set my nose running from a hundred metres.

"Delicious," he said, piling the bones onto the plastic plate and passing it back to the proprietor, who took it, and flung the bones and the last bits of rice onto the sand behind the table.

The effect was terrifying. The boys converged on the naked drumstick and residue of Karl's breakfast. There was a maelstrom of arms and legs, grunts and punches and shouts. One child was flat on his back with a bloody nose; another hopping away hugging his knee. The tough ones remained where they were, prepared to struggle to the death for those leg bones.

The cafe owner had ignored the fight until he saw our faces.

"Someone's going to get seriously hurt," Karl said. The owner headed towards the brawl with a stick raised. I heard the "thunks" as it landed, but did not look. There was a horrible feeling in my stomach, which I attributed at first to the coffee.

As we drove away, I realized the unpleasant sensation had become a sharp pain in my right side.

The flat scrub gave way to reddish moonscape as we approached Niamey, and on top of this were perched plucky little villages surrounded by rocks and red gravel.

"How do they survive?" I asked myself, aloud.

"In the rainy season they can grow a little millet here," Karl said. He paused and glanced at me. "They're tough."

It was late afternoon when we reached the capital, and the Terminus Hotel where we were to stay. The hotel is one of a chain that stretched across West Africa from Benin to Abidjan, and was built — prematurely — to serve train passengers on the line that was planned in colonial times to link Cotonou in Benin with Abidjan in the Côte d'Ivoire. The railroad, Regie Abidjan-Niger, like so many great dreams in Africa, fizzled out before it could be realized. The hotels, however, were there and at the service of low-budget travellers.

In spite of the comfortable bed and the gallons of water I swallowed, the pain did not subside. In the morning Karl took me to the hospital for a diagnosis. I was convinced I had contracted hepatitis at last. Karl indicated, with very few words, that he suspected the pain was psychosomatic, a reaction to leaving my safe home in Zinder.

"Nerves," he said. He said he'd been through that his first year, and come out of it. He seemed to think I should go through the same initiation he'd undergone: toughen myself up to the realities. On the way to the hospital all I wanted was a little sympathy. But sympathy, he said, wouldn't help at all. It was part of my problem, he said. The pain grew worse.

Typically, there was immediately a helpful man who welcomed us at the hospital. He led us to a clinic where outpatients were received. I was having trouble walking, and lurched from side to side each time the pain hit. Karl offered me an elbow to lean on as we approached the clinic. There were already over a hundred women sitting there, most of them on the ground as there was bench space for only a dozen in the shade of a single tree.

There were people with bleeding wounds, oozing sores, rasping infants in the final moments of their lives and stoic mothers, sitting with impassive faces, waiting for fate to take its course, as it surely would before a doctor would be available. I had trouble breathing.

Next to the people sitting and lying there that day, I was well-fed, pampered and healthy. If only the pain would stop.

A male nurse appeared from inside to greet us. He asked about "Madame's injury" and said he would take us "immediately" to see the doctor. I looked at Karl, who was looking at the long-suffering patients around us.

"No, look," he said, "she's just got a little pain. I'm sure it will go away. Thanks anyway. These people need the doctor more than she does."

I staggered against him as he escorted me firmly back the way we had come. In the end we went to a private French clinic where the walls were moderately clean and the ratio of doctors to patients much better than the national average of 1 to 55,000.

After a long and thorough examination, the doctor made a reassuring "A-ha" sound and told Karl he would give me an injection and keep me under observation for a few hours.

Nurses wheeled me into a green ward, and Karl took advantage of this to escape "to meet with some friends." I wondered if the doctor went with him, because he too disappeared.

"Do you know what is causing the pain?" I asked the nurse who was preparing the needle.

"No," she said.

"Then what are you injecting?"

"The doctor says."

"But I want to know what I've got. You can't just give me any medicine, without knowing what I've got." I had read my copy of *Where There Is No Doctor* by David Werner, an invaluable publication sponsored by OXFAM for village health workers, which specifically advised against injections when oral medication could be used.

"Voilà," she exclaimed, inserting and removing the needle with a clucking sound that sounded like a champagne cork popping.

"Look, what is that stuff?" I repeated.

"Oh, no problem now," she said, removing a box from the wastepaper basket and handing it to me.

The drug was already taking effect. A warm glow of happiness was spreading peace and goodwill throughout the world. I had to concentrate to focus on the fine print on the side of the green box which had worked this miracle.

Before I was swallowed up by a new and all-encompassing love for mankind, I made out the word "Morphine."

The clock told me that four hours passed before the bliss began to dissipate. Mental images of Niger, which had suffused me with immeasurable joy minutes earlier, began to fade and lose their lustre. My misanthropy and reality were returning. However, the pain was gone and we could continue on our way.

A guard at the Niger–Benin border neglected, after tedious negotiations on everything from our identity and the purpose of our trip into Benin, to stamp our passports. We discovered this the next day, and six hundred kilometres from the border when the hotel receptionist said our passports had not been returned by the police after routine inspection.

In Benin in 1983 words like "democracy" and "elections" were still profanities uttered only at great risk. This was the heyday of ex-President Kerekou's rule and the Cold War which was being played out by the super powers in Africa and "state security" acted like a strait-jacket on almost every aspect of life. Travellers were required to give up passports to hotel receptionists, to be handed over to police. Check-out was when the police decided to come and return the documents.

Nine years earlier, Kerekou had declared Benin a Marxist-Leninist Republic. While this had not brought about the expected prosperity, it had overlaid the country with a tangle of security regulations and bureaucratic obstacles that added intrigue and complications, transforming even the simplest of tasks into exercises requiring infinite amounts of patience, understanding and temper control. We had driven past a giant bronze statue, a monument to the struggle for independence, which depicted a triumphant man holding the broken links of chain in two raised fists. It seemed an ironic statement on the freedom the people of Benin were experiencing, where any political activity could be construed as subversive and result in imprisonment. Almost a decade later, Beninois could finally appreciate that statue; the country was the first in West Africa to oust a long-standing military dictator through the ballot-box.

But back then, when we were struggling to retrieve our passports and allegations were being made about "foreign spies," Kerekou's demise and the dismantling of the security apparatus were not in the foreseeable future. According to the policeman at the desk who was still holding our passports, we had no choice but to retrace our steps, go back to the border a day's drive away, and request the missing stamps. This was final. Yes, we could try and see the police chief, but he was attending a funeral and would not be back until tomorrow, or maybe the next day. The funeral was important, the deputy chief was also there. No, he was sorry, there was nothing he could do for us. We were to blame, after all. We had not ensured that we got the required stamp.

We chose to wait. The next afternoon the police chief showed up, passed our passports to us, and urged us to enjoy ourselves in his country. He saluted and said, "Prêt Pour la Révolution," to which Karl had learned the correct response. "La Lutte Continue." "Ready for the revolution. The struggle continues." These were passwords to safe and easy passage through Benin, and as meaningless to us as they were to the civil servants who were instructed to use them when answering telephones or greeting the public. We spent only one night in Cotonou, Benin's unofficial capital city, before heading east to Togo.

Togo is a narrow strip of a country wedged between Benin on the east and Ghana on the west. Until fairly recently, when political turmoil set in, it was a favourite vacation-land for tourists from Europe and for expatriates from neighbouring countries where amenities and luxury hotels were in short supply.

Togo, under the iron hand of its leader of almost three decades, had made itself very attractive to tourists — with reasonable roads, communications that worked and splendid restaurants and hotels. A solid two-tiered society existed. There were those who could afford the finer things of life, and the ninety-nine per cent who couldn't. President Eyadema had developed his country without disturbing the quaint and picturesque life of the villagers who continued to be among the poorest on the continent, and Togo maintained the dubious distinction of being classed one of the world's "Least Developed Countries."

This iron-fisted peace and stability seemed to appeal to foreign investors and aid donors and tourists, until at last the bubble burst and all hell broke loose in 1991, and is still breaking loose today.

However, in 1983 Eyadema, like Kerekou in Benin, was still firmly in control and tourists flocked to Togo. In the capital, Lomé, tourist brochures displayed in lobbies of luxury hotels promoted fine mountain vistas, waterfalls, national parks with abundant wildlife. But we needed a map. The man in our beachside hotel, a bargain-basement affair with no brochures or maps or even a reception area, told us we would find the tourist office beside Marrox.

We found Marrox easily enough. This German shop and restaurant was in the hands of the Maerz Group from Rosenheim, Germany, which was partly in the hands of the late Franz Joseph Strauss, Bavaria's spiritual and political leader from the 1940s until his death in 1988. It served up Bavarian dishes and beer by the truckload. At the "stammtisch," the German and Togolese clientelle told us that Strauss and General Eyadema were good friends. Strauss came for hunting expeditions in the northern wildlife reserves, and had over the years earned himself the nickname "Idi Alpin" in Togo, which translates poorly into English but refers to an Alpine version of the notorious and disgraced Ugandan leader of years past.

Marrox obtained its beef and pork from a 27,000-hectare ranch leased to the Maerz Group for $4,000 a century. The displaced villagers were not permitted to trespass on the ranch, and were unable to get at rivers that had once been their water supplies, or the fruit trees and fields which had once been their livelihood. The land belonged now to 2,700 head of cattle and 2,300 pigs which supplied Marrox with delectable cuts of meat, to feed people like Karl and me, in the Lomé restaurant.

As we ate, we asked around about the tourist office, and the possibility of a map. A Togolese man suggested we try the "Party House," a clearing house for party documents and information of Togo's only political party and its creator, General Gnassingbe Eyadema.

No map. Instead we acquired souvenirs which revealed much about the country's political geography, and little about the physical landscape and roads. The first souvenir was a Party watch with a band that mimicked the Togolese flag. Every twenty seconds its black face began to brighten, a luminescent green face — General Gnassingbe Eyadema's — appeared and glowed for twenty more seconds, before fading into blackness again. It cost about $10 and was guaranteed, said the Party man, for life. It was made in Switzerland, he said. I keep it in a drawer, and continue to check on it from time to time, wondering if it will stop, never to go again, when the great man falls.

There was also an Asterix-style comic book, printed in Belgium, called *Histoire du Togo, Il Etait un Fois...EYADEMA*, a once-upon-a-time story about Togo's history, which began with the birth in 1936 of the humble, brilliant, hard-working peasant boy belonging to the Kabye tribe, Gnassingbe Eyadema, in a small village in the north of the country. It documented his rise to stardom and fame, via the French army in Southeast Asia, his history-making coup in which he shot and killed his predecessor — a precedent in independent Africa — and his efforts as President for the Republic of Togo.

But, no map, except the one on the first page of the comic history book, which featured Eyadema's birthplace with a red square and a white arrow bigger than the country of Togo.

We were just a block from the seaside, and the picturesque walkway from German colonial rule, before the French inherited the colony after the First World War. I wanted to photograph some fishermen pulling in their nets, under the palm trees, on a beach strewn with dug-out fishing boats. The ocean had had an effect on me, after all those months in Zinder. This was nirvana, this tropical and romantic paradise, and this was our honeymoon.

"Don't go on that beach," Karl said.

"What do you mean? Why not?"

"I'm not going. There aren't many public toilets in Lomé," he said mysteriously, "or private ones either, come to think of it."

"It's the ocean. The tide washes everything away."

"You go ahead," he said, with an annoying grin as he stuck his hands in his pocket and continued down the walkway. I was tired of what I called his negative attitude, which I felt was for the most part unwarranted. He called it simple realism. I told him he had no fantasy left. He said he did, but not when it came to matters of sanitation.

I was madder than the red sun which was melting into its watery horizon. I had gone a few steps, when the smell got past my anger, and I recognized the composition and consistency of the lumps of sand I was kicking up with my flip flops. I eased onto my tiptoes, and moved backwards. Then I turned and ran. My flip flops were coated with the stuff.

Karl was smiling when I threw the flip flops over the white balustrade. He bought me a new blue pair from a woman who had a broad selection of plastic footwear on the platter she carried on her head.

Further down the beach a giant culvert emptied on the beach, about thirty metres from the high water mark. A skull and crossbones had been painted on the concrete abutment which supported this great and smelly pipe, which caused a lake of green effluent to form and to fester on the beach, beyond the reach of the sea's natural flushing system. It struck me as odd that a sewerage pipe would be constructed on the beach, rather than a little offshore where the effluent would be out of sight and mind; certainly that was the way we always did it in eastern Canada. I was told by a German engineer that the pipe had been built before currents in the Bight of Benin began to play havoc with the shoreline.

When we passed, there were a dozen small boys splashing merrily in the sewerage. So there it was, a man-made swimming pool for the local people who could not afford the hotel pools or withstand the crashing surf of the ocean.

I held my nose but could not keep my thoughts in check. To prove to myself that I was not hallucinating, I photographed them and they shouted with glee.

The Ghanaian border marks the eastern boundary of Lomé city limits. A few months before our arrival in Lomé, Nigeria had expelled about three million Ghanaians from its territory, partly because it had been swamped by foreign workers who had gone there to partake of the oil boom, and partly in retaliation for the expulsion of Nigerians from Ghana in the 1960s. Many hundreds of thousands of the refugees had camped out on the strip of waterfront and road that led to the barbed wire of the Ghanaian–Togolese border for weeks while "papers" were processed. Some had died, all had suffered. Ghana had eventually re-absorbed her citizens, and all that was left of that terrible episode when we ventured into that part of town, was the debris — plastic, tins and faeces, which those millions of people had left behind them.

The bars in this section of town, while not as enticing as the ones frequented by Togo's elite and expatriates near the seaside on the other side of town, were full of action. Karl and I had given up our search for a map for the day, and had stopped in a small bar in a back alley for a drink.

We were immediately joined by four men. They had heard us speaking English, they said in their own heavily-accented English.

"Please sit down," Karl said, very clearly and slowly.

"Thank you. You are welcome," they said, very clearly and slowly. "We are from Ghana. You are from England."

We corrected them, got them to promise to speak very slowly and clearly, and they ordered a round of beer. It was growing dark, and a funeral procession rounded the corner. The mourners carried flaming torches, and were shedding bits of their patchy cloth costumes as they danced their way through, following drummers who were setting a frenetic and hypnotizing beat. There was something dreamlike and chimerical about the procession, led by magnificently outfitted fetish priests, set against the backdrop of a red-light, black-market slum.

The drums died in the distance before Anthony, the most boisterous and outspoken of the Ghanaian group at our table, started to speak. He was eager to fill us in on the history of his Ashanti nation, which to him was synonymous with Ghana.

These were the early days of the revolutionary regime of Flight Lieutenant (now retired) Jerry John Rawlings in Ghana, the post-classic years of non-revolution in Togo. Political relations were extremely cool between the two countries, not just for ideological reasons, but also because Rawlings' regime was heavily dominated by people of the Ewe ethnic group that populated the southeast of Ghana and the southwest of Togo, where they were Eyadema's greatest political opponents.

Land borders, barbed wire fences just metres away from us, were officially closed between the two countries. There were always ways of crossing though, Anthony told us. "There are boats and there are green borders." Anthony was a trader. "I do small small business," he said, flourishing a wad of bills the width of Togo, and ordering enough beer to flood it.

"How do you get your wares into Togo from Ghana?" I asked him.

"That's no problem," he laughed, flashing a knowing smile and a handful of gold rings.

In Benin, in a similar setting, I had met a man who declared that he also did "small small" business, which involved trading French perfume, by container load, between Togo and Nigeria.

"Do you sell perfume?" I asked Anthony.

The group laughed. They had been filling our glasses with a strong dark drink, called Awoodoo beer, which combined with the dark close atmosphere in that seaside bar to make my head swim. The muddy ground was soft and slimy and our benches seemed to be sinking. None of our Ghanaian companions was tall, and to see them I had to peer through a forest of tall, green beer bottles. Once in a while, when silence descended as someone performed first aid on the ailing stereo system behind us which intermittently belted out distorted reggae and screeching sounds, I could hear the waves crashing on the beach a block away.

"No, we sell gold. Diamonds. Small small." More laughter.

"I see," I said. "There are still lots of diamonds and gold in Ghana?"

They launched into a discussion on the mineral resources in their country, arguing occasionally in Akan, their own language, over certain points before resolving an issue and returning to English to make their point to us. They spoke of the Ashanti kingdom and the golden stool which had gone missing, said the Ashantis were the best warriors in the world apart from the Germans. They also sat on land filled with gold.

"You have a new leader in Ghana," I offered, tentatively.

"Yes, the Flight Lieutenant," Anthony replied.

"We hear a lot about him," I continued. "He's, well, he sounds like he's quite a revolutionary." In his first coup in 1979, Rawlings' temporary military council had put to death three former heads of state before handing over to an elected civilian government, and then, eighteen months later, staging another coup. Most recently, three judges had been put to death.

"He's making a name for himself. He's not Ashanti, though."

"I see," I said.

"In fact, he shouldn't be Head of State. His mother is Ewe but he doesn't know who his father is. His father is a white man, but no one really knows whether he's Russian or Scottish. How can someone who doesn't know who his father is pretend to be Head of State?"

They then discussed the various rumours about Flight Lieutenant Rawlings' paternity. One said that his father was Scottish but the father had disowned him. Another said his father was Scottish, and had not disowned him so Rawlings was really a Scott, not a Ghanaian. Another said the mother was a prostitute, and Rawlings' father could have been anyone. In the end they all agreed that the man was a "bastard," indeed Rawlings had said so himself in public speeches. Thus, they concluded, he should not be Head of State.

Nine years later, I was living in Ghana just before Rawlings contested the first presidential elections in that country since coming to power in his second coup in 1981. This same question — was Rawlings a Ghanaian and therefore fit to contest the presidential elections — was taken to court by a zealous political opponent. Days before the elections, which Rawlings officially won, the court finally dismissed it saying it had no jurisdiction over the matter. I recalled, so very clearly, that discussion I had overheard in a roadside bar in Lomé — so long ago. Ghanaian politics had not progressed all that far in the interim.

The Hotel Tropicana catered to tourists on package holidays from Switzerland and Germany. Erosion on the West African coast, which had resulted in that beached sewerage pipe, was due partly to the construction of the Akosombo Dam in Ghana in 1965 which altered the Volta River estuary and to the construction of container piers in major ports, and it had already caused two of the Hotel Tropicana's swimming pools and much of the hotel's gardens to be submerged under advancing seas. However the resort still offered tourists a tropical respite from European winters.

It also offered maps of Togo.

Map in hand, one Saturday afternoon we were sitting at the pool-side bar in the hotel when a flight full of Swiss travellers arrived from Zurich. They emerged from the bus, quickly deposited their baggage in their rooms, and moved en masse to the area around the pool — the women were topless, the men pasty and podgy.

One among the group had done a lot of drinking on the airplane. He staggered into the bar, with an over-sized elderly woman on his tail. The man was not only blind drunk, he was also blind. The woman behind him tucked in his shirt and berated him for not having let her change him into one of the new shirts she had bought him for the trip. He ignored her, and downed three mugs of beer in quick succession. "Son," boomed the woman, "how can you behave this way. Your father. Your poor father. How it must hurt him in his grave."

The son appeared to be working on his own kind of oblivion.

"You promised me that when we came out to Africa you would stop this."

Her son ordered another beer.

"You can't just drink our holiday away."

The blind son looked as though he thought he could.

Two days later on our way north, we encountered a blue Hotel Tropicana Volkswagen, crushed and mangled at the turn-off to Fazao National Park. The bus had overshot the turn-off and rolled several times before coming to rest against a tree. Twelve passengers, hotel guests who were making a day's outing to villages and to the park, were killed. The driver ran away, and some of the victims who had not died instantly in the crash, had died in the interval that followed when villagers, anxious to help, had begun dragging the injured persons about wondering what to do with them. By the time the authorities had arrived, it was too late. The bodies were taken back to the Hotel, for repatriation to Switzerland.

I thought about the blind man. Was he still leaning on the bar beside the pool in the hotel with his mother standing behind him reminding him of what a failure he was, reminding of how he had failed his deceased father or had both of them perished in that blue Volkswagen, and gone to join him in his grave?

Sarakawa is the name of Lomé's most luxurious beach-side resort — it was also the name of a historic landmark in *Il Etait un Fois*, the history of Togo. That comic dedicated four pages of cartoons and captions to the plane crash of President Eyadema in Sarakawa; in these, leering white men in cahoots with the evil opposition forces were supposed to have tried to kill or kidnap the president by crashing the DC-3 in which he was a passenger. The pilot and co-pilot had died in the crash. Eyadema was not among the victims and the "masses had begun to weep" when he suddenly appeared proclaiming, "I am again among the living," leaving the clear message that he had returned from the dead by some supernatural forces, in Sarakawa — close to his native village in northern Togo.

Sarakawa had been turned into a shrine to Eyadema's salvation and rebirth.

It was not difficult to locate anything that had to do with the president in the north of the country. The closer we got to Eyadema's native village of Pya, the better the road became. Roadsigns imported from Paris made our long-sought map unnecessary. Just north of Pya, in a barren windswept region of tiny mud and thatch villages, we came across the Niamtougou International Airport, manned by French military officers. This was Eyadema's stronghold, where the Togolese army that was primarily made up of men from Eyadema's ethnic group, were in obvious control. It was also Eyadema's emergency escape route from the country, should the southern opposition ever do the impossible and threaten his life.

In Pya itself, construction had begun on the president's new mausoleum and palace topped by a golden dome, on a hilltop overlooking his quaint native village. The national highway, built before the palace, passed too close to the president's new palace for his own comfort, and we were forced to take a twenty-five kilometre detour over a dusty rutted road, to continue our journey north and then west, to Sarakawa.

A four-lane boulevard led through deserted scrubland to the site, which was marked by those Parisian road signs. We knew we had arrived when the boulevard ended, opening onto a paved parking lot that would have served a North American shopping mall at Christmas rush. In the centre of this deserted and eerie parking lot, stood a statue of President Eyadema, four times larger than life, one arm raised in a Nazi-style salute.

I got out of the car slowly, bewildered by this monument in the middle of nowhere. An oval, multi-storeyed building stood alone and inexplicably on the edge of the pavement. We moved towards it. There was something reminiscent of an ancient temple in Greece or Mexico, in the hollow sound of the place with the dry hot wind whistling about our ears.

Our approach woke a man who was stretched out flat in the shade of the building. He said he was an official guide and he seemed very happy to see us.

"You've come on a quiet day," he said. "Most days I am busy with students. They come by bus, thousands of them, to study this glorious site where our Founder was reborn." He led us into the amphitheatre and we climbed to the second level.

"Voilà," he announced, pointing to the dwarfed and disintegrating wreckage of a DC-3, gleaming in the sun in the centre of the oval. He told the same story as *Il Etait un Fois*, about the evil white men who had plotted to sabotage the airplane and tried to kill President Gnassingbe Eyadema. He paused for dramatic effect. "Our Founder was dead. Then suddenly he emerged, unscathed, from the wreckage."

No, I was not permitted to take any pictures. That would anger the gods who had taken and then returned Eyadema and erected this monument to his rebirth. Karl gave him a huge tip for his efforts and his undying faith in his president.

## Chapter 7

# Avenue of Fortune

Our last stop in Togo was at the Paradise Bar near midday. I asked the man behind the bar what he had in the way of cool drinks. He had only beer. There was a boisterous group of young and beautiful Africans at a neighbouring table, very European in their second-hand European clothes as they behaved like people in a beer commercial anywhere. A loud, crackling stereo system belted out African dance tunes from Zaire. Directly in front of the speakers a drunk and toothless man was dancing. When he turned around I saw that his t-shirt, faded and torn at the shoulders, had the words "I'm an alcoholic. In case of doubt, buy me a beer," written on it in white letters. I guessed that this was mere coincidence — it was unlikely he could read.

There were Christmas lights blinking on and off. I would have given anything for a glass of cold water, but even without it the Paradise still felt like a refuge to me. There were no children shouting at us. "Yobo Yobo," heard at every village, the length of the country. Mobs of children gathered at the roadside as we passed, chanting "Yobo Yobo, bon soir, ça va bien? Merci. Donne moi cent francs." White man, white man, good evening. How are you? Thank you. Give me one hundred francs.

Sometimes they varied the rhyme, leaving off the demand for money and asking "What do you want?" Both refrains bothered me, and went round and round in my mind. I was trying to decide if there was any taunting there, or merely childish enthusiasm, curiosity and opportunism.

I was staring through the open door, at the blind glare of noon outside when the old beggar woman stumbled into the Paradise. She was in colourless rags, and held an enamelled metal bowl in her hand, much like a blind man carries a white cane, or a diviner a doodle bug. It led her straight to us. Her eyes were covered with a milky film, and I glanced down into the empty bowl, which had not seen water for many years. Like her feet, her hands and her face, it was aged and worn. She tilted her head to one side, much as a dog would do when pleading with a temporarily recalcitrant master for a bone. She whimpered. I turned my head, furious that she had evoked another wave of guilt in me.

She mistook that as a definite no, and moved to the next table where the robust and boisterous Togolese men and women were tucking into large bowls of rice, and guzzling beer from large bottles. She held out the bowl. One of the men pushed it away with his beer bottle, then drank long and deep. A woman at the table shouted something in a language I did not understand. The second woman at the table, with upper arms as thick as rump roasts, echoed the shout. The old beggar woman began to shuffle away. But the men called her back. One of them reached for her bowl, and poured in a draught of beer, laughing. The old woman drank, spilling most of the beer down her dress and onto the concrete floor. She held out her bowl for more. This time, all at the table shouted at her. The proprietor moved out from behind the bar. He was tall and attractive in sleek Wrangler jeans and a t-shirt adorned with Bob Marley's face and the words "Black Survival." He was holding a horse whip over his head.

I was sure he had no intention of hitting her, but he lunged towards her feinting with the long whip and the group at the table roared with laughter. The laughter had had no effect on her, but she cowered under the horse whip and scuttled away, and out of the bar. I was disturbed by the small drama I had just watched, mostly because I could have saved her the ridicule if I had given her a coin when she begged for it.

In the car, on the way north, I replayed the events carefully, again and again, wondering why it had bothered me so much. Near the border with Upper Volta, as we moved from one border post to the next dealing with all the tedious formalities of border officials, I admitted that I was much more vulnerable than that hardened and tough old beggar woman who knew, at least, how to survive.

It was almost Christmas. We were deep into the dry season with its Harmattan wind that, for three months a year, covered most of West Africa in a thick haze of sand reminiscent of London fog or Berlin smog. To compound this, most of the sub-region went (and still goes) up in smoke at this time of the year. The fires were lit deliberately, despite laws and warnings from officials. Sedentary villagers blamed nomadic herders who they said burned the bush to get rid of dried grasses and to make way for early green grass to feed livestock. Urban environmentalists and government officials blamed villagers, who were frequently setting the fires to scare up bush rats and other bush meat to supplement their protein-poor diets. Blame was laid everywhere; traditional rulers were begged to persuade their people not to set bushfires, foresters and local councils held anti-bushfire campaigns and called for drastic action, and the bush continued to burn year after year, killing saplings, destroying organic matter needed to prevent erosion and nourish the soil. Remnant populations of wild animals were decimated. United Nations reports have said that bushfires in savannah lands from Congo to the West African coast send such massive amounts of carbon dioxide and methane into the atmosphere that they are a leading cause of global warming.

As we drove north through Togo and crossed over into Upper Volta in 1983, we saw nothing but blackened charred country. In addition to the hot blasts of Harmattan blowing through the car, there were occasional blasts of flames and heat which felt like the furnaces of hell. By the time we reached the White Volta River in the early afternoon, we were both choking, sneezing and sweating, sharing a mutual bad mood which did not auger well for our journey to Ouagadougou, capital of Upper Volta where we were planning to spend Christmas. I had begun to daydream and to blinker myself to the burning countryside out there. I recited *The Night Before Christmas* to make sure I was not hallucinating and that I was still sane and then decided it simply made me doubt my own sanity. I couldn't help imagining overloaded and over-decorated shops in Canada, and people on city sidewalks dressed in holiday style as visions of sugarplums danced in their heads. Then I would wake, look out the window of the car, at the tiny villages, their mud walls and round huts, surrounded by acres of sand where millet would be planted in a few months. I didn't want to be where I was, but I couldn't imagine being in Canada either. Not at Christmas, when so much of the sentiment was so hollow and commercial. My guilt would follow me there too.

We pulled over at a collection of roadside stalls, where rickety stools and tables comprising the market offered half-hearted pairs of onions or a Maggi cube or small piles of peanuts. Apart from that market, a few thatch huts and the almost dried river-bed, the village had a small mud-walled bar which stocked bottles of warm Fanta.

I gulped down two of these before wiping my brow, taking a breath and looking around. We were surrounded as usual, by children, although to my jaded eye, they were barely recognizable as such. Swollen bellies and eyes, bent and twisted knees, a few tatters of brown clothing wrapped and hanging here and there. Village children. It was all I could do not to run screaming from the place.

"What's that on their legs?" I asked Karl.

"Guinea worm."

"What's guinea worm?"

"A parasite. They take in the eggs when they drink infested water, and then the egg grows into a worm over the next nine months and then it migrates to the body's extremities and sores form as it burrows its way out, usually back into a pond or stream, to lay more eggs. I've seen people with seven in one leg."

Well, I had asked.

The children stared blankly at us, and I stared at the sores on their legs and feet.

"What's that?"

"What's what?" Karl grimaced after a gulp of Fanta.

"That sound. Music." The children had lost interest in us and were headed, on the run, across the highway.

A shining white station wagon, speakers on the top blaring static and music and voices simultaneously, screeched to a stop opposite. It was immediately swarmed by the children.

"What is that?" we asked a young and dapper man sitting beside us on the bench. He wore neatly pressed dress slacks, a clean white shirt with the familiar crocodile label over his heart, probably from the "bend and pick" stands of second-hand clothing imported into Africa from Europe and North America to clothe the continent. A brand new Walkman hung from his belt. The headphones were around his neck, like a necklace. Karl had asked him earlier what he was listening to, and he explained that he wasn't listening to anything because he had no batteries, and they were too expensive to buy these days.

"That's the 'Tombola Minute'," he answered. The National Lottery. Scratch and win.

By now the entire roadside village had congregated around the lottery car, and glossy bits of paper, the Lotto tickets — were going like hot-cakes. The lottery logo on the side of the vehicle looked familiar, and I realized it adorned all the traffic signs in the country that warned drivers of bumps in the road. It might have been more useful to advise drivers of smooth stretches; they were fewer.

"How much does it cost?" I asked.

"Cent cinquante CFA," he said.

"One hundred and fifty CFA! But that's a lot of money for these people. They don't see that in a week."

"Oui," he said, getting up and moving slowly towards the vehicle. Adults were starting to arrive from too, coming out of their huts and moving across the highway.

"I can't believe it," I said. "There's nothing to eat, nothing to drink, and they're spending their pennies on a lottery."

"Just like in Germany. Or Canada," Karl said.

We waited long enough to see if there was a winner among the villagers. There wasn't. The lottery vehicle departed again, with its loudspeakers blaring the advent of its coming in another village. I noticed, as we drove away, that the mood in the village seemed to have picked up. People were laughing and slapping each other on the back, making light, apparently, of their collective misfortune. Small white discarded tickets littered the road, as sorry as confetti after a divorce.

Ouagadougou seemed to spring out of nowhere. The capital had no clear reason to exist — there was no river, port, mountain or major geographical landmark to legitimize a city of half a million people. The glass-fronted government buildings, particularly the Ministry of Administration, struck me as ludicrous. The city stretched for about thirty kilometres, as though mud-walled villages and compounds had begun to clone themselves and replicate, and spread. In the centre of town there were some patches of green in front of French restaurants and the old colonial streets — now called Avenues of Liberty or Independence — were lined with enormous mahogany trees. Apart from selling — market produce, trinkets, souvenirs, cheap consumer goods or bundles of second-hand clothing, and two-wheeled vehicles, I wondered what people actually did there. I wondered to what jobs the thousands upon thousands of people on mopeds were heading each morning at seven, and again at three in the afternoon after the official sieste. Ouagadougou's greatest claim to fame seemed to be its nickname "City of Two Wheels."

Almost directly across from the country's largest hospital, Yalgado, we came across a small crowd of people assembled around a victim of an accident. His moped was twisted and broken and still lying in the middle of the road, but he had been dragged onto the shoulder of the road. Someone had put a white scarf over the wounds on his head, and it was bright red with his blood. People seemed to be waiting for someone to take charge, perhaps for the hospital people to come and take him across the road. Two hours later, we passed again. The crowd was smaller, the moped was still there, and so was the victim. Only now his entire body had been covered, with a length of grey cloth. I turned away and tried to think about my parents' house, and the tree they might at that moment be decorating with Christmas lights.

There was a large population of "market lunatics" in Ouagadougou, or "marché foux" as they were called in francophone Africa. They were, people said, insane. Or they had become insane when they were cast out of their homes for any number of social crimes or on spiritual grounds, after which they died a social death. Without family, a person might as well be dead.

I had trouble coping with the picture of these men and women who roamed the streets, in rags, or naked, or ornamented with bits of rubbish they found on the roadside. There was one woman who had collected scraps of cooking pots, hundreds of them, and using twigs and bits of litter, had set fires underneath each of them as though she were cooking for a large family of elves that dwelled somewhere in her brain. There was another man who played with sand, who lived under one tree in front of the central market. He used both hands to heap up a pile of sand between his legs, then took a rounded stone and smashed it down again. He did this all day, and may have continued into the night too — I didn't go out to check.

One man spent his days strolling aimlessly about the market, much as we were. One of his testicles, both of which were fully exposed, hung like a balloon between his legs and reached his knees. The other was only slightly swollen, festering and covered with flies. Perhaps it was being eaten by leprosy, or by yaws, or it was just one of the infections people called "tropical sores." He carried a few items in his hands, a piece of bicycle chain that he was swinging to a rhythm I couldn't hear. We didn't mean to be following him, but he always seemed to appear when we rounded a corner of the market, moving ahead of us, heading often in circles in the labyrinth of that market.

He greeted no one, looked at no one and only broke his stride occasionally to bend down and pick up something from the ground — a broken sandal or a piece of plastic.

I was weak and hungry. I told Karl I was ready to stop "discovering" the market which was crisscrossed with open sewer canals. But he was fascinated by African markets. They said a lot about the economies of the continent which acted, more often than not, as dumping grounds for inferior products from Europe, and as an invention ground for devising new ways of putting rubbish to use, and sale.

The lunatic was just in front of us, and I didn't want to pass him, or come close to that bloated testicle that looked like a skin bag someone had tied to his waist.

We were walking beside a deep concrete gutter, an open and reeking sewer with a virulent green stream of waste, beside which vendors were selling tomatoes and rice to passers-by. The stench was inconceivable, and I glanced at Karl to let him know what I thought of our honeymoon pastimes.

At that moment the market lunatic in front of us suddenly leapt down into the sewer canal, knelt on his hands and knees and began to lap at the semi-liquid in the bottom with his tongue.

My legs buckled, I swam in darkness and I collapsed into Karl's arms. He caught me before my swoon landed me in the gutter with the lunatic, and dragged me towards the nearest restaurant down the street. There I found myself slumped in a chair as I sat up blinking and drank, in one gulp, the Coke in front of me.

Karl began trying to soothe me, saying it was the heat, lack of food, maybe some shock too. He suggested that he was better able to take these things because he had undergone obligatory military service in the German army that had stripped away his illusions about the world, and because he hadn't been raised in a country that coddled its youth. I didn't answer.

Next to our table there was a tall fence, freshly painted in gleaming gold. A large arching gate separated the filth on the outside from a lovely garden and lawn, awash with sprinklers and behind that, a magnificent white-washed villa.

"Who do you suppose lives there?" I said.

Karl squinted at the sign posted on the impressive golden gate. "It says Tombola National," he said.

When we left we paused briefly to read the small print underneath the National Lottery sign. "Avenue de la Fortune," it said — The Avenue of Fortune.

*Chapter 8*

# Sardine war

After a three month interval in Canada and Germany, I was glad to be back in Africa when we landed in Yaounde in 1984, surprised at how glad. Cameroon was much more lush and varied than Niger, and I no longer felt so terribly new and foreign. I was looking forward to two years in Cameroon, providing Karl was able to work something out with the coffee cooperative which was supposed to have requested a volunteer. He was somewhere in the west of the country, trying to find out if there was indeed a job for him there. The Volunteer Service had not done much homework.

I landed in Yaounde, capital of Cameroon, at dusk on April 5, 1984. The attempted coup began about six hours later, about five hundred metres from where I slept.

The persistent whining sound that started at 3 A.M. only partly woke me. Mosquitoes had been buzzing around my head all night, and I had covered my head with the pillow. I slept on until seven. In the bright light of the morning, the whining sound could have been a fire engine.

I moved to the living room and out onto the balcony of the house where I was staying, which belonged to the country representative of the Volunteer Service. There was a thick mob at the railing, staring across a green valley at the presidential palace; there was far too much commotion for that hour. Most people were speaking German. The radio was blasting military music.

My host was huddled beside it, with his head cradled in his hands. On our long trip from the Western Province to Yaounde the day before, he had been complaining of painful swellings in the glands in his neck. His wife had already diagnosed mumps.

"Guten morgen." I looked up to return the greeting to an official of the volunteer service who was on a working visit from Germany.

"You seem very calm," he continued.

I smiled.

"It looks like the putsch has succeeded," he said, in German.

"Mmm," I said.

He stared at me for a couple of moments. "A putsch. Do you not know what a putsch is?" He paused. "A coup d'etat?"

So that was it.

A series of muffled sounds came from the valley below us. It sounded like popcorn in a popper.

"Hear that?" he said. "They're trying to take the palace. Hold on...."

The martial music on the radio suddenly ceased, and the noise in the house died. An angry and tense voice on the radio announced that the coup d'etat had been launched by patriotic forces in the presidency, and had brought to an end the "darkest days" in Cameroon's history. The "traitor," President Paul Biya, had been deposed. Corrupt and foul leaders had to be removed. All telephone and telex lines had been cut. International travel had been stopped. Political parties were banned. The consitution had been suspended. There were papers rattling in the background. It sounded like the announcer was being handed the statements, one by one. His voice was rigid and conjured up pictures of a man with a gun at his head. The music resumed.

I glanced at the palace, shining white in the early morning sunshine. The night before it had been enshrined in an orange glow cast by spotlights which soared into the heavens and appeared to levitate the magnificent white building off its rocky hilltop, so that it seemed to be floating slightly above the earth, and the mortals stuck down there on the ground.

The flag was not flying, meaning Paul Biya, the "deposed" president, was not there, or was there but didn't want to announce it to the public. Twelve hours earlier I had gazed in awe across the valley at the palace and the waterfall that had been cascading under coloured spotlights down over man-made terraces. This morning it had been turned off. There was no one manning the gun turrets spaced at intervals along the palace wall which sealed off the presidential palace from the rest of the city, and the world. Modern medieval were the words that sprang to mind each time I looked at the Swedish architecture in its distinctly African setting. The figure of $60 million had been bandied about the table as the cost of constructing that palace.

A buxom and whey-faced French woman who had draped herself over a pleasant young Cameroonian man introduced herself.

"I'm Jeanne. My husband is also with the Volunteer Service. This is Vance."

We communicated in a mixture of French, English and German — a feat which impressed me until I stopped to recall West Africans I had met who were able to speak a half dozen, or more, African languages on top of a handful of European ones. (They would often dismiss the African languages as not really "counting" if you asked them how many languages they spoke.) Vance had a sister in Berlin, married to a German and he had been hoping to receive permission the day before to leave for West Germany. He said he had tried forging his own exit permit, but it hadn't worked. Now he expected he would have to come up with 100,000 CFA (roughly $270 U.S. at the time) to pay the many officials who would demand a little something extra for making him up a permit to leave Cameroon. He was afraid. He said anything could happen now that the political tension had broken open.

Jeanne said she was working voluntarily as a nurse's aid in a nearby clinic; her flat was large and spacious and her German husband had travelled to Douala. As we stared at the palace, she said I would be welcome to come and stay with her and Vance, to whom she was glued like a Siamese twin.

Grey clouds and thunder added oppressively to a surreal day that needed no props. The air was very still, except for the occasional bursts of machine gun fire.

A bulletin on the radio reminded listeners of the dusk-to-dawn curfew. Then the tired martial music continued. "It won't be nice for you to stay here and wait for your husband. It won't be nice with him coming down with mumps," Jeanne said, nodding toward the director who was shaking his head and moaning about the effects of the coup on the ongoing development projects in the country.

"The volunteer guesthouse has been evacuated," Vance said. "It's right beside a military camp. There's been shooting."

I accepted Jeanne's offer, as did a half-dozen other people, one of whom had a car and thought we should move fast, before soldiers blocked the roads.

As we drove towards town, and Jeanne's apartment, I looked at the Air Canada baggage tag hanging from a broken strap on my suitcase, and felt I had stepped into a new life too far from that country to be real.

The sound of machine-guns firing had become continuous.

Jeanne was one of those gregarious young women who needed gangs of people around her at all times, to entertain her and to be entertained by her when she was in the mood for chatter and laughter. There were eight of us in the third-floor apartment. Sliding glass doors on either side of the large living room were opened, allowing some of the clouds of cigarette smoke out, allowing the sounds of the battle in.

The water went off during the day, raising speculation that the rebel forces had taken the city's water works. There was also speculation on how to eliminate solid wastes from a flat full of guests, with no water in the toilet. The only solution was to keep the door to the lavatory closed, firmly.

Jeanne and Vance disappeared frequently into the master bedroom for little "siestes." The rest of us would escape the poorly sound-proofed apartment, and shuffle like a millipede onto the third-floor balcony that provided the best view of the ongoing war.

The radio announcement that the coup had ended the "darkest days" of Cameroon's history had been premature. The battle raged on below us, in a broad valley of sewers and mud houses. The power had gone off. At dusk the curfew settled over Yaounde, and we were plunged into total darkness, broken only by the jagged flashes from the muzzles of guns. We slept on the wooden floor, using cushions from the sofa to make our beds.

By the next morning the drinking water in Jeanne's water filter had dwindled to two litres. Jeanne and I decided to make a foray into the streets to find some bottled soft drinks. We did some reconnaissance from the balcony first. There were large crowds of bystanders gathered on the roads, inching forward en masse at the sound of a skirmish — there was one going on in front of the radio station — and then the crowd would scatter pell-mell in retreat when soldiers advanced on them, chasing after fugitives.

"They've seen too many movies," someone said. "They don't know how real those guns are." I nodded wisely, before Jeanne and I made our way, giggling and unwisely, down the steep circular staircase which wound its way from her apartment to the enclosed parking area. We could hear shooting from the alley and we scooted out the front, over a wrought iron fence, up a rutted alley to her regular supplier of soft drinks and beer.

The heavy wooden door was closed, but Jeanne — using many words which were not included in any school French classes I had attended — eventually convinced the owner to open it a crack and let us in. This being "war-time," he said, "the prices have gone up." They had increased ten-fold, and there was nothing left but Guiness Stout. He sent us scurrying with a warning and one case of Guiness.

There were soldiers in fatigues charging up the road towards the apartment building. We darted to the right, leaping like caged lizards at the iron fence. Jeanne was over and gone, and I remained hooked by my skirt to a sharp spike. The cotton gave way with a loud tearing sound and a hole which exposed my backside. We sped up the stairwell, laughing and crying, while shots ricocheted back and forth within the parking lot.

In the living room everyone was on their bellies, slithering about the floor. A heavy wooden table, a slice of an enormous tree, had been turned on its side as a shield. We dove to the floor and I began to count the rings as I had been taught in ecology classes years earlier in the Annapolis Valley. It was over two hundred years old when it was felled.

A bullet bounced off the bottom of the balcony; another embedded itself in the plaster on the living room wall. A German doctoral student, who had grown up in Africa the son of a World Bank official, claimed to have seen a dozen similar coups on the continent. He suggested we photograph the bullet, and we did, using a piece of graph paper for scale. He said we would value the photograph in later years. He had seen much worse fighting, though.

BBC was bringing reports from their correspondent in Abidjan. "It is still not clear what is happening in Yaounde, capital of the West African country of Cameroon."

However, according to "western diplomatic sources," it seemed the presidential guard, still loyal to former President Ahidjo, had rebelled against current President Paul Biya. Communications were still cut.

In Jeanne's apartment, people were coming and going during each lull in the fighting on the streets. They brought reports from "Radio Trottoir," the street information service, Africa's most prolific producer of news and rumours. Rumours in West Africa caught and spread like bush fires in the peak of the dry season. Without a reliable and believable press, the people resorted to rumour-mongering. Behind the fire and the smoke, there was often some grain of truth. But one could get burned trying to find it.

Separating fact from fiction, truth from fantasy, the absurd from the mundane in Africa was like an exercise in mathematical theory. Logic and law said it should be fiction or fantasy, too absurd to be possible. But whose logic and whose law?

A lot of rumours came our way in that apartment.

1) The former President Ahidjo, who had stakes in the Moroccan fishing industry, had been sending arms to the Presidential Guard in shipments of sardines. The sardine cans had been filled, not with fish, but with armaments.

2) Ahidjo, living in France since handing over to Biya, was already in the skies, Cameroon-bound, and would be landing in his northern home town of Garoua within minutes, or hours.

3) A plane was underway but it was full of Moroccan mercenaries, and Ahidjo was still sitting in his castle in France, orchestrating the coup from a position of safety.

4) Ahidjo had relinquished power to Paul Biya not because of his desire to be the first African president to hand over power peacefully, but because he had been tricked by a doctor who was (a) French, (b) Moroccan, or (c) bankrolled by Biya, to convince him that he was too old and ill to continue as President. This coup was his comeback.

5) The coup was really an explosion of ethnic, regional and religious hostilities pitting north against south. Biya, a southerner from the French-speaking part of the country, was doling out privileges and positions to his tribesmen, which angered northerners who had formerly received these from Ahidjo.

6) The coup was an explosion of hostilities over oil wealth. The billions of dollars that were being pulled in by Cameroon's fledgling offshore oil industry were in private bank accounts belonging to (a) Ahidjo, (b) Biya, or (c) both of the above.

7) The Presidential Guard, the rebels, were being supported by the French or President Biya and his loyal forces were being supported by the French.

8) President Paul Biya was (a) sitting in his bunker, a bomb shelter carved out of the rock underneath his palace, hoping to save his own skin, or (b) had fled the country, or (c) was already dead.

The main sources of this intelligence were young ladies of the Yaounde streets. They seemed to have received their own intelligence reports from Jeanne's apartment, that there were several young and unattached white men (i.e. men with money) holed up inside, and they made their stilettoed way up and down the stairway to do their own reconnaissance. There was Michel, a slip of a woman under a broad-brimmed straw hat, her curves barely contained by tights spotted like leopard skin, her nails freshly painted blue and green. Four of the men were clustered around her while she giggled and waited for one of them to take her under his wing. Then they turned bashful — maybe there were too many witnesses, and the only business transaction was the exchange of "news" reports for a bottle of Guiness.

Radio Cameroon was no help at all. From the balcony, we watched battles being waged in front of the radio station, but it seemed no one was yet in firm control. At first D.J.s had been playing bouncy African music, interspersed with promises that the Minister of Armed Forces would soon address the nation and assurances that "the loyalist forces were still in control," but none of us knew which loyalist forces they were. One D.J. went so far as to apologize for the "small interruptions" in normal broadcasting. Then the radio went dead before someone inside that besieged building found Gerry Rafferty's *Baker Street* tape which played non-stop for eight hours.

On Saturday afternoon, helicopters appeared over the city and began dropping explosives on the slums in the valley. Black smoke billowed from the red huts. A couple of jet fighters buzzed the city. Tanks moved in on the Yaounde préfecture and the corrugated tin roof had one gaping hole through it. We watched as men stripped to their underwear came running out of the grimy, colonial structure with their arms in the air. The calm and impartial news reader at Bush House in London began the world news with the words, "It appears that fighting is continuing in the West African state of Cameroon."

"They've thrown away their uniforms so no one will know which side they're on," said Vance, who was a student of law at the University of Yaounde. "You see why it's best not to get involved in anything political in our country. You can't win. There are security forces, armed forces, gendarmes, police and special forces for every big man. With that many law-enforcers interpreting the laws, there's inevitably trouble. The best thing to do is to keep your head down as low as you can, hoping that one day no one decides you're on the wrong side. All we want is a roof over our heads and something to eat when we're hungry."

He spoke some more of his dreams to go to Germany, or any developed country, to study law. His sister in Berlin was, he thought, pulling strings for him. Years later, in Ouagadougou, I would run into someone who was there in Berlin when Vance finally managed to get to Germany, and began his stay by getting lost as he tried to get from one side of Berlin to the other on the underground system. Even in Europe he had not escaped the ubiquitous "security" officials and that problem of being on the right side.

Below us on the streets, men in fatigues — momentarily on the right side — ransacked dingy hovels, dragging weeping men and women onto the street and forcing their terrified victims onto their knees as they questioned them at gunpoint. Others turned the houses inside out, making off with prized possessions such as sewing machines and radios tucked under one arm, machine guns under the other.

I pointed my telephoto lens out a bedroom window, and took random shots of this with a loud and indignant running commentary. The apartment commander, that German doctoral student who had grown up in Africa and was doing his dissertation on coffee cooperatives, removed his pipe from his mouth long enough to offer me some seasoned advice.

"They're going to see that lens and think it's a gun. Why would you risk all of our necks for a few photographs?"

I removed the lens, snapping just one last picture as a white ambassadorial car sped past, the Canadian maple leaf flying over the front fender.

Françoise, a tall and sturdy police woman who knew someone in Jeanne's apartment, came barging breathlessly through the door. She said she had changed out of her police uniform in the taxi as they sped away from her police district office, and begged a passing woman for a layer of her cloth wrapper, which she put on to disguise herself as a civilian. "It's very serious," she said, echoing my thoughts. "It's a catastrophe. This is how it started in Chad. They took the students from the police academy, the national guard and the gendarmerie and made them fight. Gave them weapons." I still didn't know who "they" were — Biya's loyalist forces, or the forces that claimed to be loyal to Cameroon and disloyal to Biya. "If they bring in the parachutists and the forces from the K Camp, we're finished. They're equipped for war. Then there's no more chance. A civil war. Just like Chad. My police commander refused to support the gendarmerie and the army and he's been removed. It's now the Presidential Guard against Biya, and the army is divided." She sat at the head of the table, in her coloured wrap with a blue woollen cap on her head. She looked scared to death. We all sat quietly, watching the helicopters on the horizon, hearing the shooting as the sun set.

We jumped when the lights came back on with a blinding flash, and Gerry Rafferty was suddenly interrupted by the scraping of the needle across the record, much like the now-fashionable backbeat given to rap music.

This was followed by a few minutes of silence, and then a voice informed the nation that President Paul Biya was in fact still in control of the country, and that he had a message for his people.

The tape was very noisy with poor edits cutting into his words. "He's still cowering in his bomb shelter," said Vance. "It's a taped message."

"Yes, but it looks like they've regained the radio station, or else they wouldn't be broadcasting the message."

"True," said the German commander, puffing professorially on his pipe.

Biya's voice was very high and gravelly.

Vance answered my unasked question. "He's had a throat operation. That's why he sounds like a lovesick frog. That's why he so rarely speaks on the radio, and so far has prevented the national television station from opening. He doesn't want the people to hear him, and to see him."

"Why, what's wrong with his appearance?" I asked.

"He's all spotty and grey from using bleaching agents," he said. More popular fiction to be sifted through. In photographs, which adorned walls in every hotel and restaurant in the country, he did look quite light-skinned, but I never noticed any grey pallor or spottiness. Biya informed the nation that his forces had effectively regained control of all the strategic points in the city. He said that citizens should continue "life as usual," return to their daily tasks in the development and progress of the great nation. He said his forces were just "cleaning up" the remnants of the traitorous rebel forces and should have completed the task by the next day.

He didn't say anything about the curfew. In Jeanne's apartment an hour-long discussion ensued. "If the president says everything is supposed to return to normal, then the curfew must be over," I said. "Besides, I want to know where my husband is. He was supposed to be coming in by train yesterday."

"I want to go dancing," said Jeanne."We can stop at the train station on the way to the disco."

"You're crazy," said the German student. "Look out there. There's no one on the streets. Nor even any lights. Biya was just bluffing, trying to keep everyone calm so no one joins the rebels. He doesn't have control, not yet. When he says they're eliminating the last pockets of resistance, he means they're still in full battle."

He reminded us once again that he was a veteran of African coups, adding pointedly that he had lived to tell us about them.

Jeanne replied with that French flair of hers that she didn't really care.

I agreed to accompany Jeanne. It did not occur to me that people like Jeanne and me were the stuff of diplomats' nightmares.

Jeanne took the wheel of the Renault Four and drove it with the pizzazz and delicacy of a toreador(ess), manhandling the horizontal gear shift as though it were a baguette for the breaking.

It was very dark, far too dark. Had someone turned off the streetlights, or had they been shot out?

Jeanne, laughing, skidded the white car around empty traffic circles. "I don't think the disco will be open," she said. "Too bad." She reached over and gave Vance a hug and a kiss.

I wished that it weren't quite so dark and the streets were not quite so empty. African streets were never empty. African life was lived on the streets. People slept, ate, cooked, sold and lived on the sides of the roads. It occurred to us a little too late that the roads were empty but the bushes were not.

A shot whizzed overhead, coming from the dense bush to the side of the road. I made for the floor in the back. Jeanne ducked, swearing profusely, in French, but still laughing. To Jeanne all of life was a game, without rules — like her life in Cameroon, like her marriage, which I assumed had been annulled when Vance moved into her husband's bed. She took to Cameroon as she had taken to Vance, with total abandon. She flirted with her life the same way she was flouting the rules of marriage, totally without fear of repercussion.

She was driving in a crouch, with her head below the gearshift. "Merde. Merde. Merde." Vance was quiet. "How am I supposed to drive this thing? I can't see," she said.

"Let's go back," I pleaded, my nose on the floor.

"No, we're almost at the train station now. No sense not checking on the trains while we're here."

"Jeanne, I think we should go..."

It was too late. The train station was in darkness and already upon us, as were a half dozen soldiers who surrounded the vehicle with machine guns aimed.

Jeanne obeyed the order to turn on the interior lights, keeping quiet for the first time in the three days I had known her. "He says sit up and put your hands in the air," she hissed at me.

I obeyed, glancing through the glass front of the train station. Inside, by the light of a single hurricane lamp, I could make out bodies spread across the floor of the lobby. I assumed they were people sleeping as they waited for the trains to start running again. In retrospect, when figures for casualties of the coup attempt slowly emerged, I began to suspect that they may not have been sleeping.

"What are you doing here?" demanded the tight-lipped soldier, his face gleaming with sweat in the light from the car.

"This woman," said Jeanne, pointing to me, "is expecting her husband on the train from Douala."

Six faces and gun muzzles shifted to me.

"On the train?" he asked, incredulous. "Do you see any trains running? There are *no trains running*. Who are you?"

Jeanne gave him the name of the volunteer organization.

"And him?" asked the man, using his gun to indicate Vance.

"He's my friend."

"Papers, all of you." We fished frantically for passports, Vance for his identity card, which, like an American Express Card, should never be left at home. The soldiers were jittery when our hands went down and they muttered to each other in a language I could not understand — of which there were literally hundreds in Cameroon.

Our papers were scrutinized under torchlight, and handed back.

"Get back where you came from."

"But didn't you hear President Biya? He just spoke on the radio. He said that everything was supposed to return to normal, that people should resume their..."

"We do not have time to listen to the radio. We are fighting a *war*. Do you understand? If you value your lives, you will get back to wherever you live as fast as you possibly can."

We did get home safely, and Biya's re-enforcements did come and re-take Yaounde Airport and he did eventually regain control. It would, however, take a long time — a lot of purging and arrests and security operations — for the country to return to normal. Whatever normal was.

Exact statistics in Africa were not always easy to come by, and usually even harder to believe. Once again in the weeks following the coup attempt, we were inundated with rumours disguised as facts, and facts disguised as rumours. We heard that hundreds of people were rounded up and shot in the days after the coup, that information coming from a friend who lived beside an important security prison, and who was blocked from visiting his home for two weeks after the foiled putsch. Many thousands more fled. Northerners filled the trains, escaping from the witch-hunting that followed the coup, a purge that pitted the revenge of southerners against northerners who were alleged to have supported the rebels.

President Ahidjo did not land in Garoua, as far as I know. Nevertheless we were hounded for months afterwards by security men on the roadside in their search for his Moroccan mercenaries. On more than one occasion, after having inspected my Canadian passport, one of these roadside security men looked at me long and hard, and then asked me if I weren't Moroccan.

Three days later I moved out of Jeanne's apartment. Her husband arrived home one night and I did not want to witness whatever scenes were overdue between them. Karl also showed up at the guesthouse, on the second train in from Douala, where he had been waiting for days, wondering what was going on. In the rest of the country the people had never known what was taking place in Yaounde.

Karl said we were moving to the town of Foumban, a beautiful place surrounded by volcanic craters and lakes.

There were some problems, mostly bureaucratic, to be dealt with first, to formalize the position. This would take some time, since the capital was still in shell shock. The bureaucracy had been shaken up, the roads of the capital and the country were covered with military controls, trigger-happy soldiers and citizens who cowered under their scrutiny.

But for a time I lost interest in what was happening around me. Almost two weeks to the day after my trip into Yaounde with the director of our service who was complaining of swellings under his ears, I came down with mumps and malaria and, semi-conscious, was taken to a clinic for treatment.

## *Chapter 9*

# Black stones and yellow men

I had always considered myself level-headed on the matter of snakes, spiders and other scaled or crawling creatures in the tropics. I had worked in Mexico in a Tropical Biology Station, and as an assistant to a herpetologist, who had strived to impart to me some of his affection for snakes and their evolutionary relatives. I refrained from buying the python skins for sale in most tourist kiosks, which sellers said could be used as wall hangings. Pythons, I lectured the hawkers who pestered foreigners with the rolled up skins, were on the endangered species list. I had no idea if this was true, but even if it weren't, at the rate the pythons were selling as wall hangings for European homes, I was sure they soon would be. I had great respect for these evolutionary marvels, and all snakes, which had been on the earth much longer than human beings. But that didn't extend to snakes in bathrooms, curling around my feet.

Discharged from the clinic, and still feeling the after-effects of the coup and long battle against malaria and mumps, I was recuperating in the volunteer guesthouse, waiting impatiently to leave for Foumban — waiting impatiently for all the bureaucratic wrinkles to be ironed out.

The evening the snake uncoiled itself from its corner behind the toilet and slithered towards my ankles, I let out a scream which had been bottled up inside me for a long time. I climbed onto the toilet while other volunteers came running. They were wielding brooms, and they beat the black snake to a pulp.

"Dead," someone pronounced.

"Did you have to be so brutal?" I asked. "I mean, not all snakes are poisonous. That's what I hate here. All the brutality. Everyone killing something to sell it, or because they assume it's poisonous. They do it to chameleons too. Some harmless snakes kill poisonous snakes." I stepped down from the toilet.

One of the Germans turned to me. "That was a black mamba."

"Oh for God's sake. Every snake you see is a black mamba. You don't even know any other snakes."

They filed out of the bathroom. The next night I entered my room and another snake shot out of the corner, heading for my left ankle. I leapt onto the bed before letting out a scream.

This time they were slower in coming. "Do you want us to kill this harmless snake?" asked Klaus, a German volunteer I had befriended during those days in Jeanne's apartment.

"Of course I do. What do you think?"

Later that night I read up in a tropical medical book what to do in the event of a snakebite. "Stay calm," it said. "After tying a cloth around the limb to prevent spread of the poison, make a cut — about 1 cm. long and 5 cm. deep into the skin around each fang mark with a sharp and sterilized instrument, preferably a scalpel." You could determine whether the snake was poisonous by the presence of two fang marks on the skin, in addition to the two rows of teeth. Or, if the snake had been killed before it had a chance to bite, its harmfulness or harmlessness could be determined posthumously, by making the impression of its teeth on a piece of paper.

Both of the snakes killed on my behalf had been mangled beyond recognition. There was no way to prove whether they had been poisonous. I decided I no longer cared. When my convictions were put to the test and found wanting, I had been shamelessly happy to see the snakes beaten to ribbons.

Then I heard about the "black stone." This stone could be applied to the snake, or scorpion bite, and would stick to the wound and suck out the venom with its own absorptive properties. I was told the black stone had been discovered by Catholic missionaries in (a) Congo, (b) Zaire or (c) the South Pacific, and that the local people who revealed its secrets to these missionaries had demanded that its source be kept a secret. White Fathers told me it could be obtained in Belgium, occasionally from mission stations in West Africa.

I searched for a black stone for years. Three times I had been convinced I had at last succeeded in finding one, by hawkers who visited my house on bicycles, dressed primly in slacks and shirts buttoned to the neck, sent, they said, from this or that mission. They had packaged the neat square stones in plastic bags with typewritten labels guaranteeing its authenticity. Three times I bought the black stones, persuaded by the young sellers that they were genuine when they stuck them to their lips and talked to me of their magical sticking and healing powers. Three times I bought bits of charcoal, which I could not even manage to stick to my lips, let alone a snakebite.

I was certainly not the only one who came to Africa with lofty interests in the wildlife and tropical botany. In Douala, we crossed paths with two young men, filled with the spirit of adventure and the love of tropical plants.

We had bulldozed our way through deep mud between Yaounde and Douala, where the road was being pushed through tropical forest. We had cajoled our way through road barriers set up to trap leftover subversive elements after the foiled coup, and had arrived at the Seaman's Mission. Besides being a comfortable place to stay, it was a veritable smorgasbord of personalities, from sailors in from Bristol for a few nights of drinking and womanizing, to every kind of weird and wonderful traveller who happened to make his or her way to Africa.

This list was topped by a genre of young adventurer, who I imagine a few hundred years earlier might have set out to explore the continent for the pure love of travel and discovery.

In 1984 this spirit was still alive and well in Johann and Wolfgang — two German biology students. They were travelling on their grandfathers' bicycles. The first time I saw them they were sitting like orphans on the front step of the Seaman's Mission. They were in rags, and their running shoes were tied together with bits of twine. Their bicycles were loaded with leafy botanical samples. Their faces were bright yellow, the colour of a ripe mango.

They said they were looking for Klaus, the German volunteer we had met in Yaounde, who was working in Douala. The proprietor of the Mission had told them Klaus could offer them free room and board. They were down to the last of their funds and could not afford a room in the Mission.

Klaus approached the two forlorn yellow men, introducing himself. "What's your name?" he asked the more lively of the pair, the one who had raised his eyes and shown signs of life.

"I am fine, thank you," he answered.

"How are you?" Klaus continued, looking for some coherence.

"My name is Wolfgang," he said. "And this is Johann. He is sick."

"I can see that," said Klaus. "You need a place to stay, is that it?"

Wolfgang nodded.

"Good, well let's see. You can stay in my house but I think you need to see a doctor first."

"We saw a doctor."

"It looks like you might have hepatitis," I said.

"No, not hepatitis."

"But you're both so yellow," I said, meaning contagious.

"We've been eating mangos since the Central African Republic," Wolfgang replied. "It's dyed our skin."

"I still think you should see a doctor. You can't drive your bicycles to my house in your condition. It's six kilometres. You can leave them here, and take a taxi after you've seen a doc..."

"No, we won't leave our bicycles. They're our grandfathers' and our plant collections are on them," said Wolfgang.

"But Johann is definitely too weak to ride. Is he asleep or unconscious?" Johann was staring at the sky. He didn't seem to notice us, or the conversation. His breath came in feeble raspy gusts from his open mouth. His lower jaw was slack.

"He's okay. We made it to here okay. We'll drive our bicycles."

Klaus shrugged and drew a map, indicating the way to his house.

They spent two nights there. Johann didn't regain what I could call a conscious state. The many volunteers and their Cameroonian friends who used Klaus' house as a drop-in centre tried from time to time to convince Wolfgang that he should get his friend to a doctor, or see the German embassy about a flight out. Then Johann would suddenly come back to life, sit up sharply, fix his wild and glazed eyes on a point overhead and shout that he wasn't going anywhere without his bicycle. Then he would resume his comatose position on his back on the floor, which made him resemble a corpse laid out for viewing.

Wolfgang said they had had enough of doctors. He said their trip had gone well through Europe and through Egypt. Their troubles had begun in northern Sudan, where they were robbed of almost everything they had with them for survival. Then they had resorted to a diet of mangos, which was all they could afford. By the time they reached Bangui, capital of the Central African Republic, they had been weak and were turning yellow. They had gone to a laboratory for tests.

There they had encountered an enthusiastic doctor, who insisted that he perform the blood tests. They told him they were biologists and he invited them to join him in the laboratory. The hunt was for a microbe that was sapping their strength and jaundicing them.

This lasted, he said, for hours. The doctor worked with a thick volume on parasitic taxonomy beside the microscope and every few minutes he would move from the eye-piece to the book, flipping through page after page with a furrowed brow. Then, at last, he shouted "A-haa," and pointed to a hairy microbe on the page he had found in the book. Wolfgang and Johann had read through the paragraph on the parasite, which was one of the rarest in Africa, and an incidence which defied statistical probabilities, one case per several million people.

It was not treatable. They spent the last of their money on a train to Douala. Wolfgang insisted that they were regaining their strength to continue their bicycle journey. He didn't worry about a shortage of money — they had between them less than one hundred German marks remaining. Anyone who could cling that tenaciously to a pair of bicycles would not easily give up the ghost and die or go home without finishing their pan-African trip.

Then they disappeared, leaving nothing behind at Klaus' house and telling no one they were off.

That evening in the Seaman's Mission, we learned what had happened. They had driven to the mission on their bicycles; no one knew why. By the time they arrived, Johann's temperature had begun to rise. With each degree it rose, explained the proprietor of the Seaman's Mission, his oxygen requirement also rose about fifty per cent. "He was passing out, so I called a doctor, who came. He examined them, and said they had very advanced cases of malaria, and that they both needed blood immediately because their red blood cell count was so low. If not, they would die."

Both were whisked off to a clinic, and a call went around the Seaman's Mission for blood donors. Johann received four litres.

A week later they were flown out by their embassy, which advanced money for their tickets and medical costs, but not for their bicycles which sat for months at the Seaman's Mission, while the lovely slips of orchids and plant samples withered and died, just like the dreams of those two intrepid naturalists who succumbed in the end, to thieves and malaria parasites.

If that hadn't happened, it is likely a customs official, at either end of their journey, might have put an end to their field trip — tropical plants used for medicinal purposes were highly valued in Africa, where there was a growing awareness that major drug firms had been absconding with them for years, and at great profit. Individuals who tried to export or import such herbal treasures, were more often than not, stripped of their wares on entering Europe.

We spent two more days in Douala. Karl had some meetings to attend, and I spent time walking about the port city that was, on one hand and in some moods, picturesque with its crumbling colonial buildings reminiscent of harbor cities anywhere. At other moments, Douala felt almost impossible for me to stomach with its lack of hygiene, its wet heat and the constant threat of thieves and security agents. I realized that for the first time in my life I was aware of what it must be like to grow up with fear — fear of unknown powers and absolute authorities who are not open to question. While the direct gunfire of those days in Yaounde had been too dreamlike and unreal to affect me at the time, the endless stories of mopping up rebels after the coup attempt, the repeated encounters with alcohol and power-drunk police and military men on the roadsides, had filled me with a deep dread that surfaced late at night when I would wake, realizing that at any time, in any place, a trigger-happy policeman or gendarme might simply open fire and I might be in the way of the bullets. I knew these were irrational fears, but I knew that in Cameroon, in the months after that foiled coup, the country was in the hands of irrational men. There was no reason why I might not be shot. There were more soldiers in

Douala alone than I had ever seen in my life. They operated with impunity, carrying out neighbourhood searches and seizing personal property at random and at will.

On our last night in Douala we were sitting in a roadside locale, watching the crowds and speculating on who had the money to buy all the cloth, trinkets, plastic goods that everyone seemed to be in the business of selling. Suddenly the crowds seemed to freeze. All heads were turned in one direction, gazing into the darkness. Some began to run, jumping over tables, others cowered inside the locale, mingling with people who seconds before had been dancing. I rose, adrenalin making me faint. We shot panicked glances around us, looking for a place to hide, although we had no idea what it was we were hiding from. I was looking for something bullet-proof, like that giant slice of tree we had had in Jeanne's apartment.

We were still standing at our table. A covered military truck pulled up and stopped in the dark street in front of the locale. Men in khaki leapt out, sprinting, their guns raised. They seemed to be chasing after everyone who was trying to flee. The waiter came over and told us to sit down, we would be safe. Around us young men were being dragged by their feet or hands towards the military truck. It was so dark, it seemed unlikely they could identify the men they were hauling away. Their seige seemed arbitrary, and designed to terrorize. When the truck was full, and all those who had dared to move were captive inside, it roared off. As soon as it was gone, the dancers inside took up where they had left off minutes earlier. The waiter, however, began packing up the chairs outside. Most of the patrons who had been using them had been taken away.

He pretended he didn't hear us when we asked him what had happened. A passing waitress stopped long enough to listen to our question. She laughed, did some fast steps to the music playing inside and moved away, wiping off tables and stacking chairs.

We walked back to the Seaman's Mission, pondering what had happened, knowing we would never know because no one who could explain it to us would feel any need to do so. I thought about Vance, and his advice about keeping your head down if you wanted to be safe in Cameroon.

We were glad to leave Douala, on our way at long last to Foumban. With our two trunks in the back of the service van, and our puppy, Putsch, whom we thought would grow up to be a guard dog, we set off. I was ready for some peace and quiet on the green plateau in the Western Province, far removed from the bloody politics in Yaounde and the chaotic humidity and heat of Douala. Karl said he had even found us a nice house to live in.

## Chapter 10

# Bosses, bugs and bogeymen

Our landlord, Alhaji Ismael, was the director of the coffee cooperative, Foumban division, making him Karl's boss. Generally this sensitive working relationship between development worker and African colleague was labelled "counterpart" or "homologue" in French, and development assistance or aid was given the egalitarian term "co-opération." Alhaji Ismael never granted this counterpart status to Karl, who was merely a volunteer. His idea of co-operation meant foreigners should provide him with funds and make themselves as scarce as possible, which in many cases might work very well.

The house he rented to us was the newest addition to his already considerable real estate holdings. It had been constructed almost entirely with materials "borrowed" from the as-yet-unfinished French-funded lycée, a few hundred meters up the as-yet-unfinished French-funded road. In that skeletal school complex, only the gymnasium was finished and waiting for an influx of students. Other materials, which had been destined for the laboratories or toilets, could be found in our kitchen and bathroom.

Apart from the moral question of whether these laboratory tiles and fittings belonged in our house, on a practical level they made a nice kitchen. The tall, rounded faucets used in laboratories for filling beakers and flasks, were equally practical in household use and especially good for filling buckets and large saucepans. They were certainly better than those faulty models from Europe that inevitably got shipped off for sale in Africa, which dribbled water everywhere but into the kitchen sink.

Many expatriates spent a lot of their time blaming poor plumbing and wiring and crumbling walls in their homes on poor African workmanship. It was true that trade schools were few and far between, and that many tradespeople lacked the necessary training and experience. However, I was beginning to realize that many of the problems originated elsewhere, namely with the manufacturers and the importers-exporters who used Africa as a dumping ground for faulty materials and appliances that could not be sold elsewhere, but could be sold for vast sums of money on a continent where there was so little quality control, and so many people desperate to buy.

Not coincidentally, in many parts of West Africa, the "disposable income" used to purchase these disposed consumer goods came from foreign assistance funds; in some countries over half the Gross National Product came from outside aid.

That new lycée, located a few metres from Ismael's own official residence, across the street from our house, had been turned into a veritable wheel of fortune by our resourceful landlord. The materials intended for the school were sufficient to equip not just our house, but Ismael's own residences as well. These materials were first rate, having been supplied directly by France.

Ismael's official residence, where his first wife and children resided, and a newer home he had just completed on the outskirts of town, where his mistresses and the princesses, members of the Bamoun royal family in Foumban, lay their heads, both boasted laboratory and washroom fixtures from that unfortunate lycée project. French co-operants in town said that the transformers and electrical fittings intended for the lycée had also "gone missing" from the school site, but these were never located. Word had it that they would eventually turn up in another of Ismael's private housing projects, or that they had gone towards payment on his new car, a silver-blue Peugeot sedan.

Not that Ismael tried to conceal these questionable get-rich tactics. He was very proud of his houses, each with three bathrooms, equipped with bidets, showers, toilets and basins. He liked to give us guided tours, happy to point out how modern was his plumbing. I often wondered if he thought we didn't know where all the fittings and financing came from, if he thought volunteers sent to work with the poor and downtrodden would really appreciate such flagrant misuse of development resources, or if he didn't really think about it at all.

In the end I decided that Ismael suffered from an affliction that from time to time colours relations between expatriates and Africans, the erroneous assumtion that the person on the other side of the cultural barrier was simple, or at least a little bit slow. While the expatriate was busy denouncing the stupidity of his or her co-workers or counterparts, those co-workers were busy outwitting the expatriate at every turn. In other cases, the expatriate became paranoid about being outwitted, often over a matter of a few coins, and turned unreasonable, trusting no one.

Another form of cultural confusion was also common. This was caused by an eagerness on the part of some Europeans and Africans to show how fully culturally integrated they were. In this odd reversal of roles expatriates could appear as odd parodies of a being they perceived as African — speaking clipped or pidgin English when their mother tongue is English, dressing in styles best suited to a mosque or a traditional funeral. Africans could appear as carbon copies of what they believed was modern, progressive, and white. It was not unusual at parties to see expatriate Europeans decked out in the most traditional garb and hairstyles they could find, while the Africans paraded about in the heat in cloying western suits and jackets, their hair ironed and greased with straightening lotions. As western liberals in the business of development struggled desperately to get in touch with rural farmers in Africa, dressing down and peddling their way to and from work, their African counterparts might refuse to travel in anything but an air-conditioned vehicle and might snub their rural brothers, whom they were being paid and trained to assist. They felt lucky to have escaped that hard rural life, proud to have "made it" in the modern world of urban Africa.

While the white women bronzed themselves under the merciless African sun around hotel swimming pools, African woman, their faces spotted grey from constant use of bleaching creams, sat inside air-conditioned bars and restaurants of the same hotels. (To my knowledge only Nigeria, the biggest producer of such bleaching creams, has actually banned their use in West Africa.)

123

This confusion over cultural identities often resulted in absurd masquerades in which an African made a great show of sharing what he believed to be modern values and scorned anything local or African, while the expatriate fervently promoted the use of local materials and traditional craftsmanship.

Ismael insisted that our house be furnished with Afrique Nouveau styles, which had their roots in discount furniture warehouses in the industrialized world, where, for a time, plastic and bric-a-brac were sewn into every easy chair. While Ismael argued for a salon of over-stuffed plastic or velveteen sofas in fluorescent shades, we said that we would prefer to buy locally-made rattan chairs which could be bought on the roadside in Foumban. He called these "primitive." We said they were very "chic et très chèr" in our countries.

He was proud of a bed he had had designed for his out-of-town village and wanted us to see it; then we could order something similar for our own bedroom. Be-decked in red satin, completely encircled by plush red velvet drapes, this round bed had a fully stocked bar and a stereo with flashing lights on the headboard. He pulled three cans of St. Pauli Girl beer from the swing-out bar underneath the bed, offering them to us.

In 1984 in Cameroon, Guiness was still advertised as the "drink for the whole family" because "Guiness is good for you," but it was canned St. Pauli Girl — St. Pauli being the name of Hamburg's red-light district — which was consumed by the people in the money and in the know. Champagne and French wines were also downed in incredible amounts; Cameroon fell slightly behind Gabon at the time in attaining the distinction of being the biggest consumer of French champagne per head in the world. It was Ismael who told us this, with pride.

His flair for real estate and construction and furniture design was just part of his repertoire. He was soon to be enthroned as a prince in the Bamoun royal kingdom. This required intensive preparation with the elders at night.

By day, if he wasn't at the palace being served whisky and meat by some of the town's royal maidens, he occupied a plush office at the coffee cooperative. There he invented novel ways of making his own profit margins comfortable and keeping the books balanced.

He often issued loans to friends and to staff, running a private credit firm with the cooperative's funds. One such case involved an employee who appeared only as a name on the payroll. The man had borrowed three million CFA francs from the cooperative, for the purchase of a car, which he crashed shortly after the acquisition. His death in the accident made repayment awkward, so Ismael left his name on the payroll and each month paid him his salary, which went towards repayment of the loan. On paper, in a few years, the car loan would be repaid.

He had other, simpler ways of making sure there was room in the cooperative budget for his lifestyle and his own sundry enterprises. Sometimes, he just withheld payment to coffee farmers.

There was concern in Cameroon's coffee industry that coffee production was dropping because farmers had lost interest in growing it, despite huge injections of foreign capital in the form of grants and loans to stimulate production. There were also calls for expatriate "experts" to determine the source of the problem of declining production and more money was spent bringing them in to perform their studies.

Ismael blamed the declining production on the low world prices for coffee, although Karl often reminded him that farmers said they would produce if the cooperative ever paid them for what it took away and sold. Ismael preferred to blame the problem on "foreign exploitation."

Alhaji Ismael could be amiable, in the condescending way of Big Men, or social giants in his community. He was robust and rotund, a man who always looked larger than life as he emerged from the back seat of his newly washed, silver-blue, official Pajero, folding his multi-coloured hand-woven bou-bou around him, while his chauffeur bowed low. Susan, a visiting friend, once complimented him on his fantastically hand-woven and hand-embroidered robe of indigo cotton. "But it looks very hot," she said. He frowned for a second. "It looks and *is* very expensive," he told her.

I was grateful to him for renting us the large house, the only accommodation, according to him, available in Foumban. I was also enchanted with the town itself. Foumban was the historic capital of the Bamoun people, home to the king and the royal lineage that dated and was clearly documented back to the fourteenth century.

It lay on a pleasant upland plateau, about 1,200 metres above sea level, flanked by volcanic craters, rolling green hills and valleys. The climate was perfect, never too hot, never too cold. There were cobalt blue skies in the morning, fresh air and almost no mosquitoes. Afternoon thunder storms and downpours cleared the air.

The house was larger than was generally deemed correct for development volunteers. Development people were neatly and precisely ranked in a strict hierarchy. The volunteers at the bottom were there out of goodwill, and vague desires to do something about the poverty and suffering on the continent. They were supposed to believe in what they were doing, which is just as well, because monetary rewards were minimal. The lowest paid of all were the American Peace Corps, Canadian CUSO volunteers and British Volunteers Overseas. Their monthly pay-cheques were meant to be enough to survive on and theoretically about the same as those of their African counterparts; a source of pride among many, grounds to quit for others. The German Service was considered by other volunteers to be the "Mercedes" of volunteer agencies, with reasonable salaries and benefits. Volunteers were also expected to have close contact with the people they were there to work with and to train and, in theory, to help.

Next came the co-operants — teachers and various non-governmental organization workers, most of whom earned slightly more money allowing them to maintain a comfortable living standard without luxuries. They tended to be serious about what they were doing. They had more money to work with than rank and file volunteers and fewer political constraints than the "experts" from bilateral or multilateral government development projects. Their projects were often relatively successful.

The "experts" were those who worked for the international consulting firms, bilateral development organizations, and most prestigious of all, those from international funding agencies such as the World Bank and the United Nations family of development operations. They ranged from devoted professionals who thrived on the challenge and adventure of working in the developing world, to the outcast professionals who could not find work or make their own lives work back home in their native countries. Some were hired to fill political quotas. In general, they were paid and lived very handsomely, and opulence was not rare among them.

Our house, however big, was almost completely empty. The coffee cooperative had agreed to provide basic furnishings months earlier. But Ismael was busy, and our furnishings consisted mostly of odd pieces he had loaned us from his own collection.

The house had three bedrooms, and the same number of bathrooms, a kitchen that would have served well as a science laboratory for a class of thirty, and a living room that could have served as a dance-hall, replete with plastic chandeliers which drooped lower and lower as the ceiling slowly caved in.

It took us weeks to convince Ismael to remove his motorcycle from the living room. I spent a week scrubbing the burned rubber from the blue tiles, where Ismael and his big machine had logged many kilometres.

We had been in the echoing villa a few months when we had our first real brush with the dark spectre of "authority" in that authoritarian country. It was a Sunday morning, still far too early to expect guests, when Putsch began to yap. Karl was still in the kitchen frying eggs and beans, so I went to open the gate and see who had driven up.

"Yes, can I help you?" I asked, looking past three men to a nondescript Landrover parked there.

"Yes," said one, leading his trio through the gate and past me without waiting for an invitation. Two of the men sported polyester leisure outfits, widely known as "political suits," one powder blue, the other sandy brown. The third slouched inside a trench-coat with the collar up. They were all tall and intimidating with their grimness.

"What can I do for you?" I asked, jogging along behind like a puppy-dog. Putsch, our watchdog, had taken the lead and was bouncing up and down in front, drooling enthusiasm. She led them straight onto the verandah, leading into the living room.

Annoyed at their lack of response to my questions, I became insistent. "Hey, would you mind telling me who you are, what you want?" Like all newcomers in Cameroon, I had heard terrifying stories of thieves who dressed up as policemen or staff from the national electricty corporation and tied women up in showers and threatened to kill them while they robbed the house. I had been warned not to take anything or anyone at face value.

The man in the trench coat pulled out a card, which he didn't allow me time to read, but flashed as a badge.

"We have reason to believe that your telephone has been linked up illegally to the president's line."

For a moment, I was struck dumb. Then I ran ahead, pushing my way past them into the living room, and turned to confront them as they entered.

"Excuse me, what are you talking about? Our telephone is linked up with whose?"

"The president's."

"The *president's*?"

"Yes, we have come to inspect it. And to search your house. We have been asked to inspect your furniture, which we believe has been acquired illegally. We believe you are living in luxury not correct for volunteers of your organization. Where is your telephone?"

"Over there," I said, pointing to a far corner and the device that had been silent for a month. "It doesn't work. Maybe since you're telephone experts, yourselves, you can repair it for us while you're checking on that line to the president. This is..."

Karl, seated now at the table in front of a plate of beans, sent me a warning with his eyes. He waved to the men, with his mouth full, indicating that he couldn't talk at the moment but would be with them shortly. They informed him they were going to search the premises.

They moved in a huddle to the telephone, where they took turns lifting the receiver. Concentration wrinkled their faces. They exchanged information in whispers. The man in the trench coat crawled about on his hands and knees to look at the telephone jack.

"Can't you see that the telephone is *dead*?" I asked finally.

No response. One examined a file in his hands, lifting his eyes from time to time to scan the room. I wondered if he was looking for electronic bugging devices in the cobwebs in the upper corners, or monitoring ones that he had once installed.

"We have orders to inspect the whole house."

"What on earth for? As you can see, there isn't much furniture in here. Besides, you have no right..."

Karl, sensing by my tone that I was in a dangerous mood, motioned to me to be quiet. He got up from the table, shook all three of the men's hands and told them they were welcome. Then he led the search committee towards the bedroom, chatting with them genially. He had a gentle and charming touch with people he worked with, and he knew how to use it with any kind of authorities. He detailed the list of furnishings in the house, all on loan from Alhaji Ismael or bought by us on the roadside. The list included a table, four chairs, rattan shelves and a bed.

It was the bed that greeted us when we entered the bedroom. The mattress, in spite of many days in the sun, soaking and scrubbing and beating, still smelled like a septic tank. Ismael had proudly told us that all of his children — we were never clear on the number — had been conceived on that mattress. It smelled as though they had also been toilet-trained on it. The three men didn't comment on the odour. They opened closet doors, looking for whatever it was they were after — bogeymen under the lamp, or bugs under the bed. The search was tedious and my temper was rising.

Apart from the bed there was a built-in wall closet system designed by Ismael. This elaborate arrangement of nooks, crannies, closets, drawers and cupboards reached from floor to ceiling, wall to wall. Each drawer, cupboard or door had its own lock and key, for a total of fifty. Many of the keys had fallen out and were on the floor. Still, they played with each key until they had searched all fifty recesses. Forty-six were empty.

The only object of interest was a portable hair-dryer that they pulled, with satisfied grunts, from a drawer full of underwear. I had to demonstrate its use, while the man in the trench coat took copious notes in a black book.

They moved onto the adjoining bedroom, asking about the lack of children in our family. A childless couple was suspect. If a wife was unable to produce children for her husband, he was likely to discard her or take a second, or third, wife, who could produce. Men were never sterile. Why, they asked Karl, did he stay with me when I didn't produce children? Or were we spies, pretending to be married?

"Look, we just got married less than a year ago," I said.

"What room is this, then?"

"It's an office." This was the place to which I escaped, to try to fathom Cameroon on paper. The desk was littered with portions of articles and stories I had been doing for Canadian newspapers, seditious notes on life and living in Cameroon. Afraid that they would spot the name of the president in those scraps of writing, I distracted them by pulling our pink wedding papers from the green metal trunk. They rummaged through its interior as though it might explode.

"I suppose you're looking for stores of weapons now, are you?" Karl jabbed an elbow in my rib. The men let the lid fall with a bang. One of them pulled open the curtains and scowled at the children and chickens in the row housing out back.

An hour after they came they were gone. I sat down at the table, ready to resume Sunday morning. Their visit reminded me of the occasional invasion of our house by hordes of ants. They marched in under doors, fanned out on walls and behind shelves, and then re-assembled a half hour later, their booty of cockroaches and insects trundled along by those ants relegated by their strict genetic order to spend their ant lives as porters. Such invasions were best ignored. The sprays on the market in Africa — Rambo, Killer, or Mobil — were not only environmentally unfriendly, they were also user-unfriendly. The trigger finger froze after a few seconds of spraying and the only effects were wheezing in the lungs which might persist for weeks. The insects might get woozy and stagger and wobble briefly, before flying or marching off oblivious to their close encounter with Rambo or Killer.

There was no creature on earth so adept at adaptation as the insects which set up home in human dwellings in the tropics. They were as annoying and immune to human sensibilities as the authorities who enacted searches of private homes in the name of the law; law in countries run by one man and his circle of henchman, was a relative term and concept. As with the insects, the best policy was to ignore them, allow them to perform their natural functions and hope that they would leave you in peace. I don't know what those three men left with, but they left us with the nasty feeling we were being watched and falsely accused of something.

At about two that afternoon Alhaji Ismael swept through our gate. I assumed that by then, everyone in Foumban knew of the visit of the security men. Word travelled fast in that town. It happened that I once crashed a motorcycle into our front wall at 11 one morning, and an hour later in the market five kilometres away, people asked me if I had injured myself in my accident. On another occasion termites began filing out of our ceiling at about ten in the morning. This was not a few stray termites, it was full scale exodus. Daniel, our "domestique," began to sweep them up by the shovelful, and dump them over the wall onto the road. Within ten minutes Karl skidded to a stop in front of the house, having heard at the office two kilometres away, that his house was being "devoured" by termites. Except for international calls, there really was no need for a telephone in Foumban.

Ismael must also have heard of the search, I thought as he swaggered towards us. Or perhaps he had instigated it?

Surely not. Ismael knew everything there was to know about us. Some of his own children lived in the row of huts behind our house and originally intended as "boys quarters." They could have told him everything about us, even what we ate and drank. We merely had to toss our rubbish out the back door for automatic pick-up and recycling. What the chickens didn't eat, what the women couldn't sell, the children turned into imaginative playthings, developing early that ingenuity and ability to make do with almost nothing which set Africa apart from the developed world.

No, I assured myself, he would not have sent those men. But he knew about them, and he looked worried. There was none of his blustering congeniality. There were rumours that Ismael was in trouble with his own director, the president of the cooperative, not because he had embezzled funds, but because he had pilfered more than his superiors. There were subtle, and not-so-subtle, rules governing corruption in Cameroon at the time, which young radical teachers loved to explain to me at length. The biggest crime was for a subordinate to take more than his superior. Some people expressed admiration for former President Ahidjo, because he had been so "clever" to make off with billions of dollars in oil revenue when he left the country. This was, some people said, his right as Head of State.

Perhaps, I mused, Ismael had something to fear from the security men. Maybe the men had been talking about the president of the coffee cooperative, and not The President of the country. That made sudden sense to me.

Ismael pulled a dog-eared piece of paper out of the many folds of his great robe.

"This is a letter I was given," he said. "It's from the Governor of the Western Province to all directors of the coffee cooperative. Because you're my good friends, I thought I should let you read it, so you will know what people are saying about you. But don't tell anyone I showed it to you."

Karl began to chuckle as he read, and he handed the letter to me. I read. The Governor had written that the volunteer couple at the coffee cooperative were suspected of being spies in the employ of the German government. They were there, "disguised as volunteers,", to see where the "money was going."The :cc list was long and impressive.

"I know you're not spies," he said. "But this could be very dangerous for you, and since you work with me, for me too. I advise you to be very cautious."

Cautious? Spies for the German government? To monitor the disappearance of development funds for the cooperative?

"It takes spies to see where the money is going?" Karl said later. The parking lot at the head office in Bafoussam looked like a dealership for Mercedes and BMW. The menu for one Board meeting would put a small credit union in the red. We had attended many official banquets where each guest received a bottle of whisky or champagne or red wine, and where there was food enough to feed a refugee camp for a day. This was 1984, when in northern Cameroon people were starving to death in the famine.

Although we were not spies, it is true that Karl had been bemoaning the corruption at the cooperative to his superiors at the Volunteer Service and to diplomats. At first, he believed they didn't know what was going on, but eventually, especially when they quashed an official letter he wrote to that effect, it was obvious they knew full well whose interests were being served by the development funds being pumped into the cooperative, and they had no intention of doing anything at all about it.

*Chapter 11*

# Rifles and bananas

After the search and the warning, we started receiving letters that had been torn open before they reached us. There was no attempt to conceal this; no one bothered taping up envelopes. That seemed to be part of the whole security process. If people knew they were being observed, it was unlikely that they were going to need observation. Fear would work on them. This principle has worked magnificently in Cameroon and much of West Africa for many years. People dared not open their mouths or engage in conversations or activities which might be construed by the authorities as "subversive." In this culture of silence, the leaders told the world their people were solidly behind them, that Africans were not "ready for" or desiring western style democracy. No, their people were too busy keeping their heads low and mouths closed, while they struggled to make ends meet.

It was, in my mind, one reason that these countries were still in need of so much development assistance, which came like a bandage to heal gaping social and economic wounds wreaked by decades of corrupt leaders at home, and accomplices abroad who propped them up. Or was it the accomplices abroad masterminding the dealing of loans and investments and sometimes aid or arms, with accomplices in high places in African oligarchies? A bit of both, I think now.

The telephone remained dead for another two months. It was unfortunate, in one way, that it ever started working. If it had remained out of order, the accounting people at the telecommunications office could not have sent us a phone bill that listed dozens of international calls. Shortly before our departure, we received a phone bill for roughly $3,000, for phone calls we had never made. We had to pay it in order to get our exit visas.

A friend in the telecommunications business in Cameroon explained how it was done. The accountants at the telephone office knew that foreigners needed exit visas to leave the country. They also knew that to obtain exit visas, foreigners were required to produce receipts for phone, water and power bills. So they simply transferred all outstanding bills to foreigners' accounts, usually when the foreigners informed them they were leaving and wished to settle final telephone bills.

In the play-as-you-go system that existed in Cameroon, we soon learned to fiddle with the rules, along with the rest. I also ran up phone bills that someone else probably wound up footing. This began during the visit of Angela, our fourteen-year-old niece, to Foumban. Blonde-haired and blue-eyed, she elicited proposals of marriage almost everywhere she went. She followed me once when I went to the post office to complain about the lack of service on our telephone line.

The local director had learned weeks earlier to make himself scarce when he saw me arrive. When I arrived with Angela in tow, he was not only in, he himself met us at the door and invited us into his office.

In his office I asked him why the phone line was still dead. For the first time he made an effort to explain it to me, all the while devouring Angela with his eyes. Then he unrolled a blueprint and launched into a very detailed explanation of phone links in Foumban. His finger came to rest on a series of squiggly blue lines which he said represented the town's main exchange

"This was flooded two months ago in that terrible storm," he said. "The manhole cover which should have protected it was broken, you know. One of your trucks ran over it."

"My trucks?"

"The coffee cooperative," he said.

"Those aren't my trucks."

"The case is in court," he continued. "We have said that the cooperative should pay for the replacement for the manhole cover. But we have received no response from your director, so we're taking the cooperative to court."

"But what about repairing the exchange?" I asked. "Who's going to pay for that?"

"Oh, we will come to that, when this matter of the manhole cover is settled."

"But other phones are working. Even Alhaji Ismael's telephone works, and he's the director of the cooperative you say should be paying. Besides, he lives right across the road from us, and his telephone works, so I don't see what this exchange has to do with my telephone."

"Indeed. Yes, we'll look into that." He rolled up the blueprint, then looked up and smiled. "Tell me, who is this lovely young woman?"

"My niece," I said. "Angela."

"And how long is Angela going to stay with us here in Foumban?"

"Only another two weeks. She's in school in Germany. She's only fourteen."

"A girl of fourteen should be married. Why don't you let me marry her?"

I glanced at Angela, who was blushing. As sweetly as I could I explained that in Germany girls rarely married before they were finished school and certainly not when they were fourteen.

"Such a shame," he said.

Still looking at Angela, he pushed the white telephone on his desk towards me. "Go ahead, make any calls you want," he said.

I made two calls abroad while he grinned at Angela and she looked at her feet. He invited us back the following week, offering the use of his telephone "at any moment."

After Angela left, the privilege was withdrawn and the director nowhere to be found. A few weeks later the telephone began to ring again. The manhole cover and that damaged exchange were never repaired, at least not during our stay in Foumban.

And we did make up for all those free calls, and probably many more, with the payment of that enormous parting gift from the telephone company.

On other occasions, Angela's presence was not a ticket to smooth sailing, especially not through the quagmire of road controls, manned by military, police, gendarmes or, sometimes, by crooks wearing stolen uniforms — although there was a fine and not necessarily clear line separating the former from the latter.

Travelling in Cameroon in 1984 and 1985 was a crash course in invention, debate and diplomacy. On one trip from Foumban to Douala there were seventy road controls on a 270-kilometre stretch. A road control in Cameroon at that time was a makeshift barricade, usually marked by a couple of boulders or bent barrels placed in the middle of the road. They could be set up anywhere, but were most often placed so that the roadside authorities could sit under the shade of a large tree and wait for their prey.

If, as was often the case, the controllers neglected to indicate their presence on the road with stones or barrels, it was easy to whizz right past and be chased by men on motorcycles, or even have tires flattened by shots. After this, hefty fines were demanded for the infraction of failing to respect the barricade.

The correct way to approach such a barricade was very slowly, with the indicator flashing your pending stop. Then you had to come to a complete stop before coming abreast of the actual control point. Failure to comply with any of these unwritten rules resulted in long discussions, loss of personal and car papers, and/or arrest.

Unwritten rules were the name of this challenging game of stop and go. The men at the barricades made up new rules whimsically all the time. A friend in Foumban, Jean-Pierre, was once charged with breaking a law which forbade driving with the ashtray full. Jean-Pierre patted the drunken gendarme on the shoulder and smiling, removed the ashtray with his right hand and emptied it onto the roadside to the left of the gendarme's foot. The officer then stepped back, unsteadily, and saluted. "Allez-y." Another friend paid 5,000 CFA to gendarmes who informed him he had contravened a new law which forbade "white men to drive without a shirt on Sunday."

We quickly learned to counter improvisation with improvisation, and to compile a list of our own rules for safe passage in the country.

Rule One: Travel only with photocopies of original papers, correctly stamped by Cameroonian officials making them legal tender. Then, if the police or gendarme could not be deterred after the mandatory pleasantries and witty parlance from seizing papers, the photocopied papers could be handed over. More photocopies could always be made. Original car papers and drivers' licenses could take months to replace, during which travel was forbidden.

Rule Two: Never stop the engine before having called the blinking indicator to the attention of the roadside controllers, or one could be accused of not using the indicator, and subjected to a fine.

Rule Three: Never be rude or aggressive, even in the face of rudeness and aggression from the authorities.

This was an especially difficult rule to obey. On a sizzling day, driving from Yaounde to Douala on a road that was still waist-deep mud, we were stopped for a control. It was manned by men in fatigues, who had spent the morning drinking strong spirits. They accused us of many things — including the crime of the year — of being Moroccan. Then they closed in on Karl, berating him for his beard. One loud and drunken soldier, sporting an uzi that was pointed into the car interior, grabbed Karl's beard with one hand and pretended to snip it off with the other.

"Cut this off," he demanded.

"Kindly remove your hands from me," Karl said.

"You stay here until you cut it off," he retorted, and he went back to the shade of a mahogany tree on the side of the road. We broiled for three hours in the sun, while more soldiers came and ransacked the car, pilfering water and pens and paper which they found in the back. Eventually Karl handed them a bundle of bills and they allowed us to continue, still shouting that the beard had to go.

I had trouble learning the rules of the road, mostly because they infuriated me. Countering them became an obsession, a full-time occupation. We were treated, and began to feel, like criminals in a country where Karl had been sent by an agency concerned with development.

On the day we drove Angela to Foumban after her arrival in Douala, we were stopped one last time about sixty kilometres from home. Angela was sitting in the back, listening to music on her Walkman and enjoying the lush green mountainous scenery.

"You better take the Walkman off," Karl told her when he saw the three gendarmes moving out onto the pavement with their arms up. Tempting material items such as Walkmans or radios should never be displayed at road controls. (Rule Four).

She slipped off the headphones and placed the miniature cassette player in her handbag, extracting a diary. This was a Holly Hobbit diary with wide lines, in which she had begun to record her experiences starting with the flight from Europe.

The gendarmes asked who she was. "Our niece," Karl replied. "She's come to visit your beautiful country for a few weeks."

"What's in those suitcases?"

"Oh, those are her clothes and personal things."

"Open."

"But it's just personal effects."

"Open."

We both got out of the tiny jeep, and the back door was opened. Three pairs of hands pulled out the two bags, yanked on zippers and began to rifle through the pretty summer dresses. One of the men seized a radio.

"Where is the receipt for this?"

"But it's her own radio. She brought it to listen to the radio, news from Germany or even BBC, while she's here."

"Where are the papers? For each appliance a receipt is obligatory. It could be contraband."

"But she brought it with her from Germany. It's not new. She didn't bring any papers for it."

The white radio was placed on the gravelled shoulder of the road.

That was when I forgot about rule number three. "Don't be ridiculous," I said. "It's her radio. Put it back now."

"Are you calling someone ridiculous, Madame?"

"Yes, if you're going to take a teenager's own radio away. I think that is ridiculous."

The three gendarmes straightened up.

"*All of your papers, now,*" shouted one.

"But you even know who we are. We live in Foumban. We come through here all the time. He works..."

Karl gave me one of his looks, and the gendarmes were puffing up in front of me. I opened my mouth to continue, but Karl pointed to the front seat and I climbed back in.

The discussion grew very heated. Karl showed them all our papers and those for the car. The subject of the white radio sitting on the side of the road was studiously ignored. I listened to the conversation with one ear as I explained to Angela what was happening. She was busy writing.

"Is that your *wife*, that woman?" I heard one gendarme ask Karl.

"Yes, but she's had a long..."

"It must be truly impossible to live with a woman like that," said the second. "Vraiment, il faut la sensibiliser. Une femme comme ça, ce n'est pas possible."

I mulled over his words which translated as "Really, you have to 'sensibilize' her. A woman like that, it's not possible."

"Yes, it's difficult," Karl said, a little too spontaneously. "But you are men, you know what women are like. They're like that. What can we men do?"

"Vraiment," said a gendarme.

I realized just then that the third man had circled the jeep and was peering through the window at Angela, who was painstakingly writing down her impressions of the airport in Brussels in a large, loopy script. I rolled up the window.

He knocked on the glass. "What's she doing?" he shouted through the glass.

"She's writing, what does it look like she's doing?" I shouted back.

"Writing what? Open this window." He rapped on the pane.

"It's her journal, her diary. About her trip in the airplane." I didn't roll down the window.

"Is she a journalist?" he demanded. I rolled my eyes. Sweat was pouring down my face. The sun pounded on my temples. Reflected in the driver's mirror I could see Karl smiling and gesticulating with the two other gendarmes. The three were moving slowly towards the radio.

"She's fourteen years old!" I yelled.

"Then what's she writing?"

"Her diary, I told you."

"Then she's a spy."

"She's fourteen years old," I shouted. "How can she be a spy or a journalist?" It was clear that, for the gendarme, spy and journalist were synonymous.

"Because only spies and journalists write. It is forbidden to write in this country."

A new rule for my list.

"Put the diary away, Angela," I said. "And give him a really nice smile."

Karl was approaching the car with the white radio under his arm. He was bantering with the two gendarmes as though they were best buddies. He got in the car quickly, starting the engine before one of them changed his mind. We sped away. I looked behind and saw the three men moving again into the middle of the road, with their exaggerated swaggers. A desperately over-loaded Toyota van, a bush taxi, was careening up the road towards them, brakes squealing with the effort of slowing the weight of the vehicle. As we rounded a bend the last thing I saw was the driver of the bush taxi climbing onto the roof of his van and tossing down loads of bananas and suitcases, for the gendarmes' inspection.

Several months later, we were in Douala on the occasion of Cameroon's national Fête de la Jeunesse. A scrawny young man strutting big in police garb stopped us a few metres from the driveway into the Seaman's Mission, and ordered us to descend and to leave the car there. I explained to him that the last time we had left the car on the roadside, thieves had punctured the rear tires with spikes, and when we opened the car to repair the tires, they had robbed us.

"So you see, we can't just leave the car here. We're turning in right here at the Seaman's Mission, so we can move it right out of your way, and it won't obstruct the youth parade."

The policeman's eyes were concealed behind a pair of sunglasses advertising Porsche in silver letters. He repeated his order that we get out and leave the car. I slammed the door as I got out. The car was full of suitcases; once again we had visitors — my mother and Susan Murray, a journalist friend from Canada. The car would now block the progress of the youth who were scheduled to march past shouting praises of the president. We would have to carry the suitcases down the long driveway to the Mission. His order was incomprehensible to me.

"You're crazy," I muttered as we moved away. Then, my temper igniting as he shouted insults at our backs, I repeated my words, only much more loudly this time. *"Vous êtes fou!"*

This time he heard me. Within seconds I was surrounded by bellowing policemen and women, who unanimously decided to arrest me. Two men seized me by the arms and led me across the street. They pushed me to a sitting position on the curb, telling me they would take me to the police station when the parade had passed.

Across the street Karl kept walking in the other direction, urging Susan and my mother forward with him, as though my arrest had nothing to do with him. He had tried, in vain, to convince me that I had to restrain my temper and show respect for authority in Africa. He seemed prepared to let me learn the hard way.

I couldn't decide whether I was angrier at him, or the police officers who were haranguing me with accusations and insults.

I soon became a much bigger attraction that the actual Youth Festival. In fact, the marching schoolchildren sporting shirts bearing the visage of President Biya never did pass. Their route took them across the road a block away. Many defected from the march to come and see what was happening with me.

The police took turns inspecting my passport.

"Would you call a policeman in Canada crazy?" asked a solid policewoman. Her uniform with the schoolgirl skirt and ankle socks, made me believe she would be sympathetic and understanding, receptive to my own foreign logic.

"Yes, well, it depends. Probably not, because in Canada I don't think they are." This had come out terribly wrong and I tried to continue. "You see, your colleague..."

She silenced me with a glare, then whistled for her male colleagues who were arguing with a taxi driver who was trying to get through their human barricade. The exchange of money in tightly closed fists was almost faster than the eye could see. Happily finished with the taxi, which had been allowed to proceed, the rest of the police officers answered the policewoman's summons. She repeated what I had said, word for word, emphasizing the part about police in my country not being crazy.

They agreed that the insult could not go unpunished. My sentence, they said, was extended indefinitely.

"*Eh, Madame!*" chanted the growing crowds of children across the street. "*La fête de la jeunesse est comme ça chez nous!*" "That's how the Youth Festival is here!" I wrapped my skirt around my knees, wishing I had something to put over my head. The children of Douala knew that the Youth Festival was a time for the police to collect money on the roads, and for them to chant unmitigated praises of the president, who sat atop this stinking system. I was embarrassed, humiliated and enraged. The sun was not as hot as the burning anger in my stomach.

Two hours later I saw Karl sauntering down the Seaman's Mission driveway, towards the scene. My mother had urged him to come and have a word with the police. She was uneasy, although Karl had assured her it was all a piece of theatre that would soon end.

As soon as he approached me, they seized his passport as well as my mother's which he was carrying, and shoved him towards me. I avoided his eyes.

A large official in brown leather boots pulled up, an hour later, on his motorcycle. He listened to the official version of my arrest and announced that we had twenty-four hours to leave the country.

"Good," I piped up. Karl cursed at me. We waited another hour on the curb. We didn't speak to each other. A woman from the Seaman's Mission came out with water and sympathized with us and with all the citizens of Cameroon who had to put up with the rotten security forces.

Finally at noon an even more important police officer passed by in an expensive sedan. He too heard a blow by blow account of my alleged crimes. He removed his sunglasses, scowled and gave us a lecture on the rules in his country, which we as visitors must respect. He ordered our release, then got back into his chauffeured car and it roared away. We were free.

I suppose my cocky indignation about our treatment at the hands of the authorities in Cameroon would be hard to justify, were it not that these roadside bandits, who paraded as Cameroon's finest, acted with such impunity for so long, making life and certainly business almost impossible for every citizen of their country. There were people who were exempt from this kind of harassment on the roads: Big Men like Alhaji Ismael, for example.

But for the average Cameroonian, the one with no political or economic connections, or aspirations larger than mere survival for themselves and their families, I felt very very sorry.

Once I watched gendarmes force a woman to lower her head-top tray of bananas so they could rifle through the yellow fruit. She looked exhausted, dressed in a faded and ragged wrapper, and had obviously walked many miles barefoot to peddle the bananas for a few francs. As the burly men in uniform manhandled her fruit, she stood silently, staring off into space. When they finished, she bent down and struggled to lift the heavy tray back onto her head, before continuing her trek. Maybe it was her silence I wanted to fill with my angry outbursts at the extortionists who pretended to be enforcers of the law in Cameroon.

I sometimes wondered whether the people at the top knew what was going on, so far below them. Did they give orders to search everyone and everything on the road? Or were they so far removed from the reality in their country, crossing it as they did in helicopters or speeding convoys of bullet-proof Pullman Daimlers, that they didn't know how the power they entrusted to those men (and some women) on the roads was being abused? It was a question to which I never got an answer.

Then again, there were those who enjoyed living in Cameroon because it was what they called "challenging." Even if the job you had come there to do was hopeless, there was always some fulfilment at the end of the day because you had managed to post a letter, make a phone call, travel a hundred kilometres without being arrested. These small accomplishments could feel like glorious triumphs.

There was, for example, the matter of rubber stamps. Stamps were needed for every document, letter, agreement. Not just one or two, but sometimes a page full of rubber stamps was needed to legalize a transaction. The men who handled such stamps in government offices were, more often than not, simply not available.

We would traipse up three or four sets of crumbling stairs, to offices bursting with faded and ragged file folders stuffed with faded and ragged documents searching for a stamp for car papers. There we found a room full of secretaries — one was filing her nails, another was gnawing on a chewing stick and a third was asleep. None knew when the director would be in, where he was or whether anyone else could help us.

After dozens of expeditions, we would give up and do as the local people did. We would retrace our steps to the roadside, and solicit the services of any one of a dozen young men who had set up their own "offices" on the sidewalks. There, amid makeshift watch repair shops and heaps of tomatoes, we would simply order the stamp we needed. The resourceful men outside ministries in Yaounde and Douala either had the government stamp on hand, or would make it in a few hours. In this way the incompetent and unwieldy state apparatus spawned private enterprise and employment. Indeed, much of the black market business in Cameroon, and elsewhere in West Africa, flourished largely because more official channels were blocked by bureaucracy or corrupt officials or had simply fallen into a state of dysfunction.

We laughed about the mess, the confusion and about the ways ordinary people got around the injustice in pursuit of their livelihoods — but it really wasn't funny. For us it was merely inconvenience. For Cameroonians it was a matter of survival. Ten years later, after seriously flawed elections in that country, Paul Biya is still Head of State. The struggle for freedom, justice and democracy still continues in Cameroon — the arrests and disappearances persist, the divisions between north and south, anglophone and francophone, rich and poor, grow bigger, and the blood still flows.

*Chapter 12*

# Bush meat and bush taxis

Cameroon presented itself to tourists as "Africa in miniature." It offered everything: steamy coastal plains, palm-fringed beaches, virgin rainforest, a snow-capped mountain, upland plateaus bathed in cool air and dotted by volcanic cones and crater lakes. Then, further north, there was the Kapsiki wonderland of tiny villages carved into hills and surrounded by surrealistic moonscape pillars of rock. There were splendid national parks teeming with elephants and hippos and there was the sensual, subdued beauty of the Sahel.

There were promises of all kinds of wildlife. In the south there were fifty species of primates; in the north the great mammals of the savannah, giraffes, elephants and lions.

We had seen a lot of this wildlife — on restaurant menus, or for sale on the side of the road dangling from boys' outstretched arms or draped over a forked stick. I had tasted boa, "chimpanzee" (which was the name given to most monkeys), bush rat, civet cat, wild pig and baby crocodile, all at traditional festivals where it was impossible to say no. I was not a fan of "bush meat." It was telling that in one form of pidgin English there were two words used to encompass all animals. One was "little beef," the other "big beef."

As a westerner schooled in the importance of wildlife conservation, I was dismayed at the slaughter of all these creatures, so many of which were on the endangered species list. Although the local people killed for "meat," much of the slaughter was to feed expatriate tastes for exotic souvenirs. Ostrich eggs were fashioned into lamps to sell to foreigners; crocodiles became purses, snakes became shoes, colobus monkeys were turned into hats and bags, tortoise shells became hair ornaments and elephant feet became ashtrays. Live monkeys were offered as pets, and if that failed were killed and served for lunch.

Then there was ivory. Despite strict game laws to protect the elephants, and international agreements with conservation groups, ivory was for sale on almost every road in Yaounde. I tried to walk past, pretending the sellers and their ivory trinkets were not there. This ploy didn't always work. The young men peddling were skilled and they knew their market. One day as I tried to sneak by unnoticed they accosted me.

"Madame, look. Ivory. You want to buy?"

"No."

"You don't believe it's ivory. Look, I show you."

Two of them held matches under the bracelet. I was, it seemed, supposed to know from the smell (or lack of smell) that it was ivory.

"It's genuine ivory, Madame. You see?"

"I don't buy ivory," I said. "You shouldn't sell it either. A whole elephant died for that bracelet." I noticed how ludicrous my lecture must sound in that context, to that audience of young men raised and educated and schooled in survival on the streets of Yaounde.

"Madame, wait." The peddlar circled in from behind, whispering. "Madame, it's not real ivory. It's just bone, look." Once again he held the burning match under the trinket in his hand. He laughed and I laughed. I told him I still didn't want to buy it. "Tomorrow, then. Madame, tomorrow." I walked away, then turned around. He was already approaching another expatriate woman, and I heard him ask her, "Madame, you want to buy ivory?"

Cameroon had a lot to attract tourists, and tourists attracted young entrepreneurs. Expatriates in Yaounde tended to gather at open-air bars, and so did young men peddling "ancient art" — masks and carvings that smelled of shoe polish. If I said I wasn't interested in those "ancient" pieces of art, they would produce a coffee-table book on ancient Nigerian art, and ask me to choose the item I liked so they could make it for me that very day. They did a thriving business. The irony of young Africans resorting to a European book on African art to peddle their past did not seem to bother anyone.

The street kids were resourceful and talented. I spent many hours watching them in action. They gathered slowly in the evenings, as the roadside bars filled up with civil servants, expatriates and business people. They were ragged, tough and full of mischief that I thought would one day turn nasty.

One evening, as I sat in a favourite roadside bar waiting for Karl to join me, I spied a boy about seven wander up the steps and sit down. He was wearing sneakers, a faded t-shirt and shorts with no crotch. His eyes moved from one table to another. When his eyes met mine, he smiled then continued to pan with his bright eyes, the rest of the clients. Next to my table a French man was deep in conversation with a Cameroonian. The boy sauntered to my table, using it as his cover as he dropped to his hands and knees. As he crawled towards the French man, his feet and ankles dragged behind him at odd angles, suggesting a birth defect which had crippled him. He paused in front of the French man, who tossed him a handful of coins without looking at the small lame beggar beside him. The boy crawled a few feet more, then to the applause of his friends who were peddling cigarettes, he leapt to his feet and skipped away, laughing. The French man looked up, glanced at the boy running down the road, met my smile and let out a hearty laugh.

Travel posters and brochures didn't mention many of the most fascinating and treacherous aspects of travel in the country — bush taxis for example. Bush taxis were the commuter vans and buses which, along with a few train lines, comprised public transport in Cameroon.

Early one morning I hopped in a blue Toyota bush taxi in Foumban, on my way to the coast. The first leg of the journey was pleasant. It was cool and I was pleased to be "moving with the people."

The short-haul drivers didn't worry if they travelled with less than a capacity crowd inside. That is, we all had a seat, and the sheep and goats had room in the back, rather than on the roof. As we wound our way towards Bafoussam I told myself this was the way to travel.

In Bafoussam, however, things began to go downhill — literally. From that provincial capital the road snaked downwards, a thousand metre drop, to the coastal plain. The bush taxis did not depart until they were truly full. By the time our van pulled out of the melee at the taxi rank, I counted seventeen adult passengers in a van with seating for nine. The sheep, goats, bicycles and sacks of edibles were stowed on top. At first I thought they had also loaded a cow onto the roof, but realized later that the sound came from the old man in the front of the van who was clearing his nostrils out the side window, using one finger and a lot of air.

I was squashed between two women and their many children on the bench at the very back. The women were southern market mammies, extremely broad in the beam. I consoled myself that their weight alone should help counter-balance the tremendous load on the roof.

The bush taxi lumbered out of town. There were a dozen stops for passengers to purchase snacks from vendors on the roadside, mostly fruit, manioc and beans wrapped in banana leaves "to go." The van ran out of gas a few metres short of the pumps in the town's last-stop gas station. The young men on board alighted and pushed the van to the pumps, where the driver had them pump in four gallons, exactly what we would need to reach Douala. Out of the sight of the bush taxi owner who sold the tickets at the taxi station, the driver took this opportunity to pick up some more passengers, whose fares he pocketed. They joined us in the rear of the van.

Neat hand-printed signs on the battered interior informed us that the van's legal capacity was "11 passengers." There was to be "No Use of Profane Language" and "No Vomiting Please." That "please" impressed me.

I counted heads. As we careened down the first steep incline, our passenger count was twenty-one. I could not see past the heads to count all the children.

The force of two pairs of meaty hips eased my leaner backside forward, until I was resting on the very edge of the seat. Villages whizzed past in a blur. The driver and a policeman sitting beside him were laughing together about something. Policemen did not have to pay and they always had the front seat with ample leg and sitting room.

I had no idea how fast we were moving, but I was sure it was a personal record. I leaned my forehead on the seat in front and closed my eyes. I prayed very hard. I begged Karl and my family to forgive me for allowing myself to be lured onto the road (and my inevitable death there) by enticing travel brochures and a stubborn desire to "move with the people."

A hand touched my shoulder. The woman beside me smiled. "You are feeling sleepy?" She was stuffing bananas, one after the other, into her mouth.

"Sleepy?" I asked. "How could I possibly sleep? He's going too fast. Far too fast." If the driver lost control even for a second, we would be hurled off a precipice, into space. I wondered if the two fat women securing me in my place with the pressure of their padded hips would act like those inflatable cushions provided in expensive cars.

"Yes, he drives fast," she agreed. "It is very good. We will be in Douala early. It is good." She nodded slowly, chewing on banana and peanuts.

Why weren't they afraid, my fellow passengers? Possibly because they assumed life and its surprises, and death, were matters which were out of the their control, in the hands of God.

Weeks earlier I had seen a similar van fly off the road just outside Foumban. We passed seconds later, just as it exploded in flames. Thirteen people had died, and their charred remains were sent to the hospital. Identification had been impossible. As we skidded around corners, overtook on blind hills, swayed around hair-pin curves which offered breath-taking mountain vistas, I asked myself why I had not thought more seriously about this excursion.

We soared over a railroad track. That reminded me of the accident we had seen in Douala a few weeks earlier. It was a Friday at 4:30 in the afternoon as we sat steaming in a short queue of cars and trucks and bush taxis, waiting for the train out of Douala to pass.

Since 1913, or thereabouts, the train between Douala and Nkongsamba had travelled its narrow tracks unfailingly twice a day. Just in case anyone had forgotten that, or the railroad crossing on the outskirts of Douala, the authorities had erected large and menacing billboards with skull and crossbones at intervals of a few metres at the approach to the train crossing. Apart from that, the train — a museum piece with wooden benches and locomotives dating back to colonial times, tooted its own horn loud and clear, as it approached the road crossing.

From our place in the line of cars on the road, we had watched the train approaching, inching its way slowly but surely out of Douala. The hundred and fifty kilometres to Nkongsamba took eight hours.

"Where is he going?" Karl said, as a blue pick-up pulled out from behind us and sped past. The back of the pick-up was loaded with yellow bananas and passengers, who waved and grinned at us as they sped past.

"No, he can't. Oh God....no..." said Karl.

It was one of those things which has replayed, year after year, like a horror classic, in slow motion in my mind. The train approaching, its warning whistles screaming, the passengers in the pick-up hooting merrily as their driver led them in a game of chicken with the train — the sound of the train brakes squealing and metal wrenching as the blue pick-up was mangled and dragged a hundred metres before the little train could come to a stop.

"Oh, my God," I said.

The traffic in front of us moved forward over the tracks. A few vehicles stopped beyond the crossing and the passengers emerged, running towards the scene. From nearby houses and roadside market stalls, hundreds of children came on the run.

"We have to stop too," I said. "We could take someone to the hospital."

"They don't need a hospital. They need a morgue," Karl replied.

We moved slowly forward. I glanced out the window, taking in the sight of the twisted pick-up, drenched with blood and bits of bodies and mashed bananas.

The passengers from the three cars on the train had gathered at the windows of the car against which the pick-up was tangled. They munched on bananas, drank Coke from cans, and stared down into the wreckage. I wondered what they thought. If they blamed anyone for the carnage. If they thought God had a hand in man's foolhardy gambles with human life. If they thought, as I did, how unnecessary the accident was. I thought that it was wrong to drive past as we were doing.

"There's a road control ahead," he said. "We can inform them and they can get help."

We drove on and came to the road control five hundred metres up the road. A gendarme swaggered towards us, already inventing a list of infractions.

"There has been an accident," I said. "You must go back. The train and a car. There are many people hurt, or dead. They need help."

The man chewed on his pink bubble gum. "Were you involved in the accident?"

"No, of course not. It was a pick-up. It didn't stop for the train, and the train hit him."

The gendarme looked up at the sky, ruminating, then appraised us sternly. "Open your trunk," he said. "I want to check for illegal goods."

If he didn't care, should I? It didn't really matter, I decided, whether I cared or not. But I did care, and the gendarme's disinterest ignited inside me, like a gun that needed firing.

And there I was, pitching toward my death in a bush taxi while this recollection froze in my mind. I stayed frozen, knuckles white, jaw clenched, on the edge of my seat. The woman beside me shifted her buttocks slightly, noticing my discomfort, and patted the plastic seat with her hand. She smiled.

"You rest," she said. "You be getting malaria?" She held out a banana. "Eat something?"

Bile rose in my throat, but vomiting was not permitted in the van. I swallowed.

At each police control I joined my palms in silent prayer that one of the authorities would force the driver to disembark half of the passengers and the load, and warn him to slow down. These prayers went unanswered. The policeman in the front seat handled negotiations at each control. The seats which drivers reserved for police and gendarmes in bush taxis were of mutual benefit.

But my other prayers, that we arrive in one piece, were answered. As I emerged from the bush taxi in the sticky heat of Douala, I felt the way Togo's President Eyadema must have felt when he came "miraculously back to life" after his plane crashed in Sarakawa.

I swore never to get in a bush taxi again.

I broke that oath. Volunteers of all denominations were encouraged to use public transport; it was part of the philosophy of being a volunteer — mingle with the masses, share their discomforts and problems and bush taxis. Live with the people, die with the people, was how I saw it.

It was also a policy encouraged by the meagre living allowances most volunteers were paid. Peace Corps, back in 1985, were allotted motorcycles or mopeds for their work and travel. However, statistics on motorcycle accidents prompted the Peace Corps to change this policy and the motorcycles were replaced by mountain bicycles, which were fine for moving in villages, but not when the volunteer was posted many many miles from a town or city where they needed to shop, collect mail and attend meetings. For these, they turned to bush taxis.

Not long after my trip to Douala, the German volunteers were summoned to the town of Bertoua, a town several hundred kilometres north of Douala. We took the train from the capital to Belabo, disembarked and sought a bush taxi to ferry us the rest of the way to Bertoua. We decided to rent a whole van for ourselves, and I coached the driver in the safety rules he was to follow before agreeing to enter. I explained to him that I was "afraid."

This was a notion as foreign to him as I was. He laughed loudly, but nodded agreeably. He put me beside him in the front. I thought it was a good place; I could keep a close rein on him.

The van moved off. I glanced at the speedometer. Thirty kilometres an hour. "This is a good speed," I said, hugging my bag and anticipating the trip through tropical forest inhabited by pygmies. The driver flashed me his gums, that were orange with half-chewed kola nuts, the ubiquitous tranquilizer, pain killer and ceremonial offering to chiefs in West Africa. He had only a few stumps of teeth left. I returned his smile.

A few minutes later he stopped the van, which we had already rented and paid for in full, stipulating that the half dozen German volunteers and their spouses would be the only passengers. He picked up a dozen women and their children, their foodstuffs in bulky sacks and their livestock, which he slung on the roof.

"Hey," yelled Frederick, one of the volunteers in the back. "We already paid you. You're not supposed to pick up anyone else. We're overloaded."

The driver pretended not to hear. There was loud muttering in German from the back. I decided not to grumble as long as he drove carefully.

The needle of the speedometer remained on thirty, as the taxi picked up speed until we were almost flying through our own cloud of dust.

"That speedometer doesn't work, does it? Hey, you promised to drive slowly. Slow *down...*" My stomach catapulted into my mouth, and I joined in the involuntary "oooo's" coming from the back as the van took to the air over bumps. The road was narrow and winding, a gravel path carved through statuesque tropical trees. The driver crouched at the wheel, and his thigh trembled with the pressure he was applying to the accelerator.

A timber truck parked in the middle of the road loomed up on us, and I yanked at the driver's sleeve, crying for him to stop.

"*No brakes!*" he shouted, pulling out at the last second and veering past the truck with millimetres to spare. He threw his head back and laughed.

Behind us the passengers had begun to scream. Their chorus was drowned out by the sound of the van's engine, and the choir of sheep and goats on the roof.

I had begun to cry.

"Afraid?" asked the driver. He offered a mighty grin. "Don't be afraid. I'm a good driver." He chuckled, and whooped each time we took a treacherous turn on two wheels.

Miraculously, we finally pulled up at the police control on the outskirts of Bertoua. The Germans complained to the police that the driver had cheated them and driven like a maniac, and should lose his license.

The authorities reacted fast. They removed all of our luggage, and sent the bush taxi on its way. They searched each of our bags, and interrogated us on our mission in Bertoua. They decided we had no good reason to be there — they had heard nothing of a meeting of German volunteers — and trundled us off to the police station. There they confiscated our papers, and disappeared with them inside. They said the police chief would deal with us.

We waited outside, exchanging comments about the squalid and stinking cells around us. I thought the black crud on the walls was dried faecal matter; someone else said it was simple grime and someone else said we were both wrong — it was obviously dried blood.

One of the officers on duty understood German. He rounded us all up into a neat line in front of him and told us that if he heard another word he would find us accommodation inside the cells and we could see for ourselves what was on the walls.

We sat very quietly on the steps for two hours while the police chief decided our fate. It wasn't until the director of the Volunteer Service arrived — in his own car — and explained why we had all come to Bertoua, that they let us go.

Cameroon was like a game of snakes and ladders; you moved forward, you moved backward and at the end of the day, you felt you had accomplished something by remaining alive and free to start the game all over again the next day.

*Selling dead monkeys (bush meat) on the roadside in Cameroon, 1985.*

## *Chapter 13*

# Swimming with Mamy Wata

While Cameroon, like all of Africa, defied generalization, there was one thing I felt I could say uncategorically about Cameroon: it was never dull. Maybe it really was an Africa in miniature as it claimed to be, a whole continent of tragedy and comedy and colour crammed inside a nation's borders. Every day brought with it something new, challenging, incredible, wonderful or downright mystifying — but never anything boring or mundane.

Or maybe I have that impression because I had got over much of the fear and guilt which plagued me in Niger, and was trying hard to get to know what was going on around me, making up for that year of second-hand stories and the complacent lethargy and introspection in Niger's Club Privé.

Even the small town of Foumban resounded with drama and pageantry. The King of Foumban, a historically important figure with a six-century lineage fully documented in a museum outside his palace, was about to celebrate the hundredth anniversary of his dead father's birth which was somehow tied together with his birthday. Donations came from abroad for massive renovations of the royal palace, built during the German colonial period in Cameroon. Journalists and foreign dignitaries, including members of the Mitterand family from France, flocked to Foumban for this royal ceremony. The town was bursting with music, champagne, fantastic dresses, drummers and mystic ritual. I had trouble trying to fathom what it was all about, but it greatly impressed me.

Two days after the event, President Biya arrived unannounced, to offer his greetings and congratulations to the King on the anniversary. While he was in the region, he also went unannounced to a nearby military camp at K. This camp was the one which had sent in re-enforcements at the last moment during the coup attempt in 1984, saving Biya's neck. It was an elite military establishment, home to the country's airforce and champion parachutists.

The Commander of the camp referred to himself as the champion of all champion parachutists and told us stories of his feats during training he had had in Pau, France and in Gagetown, Canada. Commander Kumba was a vivacious and witty man, with whom we often shared Sunday afternoons at a small restaurant across from the military airport. One such Sunday afternoon, a couple of weeks after the King's anniversary, when he tired of the beer in Madame Dorotie's restaurant nearby, he invited us to his house for more refreshment and entertainment.

Kumba said he was put out by the president's visit to his base, and accused President Biya of having rifled through the documents in his office, in his absence. He was in the mood, he said, for a coup. This time, he continued, he would not go and save the president as he had in April 1984. He stood. We were waiting for his cue to follow him out.

"I will be president," he boomed, pointing to his chest and leading a round of boisterous but nervous laughter. Since the coup attempt almost a year earlier, we had heard politics mentioned only in whispers. He held up a miniature whisky bottle, the kind given out on airplanes, and placed it over his right breast pocket. "This is my seal of office," he shouted. "Let's go."

Although I liked the Commander, I didn't fully trust him. There were times I thought him quite mad. Or deadly sane, feigning madness to trap would-be dissenters or subversives. In Cameroon it was hard to know whom to trust. This was another effective way to control the people, and to subdue any opposition. Plant rumours, plant people everywhere and soon no one trusted anyone any more. The culture of silence settled in; outsiders often mistook it for political stability.

Karl and I discussed this as we followed the Commander's jeep through the security gates of the camp and pulled up behind him in front of a small shuttered bungalow that would have suited a Canadian lake-front property.

"You like my Canadian house?" the Commander asked me, as he emerged from his army jeep.

"Yes, it really does look Canadian," I said.

"It is Canadian. Canada built this camp," he replied. He seemed surprised that I was surprised.

"Canada has always helped our army. This is all Canadian," he said, sweeping his arm to indicate the spread of officers' bungalows and military barracks. News to me.

"We greatly admire your country," he said. I smiled.

He ushered us inside and introduced us to his wife, a quiet and very shy woman of mixed European and Cameroon parentage. He immediately pointed this out to us. Then, as she stood there before us he began to berate her for her failings as a wife. He was, I realized, drunker than I had thought back at Dorotie's.

"I'm going to send her to you," he told me. "She needs training. If she can't learn from you, I'll send her back to her mother." He laughed and slapped her on the back. She tried to smile for our sake, but she looked close to tears. "She doesn't know how to cook like the whites. I want her to learn how to make your cakes."

"Cakes?" I asked. He and some of his men had once roared up to our house, late at night, after a drinking spree in Foumban, and I recalled that in an effort to be hospitable I had offered them the only thing I had in the house to eat — a week-old pound cake.

"Yes, cakes like the whites make. All white women know how to make cakes." His wife cowered as he spoke, and nodded sadly at each one of her failings he listed.

Magnums of hard liquor were produced, and tumblers filled to the brim. Commander Kumba proposed a toast to us, then ordered us to drink. His wife sat timidly on the edge of a chair in a corner, staring at her hands folded on her lap.

He suddenly decided we needed some music, and began searching through a pile of record albums stacked on the floor. He had downed two full glasses of pure whisky, and he had trouble placing the record on the turntable and the stylus on the record. It came to rest with a loud popping sound as it landed in a groove. I had been watching him, wondering what he really thought — about the coup, about the president, about his wife, about us. I wondered if he had been sober when he sent in the troops to save Biya during the coup attempt.

I was still wondering, when the unmistakable sounds of Cape Breton fiddling filled the small room, in that Canadian-style bungalow in the middle of a military camp on a remote plateau in western Cameroon.

"What is *that*?" I asked. He handed me the album cover. I had not heard of Charlie McKinnon before, but there he was in full colour on the cover which read, "Cape Breton's own Charlie McKinnon."

"He's one of my favourites," Commander Kumba said. "When I was training in Camp Gagetown we used to listen to him at parties."

"Amazing," I said, my mind leaping to link continents and lives that defied links. Leaping to connect this man, so busy trying to please and amuse his white guests, with a man who was prepared to divorce his wife on the grounds that she couldn't bake a cake like the whites.

We sat in that Canadian bungalow swallowing one after another of the Commander's incredible tales of intrigue and mystery in Cameroon's army. In coming weeks, in Madame Dorotie's restaurant, we would meet again to discuss with Commander Kumba a series of mysterious tragedies which were about to strike the Department Noun, of which Foumban was capital.

Foumban was on the main north-south route joining the coast of Cameroon with the north. In 1984 and 1985, during the drought, this road was the crucial lifeline between food supplies coming into Douala and famine-struck northern Cameroon and Chad. About sixty kilometres from Foumban there was a bridge over the River Noun. It had been built, according to the date engraved in the concrete abutment, in 1939. It was built to handle small vehicles and pedestrians. Forty-six years later the bridge was taking bulldozers and eighteen-wheel trucks carrying tonnes of food aid. The bridge was starting to show cracks under the stress of the modern world.

One morning we arrived at the edge just as an earth-mover was starting across. The earth-mover was not only too heavy for the bridge, it was a few centimetres too wide for the structure. A stocky white man stood in the middle of the bridge, urging the driver of the machine across. As it inched forward onto the span, the bridge began to dip and the railings along the side snapped, making loud and regular pinging sounds. I hopped from the car with my camera ready. Security rules in Cameroon forbade photographs of "The Presidential palaces, airports, military zones and installations, security and military staff in uniforms and other aspects liable to cause moral decline and tarnish the country's reputation." Bridges, I had been warned once in Douala when I tried to take a photograph, were considered strategic points and were prohibited as well. Still, if I were quick. I snapped two photographs and hopped back into the car, quickly zipping up the camera bag. When I looked up, there were six burly fellows at my window. I suspected that the white man, who appeared to be in charge, had sent them. The earth mover was approaching the other side. The men had their fists raised. They said they wanted the camera. They knew that the photograph would incriminate them in the damage of the bridge. I had no intention of incriminating anyone. I simply wanted that photograph. I urged the earth mover forward with telepathic messages. With just a second to spare before those fists landed on our car and my camera bag, we roared off in the small Suzuki. The men were still shaking their fists in the air as we passed the earth-mover and rounded the next bend.

A week later the bridge over the River Noun collapsed just as a semi-trailer nosed off the span. The driver escaped. His cab reached the far side, but the trailer tumbled fifty metres into the river and lay upside-down, beside the remnants of the concrete bridge, in the rapids below.

This in itself was only a minor tragedy. For us, it meant that a shopping trip to Bafoussam took six hours rather than one and involved a long and dusty detour through treacherous mountain roads. It meant that the convoys of food aid trucks took a few more hours to reach their destinations in the north, and occasionally over-turned on the steep curves of the back road.

But no one had been killed when the bridge collapsed, and people agreed that this would spur the powers that be to build the new bridge they had been awaiting for ages. People said that funds for a new bridge had already been dispensed six times over the past decade, but that each time they had mysteriously disappeared, which was a euphemism for being "chopped," the popular term for stolen. This time, they were sure, no one would dare chop the money for the new bridge.

The next tragedy was more serious. This time a lake in the Department Noun exploded. A year later in 1986, a lake in the Northwest Province of Cameroon would explode the same way, killing thousands of people and attracting international attention as scientists and newshounds swarmed to the area to photograph the swollen bodies and determine the cause of this "unique" natural disaster. However, when the lake in the Noun Department exploded in 1985, the story was hushed up. There were thirty-three casualties. The bodies were taken to the hospital in Foumban, where the doctors could not peel the clothing off the burned skin. The bodies were hastily and quietly disposed of, without further official discussion or fuss.

The rumours took up where the official and terse news reports in Cameroon left off. Commander Kumba maintained that it had been a bomb, intended for his military base. Others said that fishermen, who used mixtures of poisons and pesticides to do their fishing in the waters of the lakes and rivers, had inadvertently caused the explosion. Others said this was a completely natural eruption of poison gas which collects in pockets under volcanic plateaus and mountains.

Then our neighbours told us of similar explosions in past years. They said that no Cameroonian wished to investigate such mysteries because they were fearful of bad forces, and the spirit of the waterways, the Mamy Wata. The lakes on the upland plateau, deep dark green pools found in volcanic craters, were the homes of the Mamy Wata, and she didn't like intruders. We often swam in the lakes. I was relieved and surprised that no one had thought to blame it on us, although people did bring up the name of a German who had become a local legend when he used ropes and mountaineering equipment to descend into some of the region's deepest volcanic craters and swim in their turquoise waters.

Commander Kumba told us that the French military were asked to come in and investigate the explosion. But to our knowledge, no one came.

Then, new rumours began to grow and spread. The Department Noun, people said, was jinxed. First the bridge over the river, now the lake. The explosion had proven to the people in the area that the Mamy Wata and other supernatural forces were at work. Someone was playing with black magic.

Then, two weeks later, a Cameroon Airlines jetliner crashed on take-off from Douala Airport. The name of the airplane? The Noun.

After this, the medicine men and fetish priests in the area went to work, trying to eliminate the curse which had been cast on their territory.

"It's just a coincidence," I used to say to my neighbours when we stood around in the evenings talking about the events.

"There is no such thing as coincidence," said a young teacher, defying me to argue further. He had a juju explanation which made my handy but meaningless explanation — coincidence — seem vague and implausible. Reality, I decided, was really a matter of perception, and I was beginning to question many of the philosophical and scientific gurus whom I had believed in another time and place.

Try as I might in Cameroon to get to the bottom of things, to sift through the rumours and the official news reports and the street versions to find some truths, some cold hard facts, it became gradually more and more clear that there were none. It also became clear to me that I was an outsider. People were reluctant to discuss the Noun tragedies with me, because I had failed to believe at first that black magic could bring down a bridge and an airplane and explode a river. Local mysteries were not fodder for foreign ears.

Just as the people took bad luck, they took and made the best of good luck too. Or maybe, when the beer truck crashed shortly after the tragedies, this was a sign that the fetish priests had managed to turn the luck around.

The truck overturned on a stretch of straight and smooth road. It lay upside down, almost in the middle of the road. How it could have done that stretched my imagination. We slowed and moved over onto a narrow and steep shoulder to inch our way past. The people in the neighbouring village weren't concerned about the physics required to flip a perfectly sound truck on a perfectly sound road. We could not get past because the way was blocked by people making merry, dancing and singing and holding beer bottles. They surrounded our car and breathed beer fumes on us, inviting us to join them for their impromptu party. The beer was free. "You are welcome to our happy village," said a man who was using our Suzuki as a support, "you are welcome." Karl accepted a sip from the beer bottle the man offered, then gently pried him away from the window. He staggered back to join the dancers who had moved off and were swaying and drinking around the beer truck. As we thanked them and said goodbye, a loud cheer went up in our wake, as though we had been the cause of this windfall accident. It looked as though a mysterious wind had put it there.

Strains of their joyful drunken singing wafted through the window as we drove off, and Karl and I burst out laughing. People in that part of the world seemed to have a wonderful gift, of grabbing hold of good luck and happiness when they had the chance.

*Chapter 14*

# Strangers in strange places

I found it difficult to get close to people in Foumban. As an after-effect of the coup attempt, many people in the town were reluctant to be seen in the company of foreigners. It sometimes led to their harassment at the hands of security police. A weekend curfew was once imposed while security men went through each house in Foumban. No explanation was ever given, but people speculated that it had to do with the traditional allegiance of the Bamoun dynasty to former President Ahidjo. Ahidjo's former driver still lived in Foumban.

I was also beginning to realize that for all the open friendliness of the people in the country, all those smiles and waves and greetings, Cameroonians, like other West Africans, were extremely private people. They lived in crowded houses, on top of each other, and cooked and ate outside their rooms in compounds or in full view of the roads — maybe that is why, when it came to feelings and thoughts, they were circumspect, especially with foreigners. Information was a cherished commodity, something so dear and dangerous that it was difficult for me to extract any from anyone.

One young teacher cum philosopher, Kissame, was introduced to me by Vera, who worked as a mechanic in the Western Province. He came to visit with Vera on several occasions, each time bringing me books, wrapped in plain brown paper, which were forbidden in his country. They were written by the brilliant Cameroonian writer Mongo Beti, who was accused by the state media of seeing things through "white men's eyes," whatever those were. Kissame would talk not just about the rotten politics in his country, but also about the difficulties of extricating yourself from the demands and conventionality of the Cameroonian family. If you tried to get ahead, he said, there was inevitably jealousy among family members. I learned, six years later, that Kissame had died, of poisoning.

Apart from these friends of friends, I had little contact with my neighbours or the people of the town where we lived. I had no job or workplace outside the house where I might have made friends, and Karl was isolated from many of his colleagues by their fear of Alhaji Ismael, and their fear that Karl could be an informer. Ismael did nothing to dispel these fears; he rather promoted them. He had grown quite cool with us. His children who lived behind us no longer came to talk to me and play. One night someone took a pot-shot at our backdoor with a pellet gun.

This bothered me, made me wonder who hated us, and why. Was it because we were foreigners? Or because of those rumours about us being spies?

The questions plagued me, and made it difficult to strike up friendships with neighbours. I wanted to get away, to reconsider. We were trying to decide whether Karl should stay and finish his contract or cut it short.

He had vacation due him before leaving Cameroon; I had a friend from Canada visiting, so we set off, using the Cameroonian travel brochures as our guide into the great hinterland that promised so much.

Mission stations were frequently the only accommodation available in out of the way parts of the country. These hostels were pleasant and provided travellers with clean beds, rudimentary bathroom facilities and even meals, on order. They were run primarily by Catholics, who had made great headway in the southern half of the country in making converts, and in building schools, hospitals and monasteries which produced the country's best jams, cheeses and coffee.

On our first evening in a Catholic mission station, we were sitting on the verandah enjoying the peace and quiet of rural Cameroon, when we were joined by Father Allen. He told us he ran the mission. He wanted to know who we were, where we came from and what we were doing in Cameroon. This was a ritual form of greeting among strangers meeting in out of the way places. After it was completed, there were seldom any further questions about personal matters. More often than not conversation circled around the subject of development, and might end up spanning the globe. But we shied away from feelings, inner thoughts and reasons for being there. I doubt if many of us could have expressed any.

Nevertheless, Father Allen was insistent on knowing, not just where I came from, but where my ancestors came from.

"As far as I know, they were all Scottish," I said. "But they came to Canada from..."

"I knew from your face you were Celtic," boomed the Father. "If I thought you had any Anglo-Saxon blood in you I'd toss you off my verandah."

We laughed politely.

"I mean it," he said. "I'm Irish, pure and pure. I'm a nationalist right down to the bottom of my heart."

I had been about to tell him my forebearers were all Scottish, United Empire Loyalists who had emigrated to Nova Scotia from the United States during the War of Independence. I bit my tongue and continued to smile.

He turned his attention to Susan, who was blonde and petite. She told him she had some German ancestry. He was particularly pleased that she and Karl were of Catholic families.

"Anyone who has fought with the bloody English is okay in my books," he said. "Two Germans and one Celt. Let's have some drinks to cool down. And some music to warm us up again." He rose and scurried inside. Maybe it was the greenish glow of fluorescent light, maybe it was the power of old suggestions, but from behind I thought he looked very much like a leprechaun.

A few minutes later the voice of the Welsh singer Tom Jones came pouring out of the building, dousing the chirping sounds of the night insects. Father Allen came out with a tray full of bottles and glasses.

"You like this music?" he asked.

"Oh yes, he's very good," I said. Susan nudged me and burst into her bubbly giggles.

Father Allen poured beer for us, whisky for himself and began to sing along. He played the hit *Delila* three times. Susan laughed, he sang and ranted, I nodded a lot and Karl sat quietly savouring what he was always looking for: strange people in strange places.

At 11, we thanked him for a pleasant evening, and said it was time for us to turn in. We had a long trip to the north ahead of us. "Oh you can't go to bed now," he said. "It's Saturday night. We're going to the disco."

"Disco? Here?"

"Oh, no, not here. Up the road apiece. I'll drive."

I hoped that God was really on his side. He was very tipsy.

Discos were called "boîtes de nuit." They were, without exception, tiny box-like rooms painted black inside, usually awash in ultraviolet light that revealed white underwear. Mirrors on the walls and on pillars around the dance-floor attracted young male dancers who would spend hours dancing with their images, so close that their breath would steam up the glass. Disco balls which showered dancers with speckles of coloured light were ubiquitous. Once inside, it was impossible to say which continent you were on. The music was generally pure disco — Madonna and Michael Jackson were making their debuts at that time in West African discos — with occasional Makossa, salsa or Zairian hits thrown in.

In the disco, Father Allen left us immediately and disappeared into the black corners, into the deafening music of the night. We sat quietly at our small black table, on small black stools and watched two boys wearing sweat suits and Walkmans on their hips displaying their athletic prowess as break-dancers. I tried to imagine the stillness outside the box, the peace in that small Cameroonian town where people were asleep on mats in their rooms, oblivious to the twentieth century.

It was impossible to talk. Occasionally we caught a glimpse of Father Allen, making his rounds. He moved from one young woman to another.

"Tell him we want to go," I screamed to Karl.

I pointed to the door. He nodded. I rose and threaded my way through the squirming bodies, searching for the Father. I found him with three pubescent Cameroonian beauties perched on his lap. I pointed to the door. He nodded, as one of the young ladies held up a bottle and offered it to him, like a mother with her baby.

I went back to Susan and Karl and shrugged.

It was 4 before we finally convinced Father Allen that we were leaving, with or without him. He was very unsteady on his feet and I asked him if I could drive.

He refused and eased himself into the driver's seat. Karl and Susan had already climbed in the back, so I sat next to the Father. I had survived bush taxis only to land up in this car driven by a drunken Irish priest. He babbled on about nothing that made any sense to me and we, the passengers, sat in silence.

At first I thought a bug had crawled up my side towards my underarm. I rubbed at the tickle, and found it was Father Allen's hand. The Holy Father firmed up his grip and began to grope at forbidden territory over my heart.

In German, I told Karl what was happening. "Do something for God's sake," I said. "Say something. You're my husband."

"He knows not what he's doing," Karl answered.

The hand stayed where it was until we pulled up at the Mission Station. I don't know why I didn't slap it away or scream obscenities at him. I have in other situations. Maybe I felt that celibate hand was somehow holy. Or maybe I was afraid he would throw us out of our rooms.

We rose three hours later, at 7:30, so as not to miss breakfast. Halfway through a pot of strong dark Cameroonian coffee, Father Allen arrived. He swept into the dining room with his cassock billowing, fresh from his first Mass. He was in an expansive mood — still rip-roaring drunk — and described his parishioners as "a bunch of cows." He sat down beside me, showering us with blessings and with the smell of whisky. I edged away a little, to avoid the alcohol fumes and his hands. But they were folded neatly on the table in front of him, as he launched into a formal blessing of the food we were about to eat, with ample thanks to the Lord who had provided it.

He had told us he had been out missionizing and spreading the good word for seven years. Next year he would be recalled to Ireland for a time, before receiving another call to another mission station somewhere else in Africa. As we drove off that morning, I wondered whether he had come to Africa as wild and aggressive and unholy as he was, or if his years in Cameroon had set him off balance. Africa had a way of doing that to foreigners who were surrounded by rural Africans so skilled in the art of kowtowing. Who, after all, in his remote parish in Cameroon would dare to question him, challenge him on his behaviour, bring him down to earth? He was a man of God.

We travelled slowly northwards, where drought and famine had struck hard. At Kousseri, the northernmost town in Cameroon, we strolled through the markets and out onto the sandy banks to stare across the Logone River at Ndjamena, the capital of war-torn Chad. River canoes were bringing load after load of refugees across the milky blue ribbon of water that snaked its way through white sandy canals. Kousseri was peopled with ghoulish figures, mostly draped in remnants of cloth, barely recognizable as human beings. They were famine victims, with their palms outstretched, their eyes glazed over. These were the kinds of television pictures the world had been watching for a year. There was no television in Cameroon at that time, and apart from some photographs in magazines and newspapers, I had not been this close to rampant famine. The poverty and squalor that had so shocked me in Zinder, compared with this, looked like prosperity. There, at least, lives and families, farms and livestock, had been more or less intact. Here, there was nothing. The town looked like a refugee camp, except there was no one there to care for the victims and nothing, except hand-outs from passers-by, for them to eat.

In a shop we found tins of beef, labelled clearly with the initial UNHCR, or United Nations High Commission for Refugees, for sale in a shop at 1,500 CFA Francs, or $4. There was also vegetable oil, a gift from the people of America, on sale there.

There was nothing much to say, or to be done. We could give a few coins to a few of the beggars, but to what end? Susan said that when she had seen the coverage of the Ethiopian famine on television in Canada, she had sent cheques off to relief organizations and assuaged her conscience. But in that setting, in the raging heat and despair of that Cameroonian town, we gave nothing; it seemed utterly hopeless.

We headed back south. We all felt subdued by the trip to the border town, and there was that persistent nagging guilt. We were just tourists, really, seeking sensational memories and photographs, taking, rather than giving.

At Waza National Park we arrived at the same time as a Bedford Truck carrying two dozen overland tourists from Great Britain, Canada, Australia and New Zealand.

"What are they doing here?" I asked, of no one. Their presence enraged me. I felt they had no right to be there. Then I asked myself what right I had. Then I tried to turn the whole thing around, to imagine how Africans felt when they saw us in their countries, pretending to be experts on the continent and her problems, writing papers and books (like this one), and going home with tales of horror and the absurd to tell to friends and family. As if they knew it all. I tried to be reasonable, to convince myself that I had no more right to be tramping through Cameroon than that group of filthy young overlanders. But I couldn't.

Overlanders were groups of young, usually unattached men and women from the industrialized countries who packed themselves into large trucks with benches in the rear and set off for continental treks through some of the least accessible parts of the world. In my university days I had read the travel posters, inviting students on such treks, and drooled over the idea of such an adventure. But I had never made it. Maybe that's why I was so unreasonably resentful of the ones I saw in Waza, who had.

This group had begun in London, and headed south. They were on their way to southern Africa.

As we checked into the hotel in Waza, they were roaming about the place, filling the pool, yelling at hotel staff, monopolizing all the chairs and tables on the look-off patio and generally giving the impression they owned the place.

Karl said he smelled comic opera, and headed off to mingle. On one hand I was envious of their journey. On the other, they showed me something about myself, my generation, the First World, I didn't want to acknowledge: self-centred arrogance. I didn't want to look in that mirror.

They wore odd assortments of African costumes, sandals, jewellery they had picked up along the road. They wore them like badges, I thought, just as the parents of my own generation had tended to plaster their cars and campers with stickers that told tailgaters monotonous tales of scenic look-offs and amusement parks they had visited.

One diminutive Irish man was passed out on a table. Two hulking Australian women picked him up and carried him off, down the hill to the camping area below. I remained in the lobby, reading a brochure on Waza National Park. Karl had found himself a seat at a table with an attractive young British woman. I heard her tell him that Danny, the "Irish bloke," was going to drink himself to death if Betty, one of the Australians who had carted him away, "didn't let him f___ her soon." He had been in love with Betty and "awfully drunk" since Tangier.

Then she asked Karl where he was from and what he was doing. He replied and asked her where she was from.

"Philadelphia," she replied.

"But you sound sort of British," he said.

"Oh," she said, curling her lips around a smoke ring. "I've decided I really prefer the British accent. Americans are so uncultured."

Karl was smiling. "Your hair looks nice. That's not British."

She patted the dark cornrows on her head. "Oh, that. I had it done in Nigeria. I think the Africans have such lovely hairstyles."

I moved away. I wondered what the woman was looking for, and where she would ultimately find it. If, in ten years, she would look back fondly on her trip to Africa to "find herself." Or if, in ten years, she would be just as lost as she was that afternoon in Waza and still sucking off bits of cultures other than her own, searching for some status and individuality in the monolith of American culture where individuality was so cherished, and so evasive.

At dusk we made our way into the park. We paid the obligatory fee for an obligatory guide, and watched elephants frolicking in a giant water hole and traipsing across the flat dry savannah in single file, biggest to smallest, as the sun plummeted in the west. When we arrived back at the park gate, several of the overlanders were arguing with the guard posted there. The American woman was among them.

She spoke no French, and was shouting at one of her companions to translate her words for the guard. "National Parks in America are free," she said. "We're not children, we don't need a guide." No one seemed to be heeding her, or even listening.

The guard was explaining to a tall, rugged Australian man that they needed a guide because some of the animals could be easily disturbed and become dangerous: lions and elephants for example. The overlanders refused to pay and said they would boycott the park. The guard shrugged and retreated to his booth.

In the evening, after dinner, we went to the bar. A very pale and dreamy English girl was poised on a stool, staring off into space. She was wearing an African wrapper of printed cloth about her thin waist and legs, and her feet dangling from the stool were bare and dirty. The Australian driver of the truck was drunk. As we came in he leapt over the bar to take over serving drinks from Charles, the Cameroonian on duty.

I took the stool beside the English girl, the one vacated by the Australian driver who was now roaring about behind the bar, slamming bottles of beer about in the refrigerator. I sat unattended for a long time. I tried to strike up conversation with the

English waif beside me, by introducing myself. In a tremulous voice I could barely hear, she introduced herself as "an artist." "I'm in love with Mike," she added.

"Mike?" I asked.

She pointed at the browned and blue-jeaned Australian behind the bar. Then she let out a few wispy sighs and turned her wide blue eyes towards the back of the bar. I decided she must be on drugs.

"Excuse me," I said after a while. "I would like a beer, if I could." Mike had been shouting with some overlanders in chairs behind me.

It took him a moment to respond to my request. "You'd f____-well like a beer, would you. Well you can f____-well get your ass over this bar and f____-well get it yourself. I've f____-well had enough of people like you." I glanced over my shoulder to see if he were, perhaps, speaking to one of his followers. "Yes, you," Mike shouted. I turned back. He was staring me down with a look of hatred, with a pair of icy blue eyes shot with streaks of red. I felt he had been reading my mind, or perhaps reading over my shoulder earlier when I had been making my nasty notes on the troop of trekkers he was leading. I felt guilty.

My face grew hot and I slid down from the bar-stool. The English girl hadn't batted an eye. I slipped out, hoping he would not heap any more abuse on my retreating back.

I decided the whole bunch of them had gone completely mad. The next day, heading south over parched plains where women were clawing holes in sandy riverbeds in search for water, I tried to imagine how we looked to those people in the villages. Flashing vehicles with flashes of white faces, flashing past in a split second.

And what did they think of young people from our countries who set out in the back of a rumbling truck, to traverse the continent, sleep under the stars, walk about unwashed like the last peasant farmer? I was struck, not for the first time, at how ludicrous the whole business really was. Around us Cameroonians were struggling to make ends meet, to keep some kind of roof over their heads, luxuries and amenities like running water and electricity and schools and clinics unattainable visions in their lifetimes, while young people from that other world left those coforts behind, for a few months at least, to bump and grind their way around the world to see how other people lived.

While they travelled and suffered, they fell in love, not with the places they visited, but with each other. The back of that Bedford Truck in Waza was, to my self-righteous mind, an incestuous nest of young white people, making their own adventure in Africa. But it had precious little to do with Africa at all. Africa opened her arms to visitors and strangers, but she did not pull them to her bosom unless they had something of themselves to give.

We decided, as we drove south to Foumban, that we would leave Cameroon. Karl didn't want to sit helpless in the cooperative for another year, and watch while Alhaji Ismael robbed the farmers.

Karl wrote a detailed letter to his employers explaining the problems at the cooperative. He expected they would take the matter up with the authorities, and see that no new volunteer was placed there until the place was cleaned up. His service refused to admit to the Cameroonian authorities that the reason he was leaving the coffee cooperative before his time had expired was because of the corruption. Rather, they filed his resignation letter away, and sent their own official notice to the coffee cooperative and government saying the volunteer was leaving for "personal reasons." They wanted to avoid any kind of diplomatic scandal or saying anything to rock the boat, although Karl pointed out to them that the cooperative was sinking under the weight of corruption.

We had no idea where we would go next, or what we would do. We had no savings at all. I thought I should leave early and look for work back in Canada. I started to prepare myself for the departure.

The cheapest way to get out of Cameroon was with Aeroflot, which did not belong to IATA. Aeroflot flew from Brazzaville to Douala, to Tripoli in Libya, to Kiev and then on to Moscow. From Moscow there were flights to Berlin.

Jan, an American friend who had told me all about the cheap fares on Aeroflot, also told me it wasn't easy to get a ticket.

"You have to negotiate," she said. "Some people are refused. But you should give it a try, at least."

I gave it a try. On a grey and muggy morning in Douala I walked into the Aeroflot office. Two Cameroonian men at a counter along the back wall didn't look up from their newspapers as I entered. I sat down in an armchair, and leafed through pamphlets embracing the shining world of Soviet technology and tourism. It was cool inside, and I was content to sit a while, studying photographs of aircraft and Aeroflot personnel with stiff smiles and uniforms.

"Excuse. Vous aidez?" The voice came from behind me, and the words were whispered almost directly into my ear. I started.

The man peered at me through thick glasses that made his eyes look filmy and much too large.

"You want fly?" He emphasized his words with arms outstretched, wrists limp like a maimed eagle. I was immediately reminded of the Russian doctor who had so long ago asked Karl and me for western stamps. He seemed so jittery, as though every word might be overheard and decoded into something subversive.

"Yes, I want to fly," I replied.

"Fly where?" he whispered. He looked about him furtively, yet the only other people in the office were the two ticket agents, who were both doing crossword puzzles in the newspaper.

"Moscow, then Berlin," I said.

He reached into the pocket of his trousers and withdrew a scrap of paper. "You write name, passport number, destination, and date," he said.

"But can't I just make a reservation? I mean, with all that information?"

"No, no," he whispered. "You write today. Come back two days time, no?"

I wrote. I was sure I failed completely. I went and made reservations with a British airline, a little sorry that it was all so straightforward, simple and, well, like home. I would almost miss the intrigue and the mental gymnastics required for such tasks when I left Cameroon.

I ran into Jan on the street the next day, and told her I thought I had messed up my application to fly with Aeroflot. "No, it's too soon to give up hope. Go back and see. He has to telex your personal information to Moscow, that's why he couldn't make a reservation. Bookings are done in Moscow. Be patient. You'll see."

I thought Aeroflot might really be onto something, a new marketing strategy — making it so difficult for someone to use your product that the challenge actually drew clients.

The next day I went back. This time I was given no time to wait in the outer office and admire the success of the October Revolution on glossy paper. As soon as I came in, the man with the glasses opened the door to his office a crack, and frantically beckoned me inside.

I had to squeeze through the opening he allowed me. When he let the door go it clicked shut. The only other place I had seen such sound-proof security doors was in embassies. He offered me a chair and moved to his own behind the desk.

"Now, what I do for you?"

"The flight. I want to fly to Moscow connecting to Berlin. I wrote that all down two days ago."

"Yes, yes. This can be arranged." He passed me a telex message with confirmation of the flights. He smiled and folded his hands on the desk.

"Fine," I said. "Well, thanks. That's great."

"You confirmed."

"Okay, well, then maybe I can buy the ticket?"

There had been rumours in Douala that Aeroflot offices doubled as spy quarters. I looked at this man, fluttering his hands and his too big eyes behind the glasses. He couldn't be a spy. He seemed, to me, too vulnerable and scared.

"I'll pay cash," I said.

"Very good. Cash."

I paused, fingering the wad of bills, waiting for him to tell me the amount.

"How much?" I prompted, finally.

"Oh, how much. Complicated. Very complicated." He went to work with a pencil and paper, which he filled with lists of long figures. I studied a world map on the wall, noting that the Soviet Union looked, from this perspective, about five times the size of Canada.

He held up the paper. At the bottom in large dark letters was the sum: 164,000 CFA francs. About half the fare with any other airline. He tapped it with the pencil. I started to say the amount out loud to confirm it, but he put the pencil to his lips. He may not have looked and acted like a spy, but then what did I know about how spies looked and acted? I wondered who was listening to us and then where, and then why. I counted out the bills, but silently.

I passed him the bundle and the wad went, uncounted, into a drawer in his desk.

"Thank you. Good flight." He smiled, for the first time.

"But I need a receipt," I said.

His eyes, large before, seemed to bounce against the glass of his spectacles. "Receipt?" he said, the smile gone.

"Yes, a receipt."

"If you needed a receipt, you should tell me. Then I must to recalculate the price. Much higher." He lifted the pencil again.

"No, then forget it," I said. I could always have one forged by one of those roadside stamp and receipt makers.

He grinned and jumped to his feet, grabbing my hand for a hearty and friendly handshake. I was a little disappointed. I had enjoyed the intrigue of dealing with a possible spy, and now I concluded all he really was a little corrupt, skimming off a little of the profits of a non-profit airline.

I went to the British airline office, where all was as it should have been, people in uniforms busy making out tickets and handing over receipts, and cancelled my alternate reservation.

I was still crying when a friendly Cameroonian customs man escorted me to the plane. He was concerned and puzzled by my tears, and insisted on helping me onto the tarmac.

"But why are you crying like this?" he kept asking.

"Because I'm leaving my husband."

"But you will see him again?"

"Of course, in a couple of months. But..."

"Then why do you cry so?"

"Because I'm also saying goodbye to Cameroon."

"Oh, but you will come back."

"Well, no, I don't know."

"You must come back. No more crying, okay?"

I felt like a child, and knew that for that kind customs man, I was behaving like one. I was sorry to leave Karl, but astounded that I felt so terribly sorry to leave Cameroon. I had been unaware of how much I had come to like the country — of which I still knew so very little, until I stood in the check-in for my flight.

The tears finally gave way to red eyes and small sighs as I climbed the steps in the Aeroflot jet that would ferry me, for the second time, out of Africa.

It was full. Most of the passengers had boarded in Brazzaville, Congo. Most of them were pale and puffy Russians, clad in tight blue jeans. There must have been a sale on belts in Brazzaville recently, because most of the women on the place were wearing the same style belt — red, white and blue stripes, with a sprinkling of white stars, replicating the American flag. The woman beside me was wearing earrings to match. I wondered whether she would take them off before we landed in Moscow. She caught me staring at her and gave me a hostile glance.

I stowed my hand luggage in front of my seat.

Over-sized stewardesses with their forearms bulging out of the puffed sleeves of their white blouses, moved up and down the aisle shouting orders in Russian. They wore heavy black shoes, with neat straps and buckles over the insteps, and upgraded for heavy labour with thick soles and what looked like steel-lined toes. Two thin and ragged men were moving into the cabin. One of the stewardesses grabbed their tickets and gave them a solid shove down the aisle. With apologetic gestures, and a stream of Arabic, they squeezed in past me and began to stow their baggage — dinnerware sets, metal pots and enamel bowls — on the floor between their feet.

I pointed helpfully to the storage rack overhead — metal bars such as those on a bus. They shook their heads and mimed shielding themselves from falling pots and pans. I began to laugh with them. We attracted stares from all around.

One of them extracted a passport from his shirt pocket, and showed it to me with pride, pointing to the picture of himself and mimicking the solemn expression he had worn for the photograph. They were Libyan.

I showed them mine. They laughed at my photograph, but didn't seem able to read. "*Canada,*" I mouthed, several times.

The plane was starting its engines and the burly stewardesses stationed at intervals in the aisle were staring down the passengers. What I guessed were safety instructions were booming over a fuzzy loudspeaker, in Russian.

As we taxied to the end of the runway, the stewardesses disappeared in their own cabin. The Libyan beside me, possibly mistaking the word "Canada" for "cigarette" reached into his shirt pocket and pulled out a rumpled package of Gauloises. He held the package under my nose.

"Oh no," I said, holding up my hands. "No smoke. No smoke."

They thought I was hilarious. Then, just as the jet picked up speed for take-off, they both lit cigarettes. As the jet titled skywards, luggage slid down the metal rack overhead, and plunged onto the heads of unfortunate passengers near the back.

Just as I had, as I cringed in the back of the bush taxi, as I drove with the drunken priest through the dead of night, as I had when I found myself facing machine guns in the height of the attempted coup — I once again appealed to higher powers to spare me one more time, so that one day, I could come back to Africa.

## Chapter 15

# Land of upright men

My cynicism and despondency about development in Africa were high when I left Cameroon. I was fed up with expatriate enclaves, corrupt dictatorships and lies, and frustrated by the layers upon layers of African complexities of which I could not get to the bottom. I had spent the first four years assuaging my own bruised sensibilities, looking inward and taking an interest in Africa only in so much as it affected me and my feelings. I had spent far too much time listening to expatriates talking about Africans and not enough listening to Africans.

In the final days of 1985 we were still in Germany; I was pregnant and we were preparing to leave for Ouagadougou. Since we had visited that city in 1982, when it was still capital of a country called Upper Volta, there had been another coup and thirty-four-year old Thomas Sankara had come to power. One of the first things he had done was change the name of the country to Burkina Faso, or "Land of Upright Men." We wondered from afar if he were crazy — what possible good would a name change do that country of mud huts? I had heard about Sankara before we left Niger: I made notes about the man in Upper Volta who had started trying people suspected of pilfering state monies in public tribunals. "Sankara will not last long," I had written in my diary in October 1983.

We waited, impatiently, for five months. There were many wrinkles to be ironed out in the contract. Karl was to be working for a German consulting firm, which had been contracted by a German development agency, to work with the Burkinabe grain agency which bought up local harvests to stabilize the prices of staple food items, and also handled storage and distribution of food assistance from a broad host of donor countries. Such contracts moved slowly.

Then a war broke out between Mali and Burkina Faso on Christmas Day, a few days before our scheduled departure. The "Christmas War" was over a disputed stretch of desert wasteland on the Malian and Burkinabe border, which both countries claimed as theirs. It broke out between customs men on each side of the disputed border. It lasted only five days and the dispute was taken up by the World Court in The Hague, but it caused concern in Germany and further delayed our departure.

We were not only anxious to start all over again in a new African country; we were also desperate to get out of Germany.

I had begun to question just what it was in Africa that development people were so busy trying to develop. There were the obvious needs on the continent — clean water, free and good education, health care, respect for human rights, which nearly all African governments endorsed officially and then flagrantly abused. Despite all the projects to improve these fundamentals, there was precious little progress. I wondered why.

I thought how often I had complained about bad roads and potholes in Africa. But was the answer the German Autobahn with its frightening speeds and pile-ups and drivers, who became demons behind the wheel of a new Mercedes or BMW, while the car itself became a reason to live?

It had only taken a couple of months in Canada, plus the five months in Germany, to make me realize I had come to love the warmth, confusion, chaos and challenges that Africa and her people offered. A couple of arguments with bad-tempered and geographically illiterate Canadian customs officials and East German border guards who told me that "there is *no* laughing allowed here," also made me realize that nasty and petty officialdom didn't originate or exist only in Africa.

A good part of my disillusionment with Africa, I realized, had been disappointment in myself and in the development projects I had previously believed were seriously meant to develop Africa. I had been traumatized by the Africa I found, because it was not what I had expected. Somehow I had allowed myself to believe, before I set foot on the continent, that all Africa needed was a fair deal and some well-intentioned development workers. It was becoming increasingly obvious that development projects rarely achieved their "goals" or reached the "target groups" they were supposed to assist. Something which was equally difficult to accept was that Africans did not necessarily want to change overnight, and certainly not into obedient puppets of some idealistic volunteers. Africa was developed — socially. There were traditional rulers and intellectuals and thinkers and writers and doers living there. There must be African solutions to the problems. And yet, those who were in a position to find them, the new African power-brokers and leaders, seemed more concerned with their own status and power than they were in finding solutions. Too many of the Heads of States, and roving African ambassadors, seemed to be in the business of bashing the west while taking from it with outstretched hand, while they bashed their own people into suppressed silence at home.

There must be, I thought as I walked the gloomy grey streets in the shadow of Frankfurt's enormous bank towers, a happy medium between over- and under-development. Where there would be enough to go around, but not too much either. Not that Africans were not as acquisitive as Europeans and North Americans. It's just that the acquisitiveness was somehow less offensive when the people scratching and scheming to get hold of some consumer item or food bargain were people who had so precious little, except all the time in the world for each other.

But in West Africa there were also the two extremes — the majority were needy; on top of them sat a new elite, no longer needy and turned simply greedy. There was almost no middle class; people whose expertise and talents would have earned them a comfortable life in an industrialized country were scraping by on perhaps a hundred or two hundred dollars a month. Their poverty was somehow worse than that in the villages. In the villages the people still functioned as they had for centuries — their horizon was the furthest water hole and their goal was survival. They hardly knew that life could be different. In the towns, among the educated, their goals for comfort and security were very much influenced by the west, and they felt the weight of being have-nots every waking and working minute. It was small wonder that, given the chance, many succumbed to the temptation to pilfer from state coffers or make small illicit deals, to ensure that they could pay at least for schooling for their children or some prestige item like a television or radio that would make them feel they were worth something. Most had large families in villages, who exerted enormous pressure on them — the schooled and employed distant cousin — to provide for them too.

It occurred to me as I sat in German coffee shops watching stylish teenagers complacently drinking their cappuccino and talking about their newest cars, that the behaviour of many of the unscrupulous individuals I had run up against in Africa, which may have seemed to me inhuman, was indeed very human. I watched and listened to conversations about a new trend in jacket colours, or about the shortage of parking places, and wondered how it was that the western world could be so hypocritical, in propping up dictators all over the world, and then sending out development people, like bandages for cancers we had helped cause.

Western democracy, for all its failings, had a healthy and necessary system of checks and balances built into its domestic policy. These had been developed over several centuries: freedom of the press, auditors beyond the control of politicians, independence of the judiciary, neutrality of the military. These could not, and were not intended to control megalomania which was thriving in every corner of the world. But they did ensure, to some extent, that no individual, or group of individuals, had total control over an entire country and its treasury. The secret to western democracy and stability lay, I thought, in a large and reasonably paid middle class, a product of industrialization. How could Africa emulate that? Still, I was sure democracy was the only way. What was the alternative? Dictators, who flouted laws and exploited. At that time, I did not believe in benevolent dictators. Today, I do, but I know they generally don't last long.

Democratic checks and balances also helped keep blatant corruption to a minimum. Those checks and balances were non-existent in the Africa I knew. Leaders had weapons — the question rarely arose as to who was supplying the weapons — and the people had nothing to fight with except words, which could cost them their lives. Those who knew how to play the system, those who had the right connections through ancient traditional power structures or modern military ranks, could grow enormously rich — often at the expense of the government department or agency they worked for. Those without education and connections or guile were kept dirt poor. Dictators imposed one kind of stability; the West knew that. But it was all a facade. Africa was seething. One day even the tolerant Africans would stand up. It was only a matter of time. The day would come.

Of course there were many other factors which contributed to Africa's problems — falling commodity prices for products from the developing world, outside political interests which might choose to support a "friendly" dictator who would vote correctly at the United Nations. There were also cultural factors. Traditional divisions among Africans, on ethnic lines, had been compounded by religious divisions and played with by both colonial and post-colonial governments to maintain "stability." There was a need for a good infrastructure of roads and communications, better and more accessible schools and medical facilities. There were as many theories about what was needed, what was wrong, as there were development projects and workers. Yet, few of the projects seemed to be truly working, or were there not enough projects to counter the overall trend? Africa was still sliding into an economic abyss. Why? The thoughts went round and round in my head. I had only scratched the surface. I longed to return.

Burkina Faso, led by its radical young president who had already been named by the media as Africa's "Enfant Terrible," looked like a very good place to start learning. It was with euphoric relief that we finally arrived in Ouagadougou in April 1986. Despite Thomas Sankara's revolution there was just as much dirt, din and poverty as there had been more than three years earlier when the place had sent me reeling and falling. But there were also "green areas" where trees had been planted, and slogans draped over roads or on freshly painted walls reminding people to "Produce and Consume Burkinabe" or that "Everything conceived by a man's brain is attainable by that same brain." There was something in the air, something so powerful it was almost tangible — hope, enthusiasm, activity. People were talking, discussing, criticizing. This was not the Africa I had known where dictatorship and despair had imposed a cloud of fear and silence. These were people who were tackling their problems with energy, enthusiasm and apparent enjoyment.

We arrived just as preparations got underway for UNICEF's and Bob Geldoff's latest media spectacle — Sport Aid: The Race Against Time. All over the world people would be running ten kilometres and the proceeds would be added to the efforts of Band-Aid, to combat poverty and hunger in Africa.

Ouagadougou had been chosen as the token African participant in this world-wide benefit run that would be covered live on television in dozens of countries. Mrs. B invited us to her home one evening, saying she wished to make the announcement about Sport Aid at a pool-side soirée in her residence in the city's prestigious "Zone du Bois." Mrs. B worked in the West African UNICEF headquarters; her German husband worked with Karl at the grain agency.

On that auspicious evening, she ushered me to a seat beside a group of eminent women seated inside a circle of roses. She was suave, beautiful and self-possessed. She broke the ice with some comments about her roses. She said she covered them each day with tin foil to ensure that they didn't burn in the sun, and uncovered them in the evening to allow them to bloom and breathe.

Unripe mangos dangling from a branch of the mango tree overhead persistently knocked at the back of my head as the breeze drifted through the garden. Chlorine fumes from the pool wafted over us. A Danish woman beside me, who had just moved to Ouagadougou from the UNICEF office in Copenhagen, talked about her daily fitness plan — thirty lengths in her pool each day at noon. I said we were still staying in a hotel while waiting for our house to be vacated by a departing German.

Mrs. B wanted to know where I was going to live.

"The house is, well, it's not far from the main sewerage canal. I don't know the name of the quarter, but it's close to the railroad monument." Ouagadougou was a showplace of monuments, each with its own roundabout and traffic snarls.

"Oh," she said, rubbing her gold rings and bracelets as though about to produce a genie, and smiling for a hidden camera. "You mean Petit Paris?"

"Petit Paris?"

"Yes," she said, letting fly a list of names or people who lived there, whom I guessed must be Very Important, and of whom I had not heard.

"I don't know," I said. She was a professional hostess, and she smiled solicitously.

"Of course, you just arrived. Tell me again where your house is?"

I gave her detailed instructions: turn left at the railroad monument, pass the shoe repair shop where the second-hand shoes with platform soles are hung on strings over the door, go through a ditch and turn right and before you reach the primary school and the sewerage canal, you find the house.

Her smile dimmed. "But," she stuttered, "that neighbourhood is mixed."

"Well, yes, I suppose it is," I said. I wondered if I had misunderstood her nationality. "But, aren't you, um, Ethiopian?"

"Yes, that's right," she said.

She picked up a porcelain bell on the table and rang for the "boy," for more drinks — individual pineapples carved out and filled with a mixture of exotic liqueurs.

The tables on the marble patio were filled with lavish spreads of fresh fish and delicacies flown in, Mrs. B said, from Lomé for the special occasion — the announcement about the upcoming Race Against Time. Mrs. B chatted some more with three Ethiopian women at the table, referring to the former leader of her country, Haile Selassie, as "our emperor" and exchanging notes on the origins or age of this or that gold armband or chain — Peru, Thailand, Ghana. They were worldly and well-travelled. They were United Nations people, a very special club indeed.

At 10, Mrs. B made the formal announcement that on May 26, international television crews would be in Ouagadougou to film the benefit run, which was being organized for UNICEF by the Ministry of Sports and Youth. She said that she hoped everyone present would participate in the run. More bottles were opened and more toasts were drunk in that walled garden of roses. She made a point of excusing me from running — I was heavily pregnant. I told her I would be there anyway. I had finally organized a journalist permit for myself and had begun to report for the BBC World Service, and I said I hoped to cover the spectacle.

Burkina Faso had been chosen for the event because it was one of the world's poorest countries, and yet everything — from telecommunications systems and air-conditioning for VIPs —

worked. It was also chosen because of Captain Thomas Sankara, a fitness fanatic and a fan of development assistance that began at home.

Like many fanatics, he liked to share his fanaticism with everyone around him. At 5 every Monday and Thursday, offices closed down and civil servants were excused to partake in forty-five minutes of sports. They could play soccer, run, join aerobics groups, bounce a ball. They could do anything but sit at their desks. The idea, according to the slogans that went up all over the city and featured large in the telephone directory, was that a healthy mind required a healthy body. This "revolutionary" idea was an old one, which has been fashionable down through the ages under various forms of government. Sankara's opponents, primarily trade unionists who reacted hotly to his honing down of the civil service, liked to compare his sports policy to that of Nazi Germany. But others, the unsalaried majority who looked with envy at the civil servants with their perks and social security and regular, if small, incomes, thought this one of the best things about the revolution. They were gratified and bemused to see white collar workers — who tended to give up physical activity and physical labour, even walking, the day they graduated from high school — sweating and puffing on the roads like the common peasant. In the developed world this had become socially correct — in West Africa it was practically unthinkable.

Emmanuel, the watchman whom we inherited with the house, knew a lot of things about class and etiquette among the up-and-coming in Ouagadougou. He considered himself a step above his friends — he worked for a white man. Some of our undeserved prestige rubbed off, as he saw it, on him. He refused our offer to buy him a bicycle. He said only poor people drove bicycles.

"But," I argued, "Emmanuel, we drive bicycles. We go out every Sunday on them. There is nothing wrong with bicycles. They're quite fashionable in our countries. They require no fuel and are less costly than mopeds."

He said nothing.

"Anyway, really poor people don't even have bicycles. They can't afford them. Most people in Burkina are too poor to buy even a bicycle."

We were sitting on the patio and it was late afternoon. Just as I finished my lecture, Karl drove up in his air-conditioned four-wheel drive Mercedes Geländewasgen, one of the perks of his having turned consultant. Emmanuel looked at the vehicle, then at me, then back at the vehicle. "Madame," he began, "everyone knows you drive the bicycle for fun. Everyone knows you are rich, because you're white. They know you drive bicycles for fun. They would know I was driving a bicycle because I'm too poor to drive a moped."

"That's ridiculous, Emmanuel," I snapped. "A bicycle is better than walking."

He gazed at me.

"Well, isn't it?"

He sighed. "Madame, if you're walking, people may think that your car or your moped is broken down. But if you're on a bicycle they know you can't afford anything else."

He was stubborn, and so were we. We would buy him a bicycle, but a moped he would have to save for and buy himself. Meanwhile, he would walk the several kilometres to and from work. Instead of the bicycle, he wanted a sewing machine so he could sew in the evenings while he "watched" the house, and that way he could add to his income and save enough for the moped much faster.

We agreed. Emmanuel was one of the people whose "modern values," borrowed from the white men he had worked for, made him believe that mass sport was demeaning.

For the most part, though, the Burkinabe took to the mass sports with good humour and dogged determination. The sport sessions may have caused a lot of grumbling, but once they were underway they looked like very good fun. Sankara, his wife and his Ministers took part.

My experience with top government officials in Niger, Cameroon, and Togo had not prepared me for Burkina Faso in the throes of its revolution in 1986.

The Minister of Sport received me in his hot office one afternoon. He apologized for the heat, and said that government offices were not to use air conditioning before the peak of the hot season, to cut down on monstrous energy bills. As he spoke he caught papers and documents, which were being buffeted about by the rickety fan which was blasting us both with hot air.

"Sport Aid," he declared, "will let the whole world know about our revolution." He was dripping with sweat, and enthusiasm. Until then, I had never seen a government minister in any country in the world whom I would have described as "dripping with enthusiasm."

"Before this," he continued, "no one knew anything about Burkina Faso, Land of Upright Men. They said we were a bunch of little communists. We're not communists. We're revolutionaries and this is our own revolution, not something from a book somewhere. We're standing up and trying to solve our own problems, not begging others to do it for us."

I thought, but didn't say, that it was doubtful that many people in the world gave much thought to Burkina Faso. Few people I knew in Canada or Germany were aware the country existed, (although it did gain some recognition in Trivial Pursuit where Ouagadougou had a question to itself). I was quite sure that the bulk of the people in the world had never heard of Burkina Faso's revolution, let alone given it a label as this or that.

"But at three o'clock on Sunday," he said, his eyes waxing with the dream he was conjuring up for me in that hot, windy office, "the whole world will know what we're doing here. We will be twenty thousand people, running to show Africa and the world that we are trying to help ourselves. We've also brought in drumming and dancing groups from throughout the country, and we've erected roadside stalls to exhibit the fine work of our artisans. Everyone in the world will know about Burkina Faso!"

The Sport Aid run was scheduled for May 26, at 3 P.M. in Ouagadougou — the hottest time of the day at the hottest time of the year in Burkina Faso. But the time had not been chosen with consideration for the runners in Ouagadougou — it had been set for 10 o'clock in New York, convenient for the runners and journalists there.

When we left the house it was $46°$ Centigrade in the shade of our verandah. The roads were already packed, mostly with young people who were barefoot and in rags, heading towards the Presidential Boulevard where the run was to start. The whole city was freshly swept. Neat stands fashioned from straw mats had been set up to display bronze statuettes, hand-woven cloth, leather goods and baskets produced by the country's artisans. There were dancers and drummers in fantastic masks and costumes, and live bands and a festive mood.

The British television crew atop the United Nations Circle, were setting up their cameras to film the event for live broadcast around the world. They were stringing wires and cables between the pale blue spikes that stretched skyward like a pair of grasshopper legs, which comprised the United Nations Monument. This would later be torn down and replaced with a revolving globe with flashing lights and floating continents.

Most of the participants had already trekked many kilometres to reach the starting line. Most of them looked slightly bewildered, and I wondered what they had been told that had compelled them to make the effort to participate in this run. Most of them looked very much like the people The Race Against Time was, in theory at least, supposed to be helping.

The starting gun was fired and the run began. I waited on the island in the centre of the United Nations Monument, hoping to catch a glimpse of the radical president about whom I had heard so much. I expected he would be making good use of this incredible public relations spectacle, and appear at the front of the mob of thousands surging past us. Until then I had only seen African leaders from behind bullet-proof glass in armoured Pullman Mercedes or on television emerging from presidential jets or in full front-page photographs in state newspapers. Surely Sankara would be surrounded by bodyguards as he ran; surely he would make use of the photo opportunities and the many international journalists present. Why else would he subject himself to an afternoon run in the blazing heat with the unwashed masses?

The roar of the runners moved past us. Clouds of dust danced on shimmering waves of heat. Then they were gone. I had not been able to spot Thomas Sankara in the great masses, and doubted that he was even running.

I noticed that several United Nations people had joined the journalists around the U.N. monument. They were dressed all in white, new white running shoes, white shorts, the white Sport Aid t-shirts and they wore white towels around their necks. They had led the pack as far as the U.N. monument, in full view of the television cameras, and had then dropped out.

I turned to Pierre, a Burkinabe journalist beside me. "Where was Sankara?"

"He's there. He was in the middle. I saw his wife too, but she was near the back."

"I didn't see him. I mean, surely he doesn't just run unprotected like that, with no bodyguards around? Surely he'll want to come in first?"

Pierre, who offered BBC English courses on Burkinabe television, laughed. "No chance. Those young boys are very fast. Toma is fit, but he's not nearly so fast as they are." "Toma" was the affectionate name the Burkinabe used for their president.

"I don't understand. You mean he really doesn't mind being beaten? The President?"

He looked at me through his thick glasses, smiling. "Yes. That's how he is. He's crazy."

The first runners were already coming back, leaping and hopping, like basketball players working on dunking the ball, as they jumped across the finish line. The television cameras swung to capture their jubilation on film, and the United Nations people in their whites strolled into focus, offering interviews to journalists who had followed the pack. They spewed accolades to Burkina Faso which was trying so hard to help itself, but would naturally need help from the outside world, and the United Nations family of development agencies. There was a lot of banal comment about the goodness of mankind and the worthiness of an event like Sport Aid, in which rich and poor alike took to the streets to demonstrate their concern for Africa's hungry masses.

Pierre led me by the hand into a throng of sweating runners who had gathered around the Monument. In the middle was Thomas Sankara, his red t-shirt and shorts drenched with sweat. He was grinning and offering short answers to journalists.

"There's our president," Pierre said, tugging at my microphone and pulling me forward to pose my own questions. But I had no questions at all to ask. Sankara had already said that Burkina Faso's participation in Sport Aid was a symbolic gesture, and that for most of the participants the run was nothing more or less than they would do every day to eke out a survival. The sweat on his face and that boyish grin were proof that he was going to prove himself a very different kind of leader, that our time in Ouagadougou was going to be unusual.

My blanket scepticism about revolutions, and revolutionaries was suddenly being challenged, and it felt...very good.

Two weeks later Burkina television aired the Sport Aid broadcast that the rest of the world had seen live on May 26. This was the broadcast that was going to put Ouagadougou on the map. We invited many people from the neighbourhood in to watch. First there were runners in New York, then Melbourne, London, Toronto, Madrid, Paris. We waited impatiently to see Ouagadougou. Many of the people in our room that afternoon had run the race. Some had been in the drumming and dancing groups. They were all desperate to see themselves on television. But the broadcast dragged on, and still nothing from Ouagadougou.

The runs in the world's capitals were shown in between publicity spots for UNICEF. These were intended, I suppose, to shock a complacent and comfortable audience in the developed world. There were close-ups of drought-stricken land, the jagged cracks in dry soil that are synonymous with African famine.

"That's just dry season," announced one of the viewers.

Then suddenly, out of nowhere, a figure appeared on the screen that showed African wasteland. She cut a forlorn picture, that waif clad in black robes fluttering in the wind. The camera zoomed in on her face, a sorrowful face from Ethiopia. She gazed into the camera with large, blank eyes. Then we flashed to a baby lying alone in a mud hut being watched by a huge vulture. The vulture cast its evil eye at the infant, who lay unmoving on the floor. Suddenly the vulture swooped down on the baby and carried it off into the desert sunset.

"Hey," someone shouted. "Is that what people in your country think we're like here?"

"Why did she leave her baby alone? We never leave our babies alone. We always carry them," complained a woman.

"You're all missing the point," argued an older man. "That was witchcraft. She was a witch. She made the vulture take the baby."

"Quiet, here comes Ouagadougou!"

The words "Ouagadougou, Burkina Faso" appeared in white at the bottom of the screen, which was filled with the hazy image of bobbing heads barely discernible through the dust and heat waves. Only the front line of runners was clear — the United

Nations officials in white. The film clip of Ouagadougou lasted only a few seconds, then faded and the announcer shouted exultantly that we were being taken to night-time shots in a rainy Australian city.

"Is that all?" came a subdued voice after a silence.

There was some loud arguing in the language of the Mossi people, Mooré, which I did not understand, before they all began to laugh, as though they thought the joke — on them — had been a very good one.

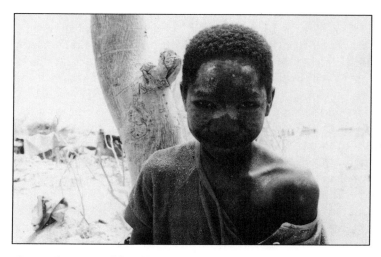

*Boy miner in gold fields at Yako, Burkina Faso, April, 1988.*

## *Chapter 16*

# When the pot breaks

I went home for the birth of my first child in my eighth month of pregnancy and returned to Ouagadougou when Anna was six weeks old. I was one of the first to disembark from the plane and the last one to get through the doors into the arrivals area, where there were passport, baggage and health controls. There was a gaggle of missionaries and several French nuns who elbowed me neatly out of their way after the plane's quota of businessmen, development experts and local VIPs had already done so. One slick French man hesitated on his way past me in the queue. He paused, peered down into the stomach pouch I was carrying. "How old is that thing?" he asked. He didn't linger long enough to hear an answer.

I didn't want to be there, where my child and I were not "special," so far from my own family and friends. As I went through the lengthy procedure of immigration controls, I experienced the first serious bout of homesickness I had had in Africa.

It was 3:30 in the morning when I finally passed through the final passport control, minus one suitcase which had gone missing en route. I was bathed in sweat and drowning in fears. For the first few days, I had myself convinced I had brought my daughter there to die. I felt I had committed a crime — taking her away from the sanctity of the developed world with its hospitals and hygiene, to the heat, squalor and disease of the developing world. The whole process of giving birth in Canada had fostered in me the certainty that babies were extremely fragile. Motherhood, as it was presented by the hospital staff and the books, looked extremely treacherous, full of pitfalls that could cost the baby its life. In the Canadian hospital I had been scolded for walking with Anna in my arms in the corridor, in case I fell down and filed a lawsuit. "Baby" was to be moved about in her special wagon, not to be taken to bed because "Mother might roll over and smother her."

New mothers were harangued by well-intentioned but insistent nurses and counsellors into attending courses on everything: "bathing baby," "buckling up baby," "mother and baby fitness," "mother and baby nutrition." There were daily lessons on breast-feeding. New mothers were rounded up like convicts by boisterous and coercive nurses, who used a lot of "How are wes?" and "We don't want to miss thats." They were pleasant, patronizing and persuasive, and did not take well to mothers who missed their courses. "Oh, we think we know all that, do we? Last year we had a woman like that here, and the first thing that happened when she took her baby home was a terrible accident while she was bathing him, and he was paralysed for life."

Breast-feeding, as it was taught in the hospital in Canada, was something so mystical and magical that it was done in a dim room and spoken about in reverential whispers. Occasionally I would try sneaking Anna out of her cot to nurse her. A nurse would inevitably discover me, yank the curtains closed and lecture me on keeping the yellow breast-feeding time sheet filled in (five minutes on each side was maximum permitted). There was some discussion about the exact colour of my hair, whether I had enough red in it to make me one of those red-heads with highly sensitive skin and nipples. I began to approach breast-feeding, and motherhood, with a trepidation I had never thought possible. Still, newly landed in Ouagadougou, I longed for those solicitous nurses.

The next morning we returned to the airport to search for the suitcase which had not arrived. As we drove through Ouagadougou I cringed. There was too much bustle, noise and dirt. How could I keep Anna safe? Sewers were open, empty lots were public latrines. The pervasive smell of human faeces perfumed the air. I thought I could smell the diseases — cholera, typhoid, polio. How could I have forgotten how filthy the city was? Anna was crying and I couldn't get her to nurse. I kept thinking about that quiet place the nurses had talked about, the dim lights, the soft music, the rocking chair, where mother and baby could relax and the milk would come.

"Look at that," Karl said.

"What?" I asked. Anna was crying more loudly now. She seemed to absorb my fears.

"That woman. On the bicycle." In front of us was a woman peddling a bicycle. On her head was a metal bowl piled impossibly high with ripe, red strawberries, which grew well in Ouagadougou. On her back, wrapped snugly and securely in her cloth pagne, was a baby.

Both of us stared in wonder as she wove her way through traffic. Mopeds buzzed past on either side, carts pulled by donkeys or pushed by young men with bared and dripping backs were nudged out of the way by speeding motorists. We were part of a symphony of squealing brakes, honking horns and Anna was still crying and hammering me with her tiny fists. The public health nurses in Canada had spoken of the dangers of dehydration. Was she dehydrated already?

The woman on the bicycle peddled along furiously. Not a single berry rolled off that mountainous heap in the bowl on her head. As we watched she removed her left hand from the handlebar, and shifted her baby around to her left side slightly. Then with the same hand she deftly removed a pendulous breast from inside the wrapper, slung it under her left arm and around behind where it was instantly snapped up by the baby, who began to nurse as its mother peddled on.

All the things I had been taught in that Canadian hospital about breast-feeding and child safety seemed, in this context, irrelevant.

I wished, as we drove through Ouagadougou in the blistering heat that first day, that I could stop picturing that pristine and sanitized hospital and the country I had left behind. The staff and advisors may indeed have bothered me, but now I longed for the caring nurses and that well-equipped health institution, which came to represent to me all that was best about the developed world, all that was wrong in Burkina Faso. The nurses had given me the impression that in Canada, everyone cared whether Anna survived and lived out a happy and fulfilling life.

In Burkina Faso, her life or death made no difference to anyone but us.

Even in the final months of pregnancy I had begun to look at the nondescript gangs of spindly, ragged, malnourished and curious children playing in the dust and wrestling on the sides of the roads and wonder whose children they were, what future lay before them, wonder how they had survived as long as they had.

At that time in Burkina Faso about half the children born would make it to their fifth birthday, one of the reasons that the overall life expectancy in the country was thirty-nine years. By 1986 it had risen to forty-one, partly because early childhood morbidity had been reduced by Sankara's vaccination campaigns. A UNICEF doctor who was organizing these vaccination campaigns, spoke to me in confidence one evening.

"The trouble is," he began, "the campaigns in Burkina are working. The immunizations are not disappearing on the black market, the vehicles are being used for the purpose they were intended. It's a time bomb."

I asked him why. He said vaccination campaigns in Africa were generally very ambitious because it was unlikely they would be even ten per cent effective. But, he said, no one had foreseen the effects of a leader like Sankara on the vaccination programmes in Burkina Faso. He said he had warned Sankara that in just two years eighty per cent of the country's children had been vaccinated against the seven childhood killer diseases. "If it continues, and if the family planning program doesn't catch up, this country's going to be in trouble."

He explained that the children were still being produced by parents who assumed at least half of them would die. This was no longer the case, but the parents were still reproducing at a rapid rate and population growth was nearing three per cent a year. The seven killer diseases wouldn't kill them, said the doctor, but malnutrition and starvation would, eventually. The country couldn't support any more people. "Sankara knows it," he said. "But family planning campaigns are quite different from simple vaccinations."

Among illiterate rural farmers, for whom a large flock of children (and wives) was akin to a large herd of cattle or goats — as signs of prosperity and well-being — family planning could barely get off the ground. It was a sign of male strength and virility to produce as many children as the woman could churn out, and traditionally, women didn't question their husbands' wishes. They were also battling the traditional odds, producing many in the hopes of keeping a few. In villages children were there to help parents, not the reverse.

On a trip to Lomé to pick up project vehicles we had met with Theophile, a Togolese acquaintance, who spoke to us philosophically about the value of human life. He related the tale of a seven-year-old boy in a village who had fallen into the cooking fire, upset a cauldron of boiling fat and suffered third degree burns to eighty per cent of his body. The German nurse who worked in the village, treating lepers, caused great furore when she insisted the child be taken to a hospital for extensive and expensive treatment. Theophile had been brought in to intervene, to explain to her why the family refused. He said he understood the family's side. Among the poor, rural farming people in his country, parents were fatalistic about the death of an infant. "If one pot breaks," he said, "we just make another." The idea that human life was sacred, and was to be saved at all costs, he called a "contamination" of the traditional African philosophy. He pointed out that "all costs" could not be taken by most Africans to save a child's life. If a child was severely injured or seriously ill, the parents were unlikely to take him or her to a hospital — even if there was one and even if they had the transport fares. They didn't for the simple reason that they would be expected to pay the costs of whatever treatment the child needed, and if they paid the costs, they might not have any money to feed the rest of the family for months. Even then, the child could die, or be weakened, and remain a burden on the parents and family forever. He said he saw both sides, that he had been "contaminated" by westerners, but that in the end he had advised the German nurse not to push the case, because it was not her child, not really her affair.

The loss of a child, I knew, was so commonplace in West Africa that it had to be treated like all the small-giant tragedies the people confronted every day. Most people were able to deal with it because of their undying faith that God, Allah, or their own gods, had simply taken it away.

One morning one of Karl's colleagues came to us in the morning and said that his wife had just delivered.

"Congratulations," I said. "How is she?"

"She's fine, now," he said. Then he chuckled. "But the baby died."

I looked at him carefully. He often chuckled when he spoke about tragedies — ethnic conflicts, the antics of corrupt Big Men and politicians. It had never occurred to me before that he wasn't laughing because he really found them funny. He was chuckling because they were terribly sad, because it was all the tragedy of life for the ordinary African. Rather than cry, he laughed.

"I'm sorry," I said, finally.

"Oh, it's okay. I'm lucky," he said.

"Lucky?" I asked.

"Yes. My wife went in and delivered and the baby was dead a few minutes after she delivered. Beside her there's a woman who is only seven months pregnant and her body was paining her. When she went to the hospital they made her stay. The man is going to suffer, paying for that. I was lucky. My wife can leave the hospital."

When the pot breaks, you make another one. I tried to imagine how I would feel if I were the mother, and could not. I was, and always would be, a product of a society which could afford to call each human life sacred and which believed that it was in our power to influence fate.

The fears began to subside in the weeks that followed. I began to relax, and Anna began to relax too. She took to Africa, to the people who didn't hesitate to grab her from my arms and bounce her around, with an ease that at first surprised me, and then seemed completely natural.

We were protected from most of the diseases by immunizations. We could afford mosquito nets and mosquito wire on the windows which helped prevent malaria. We were cushioned by our relative wealth — a standard western income — from most of the hazards to life. This was comforting, but disconcerting too.

And there were advantages to being a mother. Children linked me to adults and I began for the first time to make friends with African women with whom I had always felt some inexplicable distance before. Women who had tended to remain mute around me, now seemed eager to discuss motherhood, child-raising, and sometimes even sex.

Of all the things that must have seemed strange to people about me, what had been most incomprehensible was that I had not, even at thirty, seemed eager to become a mother. Stranger still, Karl didn't seem to mind that I had not yet made him a father. In Cameroon, the motherly Madame Dorotie had given me potions to drink and a black and white colobus monkey skin to hang on the wall over our bed, to help me conceive. She warned me that Karl would leave if I didn't bear him a child. I thought about her concerns now, and wished I could tell her that I had finally become a mother.

With a child, it seemed I had at last joined the world of women. People started to refer to me as "Anna's mother," as though it was through my daughter that I finally gained an identity.

I was slowly learning how important and cherished children were in Africa, not necessarily as individual personalities whose growth and development were of utmost interest to parents, but as God's gifts. They provided an extra dozen or two dozen pairs of hands around the house for the many and heavy daily chores. They were also a new life, in which an ancestor had returned from wherever it was that spirits went when a grandfather or great-grandfather died. They were also a form of insurance for parents, when they became too old and feeble to farm and support themselves. They were a new link in the chain that united the people with their past, their ancestors, their history, themselves.

We lived on a quiet lane, without much traffic and surrounded by Burkinabe neighbours. Emmanuel, the night watchman, liked to come in and talk to me in the evenings, especially if Karl were away.

Anna was only a few months old when he asked me when I was going to have some more children. His wife was pregnant, and he seemed to think I should be too. I only had one child, he said, a mere daughter.

He had one wife; monogamy was something found almost exclusively in urban and non-Islamic households in Burkina Faso, although Thomas Sankara was drawing up a "Family Code" which would, if it ever went into effect, ban polygamy and promote wives to co-heads of households along with their husbands.

"You're doing well with one wife," I suggested to him one day. "That means you won't have too many children. You'll be able to send them to school." He nodded at this unsolicited advice.

At this time Emmanuel had four children. Two were daughters, his own. The other two, a boy and a girl, belonged to his wife and another man. He told me the boy did not count as his own son. While he paid to feed and clothe his wife's two children with another man, their allegiance would always be to their birth father's family.

One evening he arrived on the run to announce that his wife had just given birth in a nearby maternité. He seemed downcast, but invited us to come and photograph the new baby. Then he said, "It's another girl."

We drove to the maternity clinic in silence. I thought some about the maternity hospital in Canada, which had been so full of flowers and grandparents and congratulations that it had been a little difficult to breathe for all the joy and happiness.

I should not have been shocked by the maternity clinic in Ouagadougou — I had visited such places before I had had my own baby and decided to go back to Canada for the birth — but I was shocked. The women and all their offspring, including the newborn, were camped out on concrete floors inside, thick as refugees. The fans overhead were not working, and were covered with dust-laden cobwebs. It was hot and airless inside, like an ancient tomb newly opened rather than the setting for new life to begin.

Older daughters tried to keep young siblings quiet as mothers, exhausted after the birth process — carried out on gruesome concrete slabs reminiscent of something in a mortuary — tried to sleep for an hour or two. They also cooked for the rest of the family. This meant that the clinic was suffused with wood smoke from open fires outside. The smell from the latrines was even more suffocating.

"Emmanuel," I whispered. "Your wife is very tired. Let's come back tomorrow to take the photographs."

"No, she's fine." I hung back ruefully as he tugged his wife onto her feet and sharply ordered her and the other four children outside. The new baby was still in the birth room. We went to watch while one of the midwives wrapped a bloody rag around the navel. Belly buttons were knotted very loosely in West Africa, which may have contributed to the formation of hernias, which could turn the navels into proboscis protuberances on children's stomachs.

An unsmiling and over-worked midwife then passed the quiet infant to Emmanuel and we went outside to find a vacant bench for the family portrait. Emmanuel held the child, working up a smile for the camera. His wife thanked us profusely, as though we had done something she could never repay by coming to see her and taking that photograph. It made me even more depressed.

On the way home I thought about how I had suffered through Anna's birth, and realized I still didn't know what suffering was. I thought about those blood-stained concrete tables on which women lay, three per slab on a busy night. I thought about the alternative methods in the country — women squatting alone in fields or in stifling mud huts. I thought about their courage, their strength and their stoicism. I was filled, once again, with awe and admiration for the African women, who unlike me, suffered in silence.

Eleven months later Emmanuel arrived at our house in the morning with the dispirited announcement that his wife had given birth yet again, to a girl. He seemed close to tears. He had not told us she was pregnant. This time he didn't even want us to come and take a picture.

"But Emmanuel," I said, "there's nothing wrong with a girl. She can still go to school and get an education and maybe she can find work to help support you in your old age. Boys don't do much work in the house anyway. Another daughter will help your wife with the chores."

I earned a withering glance. "I have to have a son. My daughters will marry and leave. They will belong to their husbands' families, and will not help me out in my old age. If I don't have a son, I will suffer. There will be no one to help me out."

"Yes, but if you keep having children, you will not be able to look after any of them. You might have ten daughters before you get a son. Anyway, your wife already has a son, so he'll look after you later. You're raising him."

"He is not my son."

"Are you sending him to school?"

"No, he is not my son."

"Are you sending your own daughters to school?"

"No, it's too expensive. They get married and go away. Boys need to go to school. I need my own son."

"Do you mean you're going to keep on having children until you get a son?"

"Yes."

One evening I was sitting alone in the house reading the daily newspaper *Sidwaya* or "The Truth Has Arrived." Karl was away at one of those many workshops which were, in theory, intended to orient the goals of the project in which he worked — and, in theory, make it more effective. The one good thing about his absence was that women friends took advantage of it, to come and visit. And to talk.

The *Sidwaya* that day carried a front-page story about female circumcision. There was a photograph, albeit blurry. I had to read the caption to realize that it was a close-up of a female circumcision in progress.

According to the article, Sankara's revolution was trying to ban female circumcision. A noise outside made me leap, then Emmanuel announced two visitors — Alia and Henriette.

Alia, a twenty-four-year-old mother of three, worked occasionally as a baby-sitter in the evenings. Her former schoolmate and friend, Henriette, was very poised and well educated. At thirty-one, she had passed marrying age, and Alia described Henriette's plight and life as "unfortunate." Alia had stopped school in her teen years to marry and start having children and train as a seamstress. Henriette had gone on to study to be a teacher. She now had no job and no husband, and lived in her family compound. I always had the impression that Henriette was more concerned about the lack of work than the lack of husband. Alia, however, thought the reverse was true.

I offered them soft drinks and we sat at the table. Alia spotted the newspaper and the photograph.

"Ooh," she said. "But that *hurts!*"

It took me a moment. "You mean the operation?"

"Yes, they rub it with iodine or sand. It is so very very painful."

"How do you know?"

They exchanged glances, then burst into laughter.

"Have you been circumcised?" I asked.

"Of course," Alia answered.

"Every girl is circumcised," said Henriette.

I tried not to look too surprised, and let it drop for the moment. But later that week I went to interview the Minister of Social Development. I asked her how many women in Burkina Faso were circumcised.

She paused. "I'd say about 99.999 per cent. It's very difficult for the government to stop it. Many girls die from infections. The operations are performed with blunt, rusted and dirty implements. In some cases not just the clitoris is cut, but so are the labia, and they even stitch up the opening to make it minuscule."

She said the operation was generally performed by older women in villages. A daughter from a well-educated and "progressive" family might allow their daughter to go to the village for school breaks, but when she returned, she would be circumcised. It was believed among old women, for whom family honour was everything, that an uncircumcised girl would be tempted to infidelity. She would also fetch a lower bride price. It was also a valuable source of income for these old women. The government intended to stop it, not because of indignant statements on women's rights in the international press which the Minister said turned circumcision into a "moral issue," but as a traditional practice which should be abandoned because it was "dangerous and unhealthy."

I went to see a Burkinabe doctor who was on the committee battling female circumcision. He said he had never in all his years of practice in Burkina Faso had a female patient who was not circumcised. He said too that his concern was their health. Women came to him with vaginal infections because the opening had been stitched so tightly that monthly blood could not pass. He described the agony of births he had attended. But the biggest problem was still the rate of infection, caused by filthy instruments.

I didn't want to pry into Alia and Henriette's own experiences with circumcision, as much as my curiosity had been aroused that evening. I had found, till then, people in West Africa were very discreet on all matters sexual and personal.

They were babbling furiously in Mooré. Finally, Henriette turned to me. "Alia wants to ask you a question," she said.

"Why doesn't she ask it?"

"She's feeling shy," said Henriette.

I looked at Alia. She was overtaken by a fit of giggles. I looked back at Henriette. "Okay, then why don't you ask the question for her?"

Henriette looked at Alia and broke into giggles. Through her laughter she formulated the question. "She wants to know what it's like. What it's like, ah, being, you know, with a white man."

"You mean marriage?"

More giggles. Alia's round face was wet with tears, and large droplets of sweat. She wiped it with a fold of her wrapper, sobbing with mirth.

"She means what's it like to sleep with a white man?"

"Oh, I see," I said, thinking very fast. "Well, I couldn't tell you. I haven't tried all of them."

I wasn't trying to be funny; I just didn't know what else to say. But I had broken them up and I sat and watched helplessly for several minutes as they slapped each other on the back and laughed uncontrollably.

"Why do you want to know?" I asked at last.

"Alia wondered what you did, say afterwards, I mean after the man is finished, and you are still not satisfied."

"Well," I began, hesitantly. "Let's say one is not satisfied. Then I think one would expect the man to notice and well, do something about it." I wondered how difficult it was to have an orgasm with mutilated genitalia, but like Alia, felt too shy to ask.

You mean," asked Alia, her mouth open in disbelief, her discomfiture momentarily forgotten, "that a white man will notice and do something if the woman is not... giggle giggle..."

"...satisfied." Henriette said.

"Well, no, I wouldn't say that a white man would notice. I can't speak in general terms. I'm not sure that there's any distinction between black and white at all. I think it's more a question of the man himself."

They were quiet, then Alia whispered in Mooré.

"Alia wants to know if there isn't something a woman can do, ah, to satisfy herself?"

"Well, there is, ah, well, you know, masturbation. I mean, when a woman is, oh for God's sake..."

They were off and laughing again, clapping their hands as though they had just won the lottery.

"When we were in Catholic school the sisters told us that if we touched ourselves down there, we would rot," Alia said. "You know, it would all fall off."

"How can it?" I replied. "It's all been cut off."

After that, the conversation was irretrievable, and when they left I could hear their mirth making its way down the dark alley that led to the main road.

The next night Alia came again, this time alone. After some polite chatter about the health of her children and about Anna, and this and that, and some greetings in Mooré which she was teaching me, she moved the conversation back to the matter that was obviously close to her heart — men, women and making children.

"Are you going to have another child?" she asked.

"I don't know. I suppose so. I haven't really given it much thought. Anna's only a few months old."

"You mean you don't plan your family? I thought all whites planned their families."

"Not all, certainly. I mean, I do, sort of. I mean, I should really have a second child but just not right now."

"Oh. How do you do that?"

"What, keep from getting pregnant?"

"Yes."

Sankara's government was launching an intensive nation-wide family planning programme, trying hard to get parents to space children by at least three years. I assumed that the methods were already well known.

Alia's youngest child was already four years old. Her two sons were already in school. I thought she had finished producing children and had taken some concrete measures. "How did you plan your family?" I asked. "I mean, Emilie is already four. You're already using birth control aren't you?"

She nodded.

"What are you using?"

"I pray to God," she said. Alia, born in a family where animism was still the strongest religion, had grown up a Muslim after her father converted. However, she had attended Catholic Mission schools, and then when she married, she had joined the Protestant Church of her husband. Since then she and her husband had switched to the Assemblies of God, where God and Jesus were more tangible and miracles were brought on by all-night prayer sessions.

Alia often brought me Assembly of God literature which was handed out to the congregation by visiting miracle-making evangelists from America. In these, Jesus appeared as an effeminate white man with blue eyes and golden curls to his shoulders. Adam and Eve, and other personalities from the Old Testament, appeared in this literature as white men and women. One day Alia asked me why God had chosen only whites for his religious tasks. She wondered if there hadn't been just one black man among them. Her faith in Christianity, as practised by the Assemblies of God was something I did not wish to taint with my scepticism, and I had avoided answering the question.

But prayer as a form of birth control was too much. "You pray to *God*?" I asked. She nodded. "And it works?"

She shook her head. "I pray it does."

"There are other methods, a little more sure," I said.

"Which ones?" she asked.

I explained a few of the methods available, realizing as I went through the options that all of them had drawbacks. She said she didn't like the sound of anything she had to insert or swallow.

She was intrigued by the condom — this was 1987 and condoms had not yet become as commonplace as cigarettes on shop and kiosk shelves as they would later, largely as part of the battle against AIDS in Burkina Faso. Alia said she had never heard of condoms.

"How does it work?" she persisted. I advised her to attend the next family planning session in her "quartier" of town. She said that it was for men and women and she was afraid to ask her husband to go with her. "Just tell me how it works," she said.

Reluctantly, I began. "When the man is ready, you take the condom and unroll it and slip it on very gently, and he will..."

Her face started to crack into planes of merriment before I could finish. The giggles began low in her belly and erupted into her hands, which she clapped over her mouth.

I was put off. "What's so funny?"

"My husband!" she mouthed. "My husband! One of those. Jamais!"

"Well, there aren't many other methods," I said. "Maybe you should just use the rhythm method."

The corners of her mouth were still twitching as she asked me what it involved. Using a pencil and the calendar I showed her how to mark off the safe days and the days of her period. "These eight or nine days here, the ones I've marked with an X, are not safe. That's when the egg is waiting to be fertilized. You mustn't sleep with your husband then."

"You mean, I would have to say *no*?!"

"Yes, your husband has to understand that during those days..."

She was off again. "Okay, Alia, forget it. Just keep praying."

A year later she told me quietly that she was pregnant again. She was beside herself. They had trouble making ends meet as it was. The children's schooling took nearly all of her husband's salary. They had bought a new moped and were making hefty payments. They lived in a single rented room in a compound house, with no water, electricity or toilet facilities.

I found no words to comfort her.

"You know," she whispered into the silence." I did take the pill for some time."

"Then why did you stop?"

"My husband. His friends were teasing him that he had dried up and couldn't even produce children any more. He forced me to stop taking it. Now I'm pregnant."

Two years later when I visited Ouagadougou, and went to see Alia, she proudly showed me her baby boy who was already toddling around the mud compound. They had made do, and he was a fat and happy child. Alia told me that her husband had allowed her to go back on the pill, and she had, although it was making her feel very ill. She asked me to send her some European mini-pills, which I did. Over the next few years I often visited Ouagadougou and Alia. Her children were growing tall and healthy and were doing very well in school. She had started working as a baby-sitter for a Dutch family which doubled the family income. Her husband, who worked with the Department of Precious Metals, was no longer posted out in the remote gold mining areas, but was living with her in Ouagadougou. Both of them now spoke openly to me about their family planning, about their own discovery of Jesus and about their faith. They referred just as frequently to Thomas Sankara, who had done so much to set them free from the weight of traditions which no longer fit — such as unbridled reproduction.

Her husband told me that the last son, Patrick, had been shown to him in a dream and he had asked Alia not to prevent his birth. But now the family was complete and they were getting by, with the help of their faith in the next world, where the rich and poor would be one.

Alia had opened up. We were both mothers and we were friends of several years. We shared stories of our children, their misdeeds, their development. We exchanged news of former friends and acquaintances — we went together to see Emmanuel who had finally got the son he had waited for, and had also adopted contraception for his wife. That was before he contracted AIDS; he died in early 1994.

Alia, like her country, seemed to have flowered. She now spoke eloquently about family planning and social justice and politics. She said she knew there would be a day of reckoning when all the wrongs in her country would be avenged.

*Captain Thomas Sankara (right) acting as a referee in a soccer match between his government ministers and visiting ministers of sport from francophone countries, in February 1987.*

*Chapter 17*

# No Garden of Eden

Physically, Burkina Faso was still as poor and apparently hopeless as it had been before Sankara. Economically, it was listed as one of the three poorest countries in the world. The capital was still a sprawling and squalid city in the middle of the Sahel, which was still being taken over by the Sahara Desert. The air in Ouagadougou was hard to breathe. It was full of wood smoke from fires for cooking, blowing dust and exhaust fumes from mopeds. But there also was something magic in the air, and in the whirlwind of change occurring in the country in 1986 and the first half of 1987.

In January 1987 Sankara called for an "Opération Ville Blanche" which entailed three phases of clean-up for every town and city in the country. First the streets and alleys were swept, and litter gathered up and burned. Then every building and wall in town was to be white-washed. When people complained that white was an inappropriate colour for the dusty Sahel city, Sankara retorted that it was just the right colour, because it showed the dirt. Next, he went personally into the gutters and drainage channels, filled with years of accumulated filth and sludge, and tackled the mess with a shovel. The whole operation was relatively successful.

By February 1987 Ouagadougou had become one of the cleanest and neatest cities in West Africa, despite the poverty and crumbling dwellings that comprised it. The worst of the garbage and filth was gone, at least temporarily, but what could be done about all the people whose homes were the sides of the roads?

There were still beggars and traders everywhere, and far too many homeless boys on each corner to "watch your car" or pick your pocket.

There was something in the frenzied ambience, in the slogans chalked up on walls, that Burkina could do it, stand up on its own feet and make "imperialism tremble," become "self-sufficient" and truly "independent," which at the time did not seem ridiculous at all. Sankara's love for his country and people was contagious. People in Burkina began to speak proudly of their nation and of themselves. They began to believe, after decades of foreign domination, corruption and poverty, that theirs was a Land of Upright People.

In Togo and Cameroon, the presidents' movements were only visible from behind police barriers, as roads were closed for hours before the great men passed in convoys of presidential sedans, led by flotillas of motorcycles and military vehicles. Their presence was something oppressive, slightly menacing and felt a little like a towering thunderhead casting its shadow over the whole country. Thomas Sankara's presence was felt everywhere, but it was inspiring, not something oppressive and menacing. His face didn't stare down at people from stiff and pompous photographs on hotel and restaurant walls; his face was there on the very streets on which everyone walked and drove. We would meet him early Sunday morning beside the city's dam, peddling his bicycle. Or we'd spot him in the front seat of the presidential Renault 5, "Le Car," beside his driver as he waited, just like everyone else, for the traffic light to change.

He was constantly on the move. His friends said he worked most of the night, coming up with new ideas for the revolution, calling his deputies at all hours to ask questions about this or that program. He did not drink or smoke, ate only local dishes and surprised (not always pleasantly) foreign dignitaries when banquets in their honour offered only Burkinabe food and drinks.

He was one of the most gifted speakers I ever heard. He spoke from his heart, without prepared speeches. He moved to remote corners of the country to interact with his people and to launch this or that environmental battle or clean-up campaign.

Some people were not impressed. A German diplomat told me Sankara was "simple and naive." French President François Mitterand, during an official visit in 1986, said "Thomas Sankara makes it difficult to sleep. He asks so many questions that he leaves no one with a clear conscience." Then, as a nostalgic afterthought, he added, "He reminds me of myself when I was young, and full of energy and idealism."

The American ambassador, a seasoned diplomat with dozens of countries under his turquiose belt buckle, told me he had been sent to Ouagadougou just before his retirement to "straighten out Sankara" and "to prevent another Cuba from developing." He paused, fingering his handlebar moustache, before continuing. "What surprised me is that I like the guy. He's trying hard and he's doing some good things here." While he could not accept Sankara's relations with other radical leftist leaders in Cuba and Nicaragua, the ambassador said, "This revolution is a real revolution. Sankara is turning things upside down overnight. He's trying to overturn the feudal system in this country. By any definition, this is revolution."

Unlike most people I had met over the years who called themselves revolutionaries, Sankara carried out his sweeping programmes with a touch of humour, plenty of dry wit and a spirit of spontaneous goodwill. He ruled with a pizzazz, vigour and enthusiasm that was unrivalled on the continent, perhaps on the planet.

In early 1987 he made a speech about producing and consuming Burkinabe. He maintained, correctly, that political independence was meaningless without severing economic apron strings with the former colonial powers. Sankara wanted Burkina to produce what it should have been producing for years: its own fruit juices, tomato preserves, liquors, cloth. A "Day of the Tomato" was held to promote products that could be produced from local tomato harvests, to replace the expensive tins of Italian tomato paste that flooded the Burkinabe markets, undercutting tomato growers. "Why," he asked the nation that afternoon, "do we import apples from France into our country that is overflowing with tropical fruit we can't even sell?" Why indeed? I thought.

"One apple costs more than a dozen mangoes," he continued. "The rich people buy the apples because they are expensive. If an apple cost not 140 CFA, but 14,000 CFA, those people would still buy them. To them the apple is a symbol of their wealth, power and their superiority over the rest of their brothers and sisters in this country who can't even afford to eat local fruit.

People buy them because they come from Europe and not from our trees here, because they can't resist the temptation to eat like a French man."

A group of friends had gathered around the radio to listen to this speech on our patio. There were some chuckles. There were a lot of mouths wedged open by incredulity. Someone said he had really gone crazy. Another said Sankara really was becoming a "banana republic dictator." Someone else said we should listen for the biblical significance of what he was saying.

"From this day forward," Sankara blurted out, "it is forbidden to import apples into Burkina Faso. Then there will be no more temptation." We were stunned. So were the government departments that were supposed to enact the new decree starting that same day. So were Sankara's advisors who told me they never knew where one of his speeches would lead him.

"This is for our fruit-growers. Let's produce and eat our own fruit. Let's feed ourselves. Let's not waste our precious currency on importing apples, the fruit of temptation."

Was Sankara trying to re-write the Bible? Sometimes, I think he was.

Many Burkinabe griped about the revolution. Few were able to understand the rationale behind or the speed of the monumental changes Sankara was pushing on them. But many took up the challenge. And many said they had been waiting for a president like this forever. The whole country was filled with stubborn courage and determination. It wasn't just magical, it was also mystical and enchanting. It was the story of David andGoliath.

The problems, however, were pressing and many. To anyone without Sankara's energy and dreams, they looked almost insurmountable. In a country with almost no resources except nine million people, what chance was there? Sankara could speak about the long and arduous road to economic independence in Burkina Faso, but most people were concerned with what they were going to eat tomorrow. The country couldn't even feed itself.

Besides the opportunities in government offices, in wealthy expatriate or Burkinabe homes as domestiques, job opportunities in Burkina Faso were sorely limited. Sankara was drastically cutting the civil service, which consumed sixty per cent of the national budget and was largely non-productive, at least in the economic sense. What was to become of all the students coming out of schools and universities? Sankara said that they had a tendency to come out of universities, often in Europe, with top marks and then come home "to rest." He said they must share their knowledge and expertise with the people. He also wanted them, and everyone, to contribute — often voluntarily — to the construction of the country.

One of his most ambitious projects which involved this volunteer labour was the "Bataille du Rail," or the "battle" to extend the railroad to the north of Burkina Faso and on into Niger, to complete the century-old dream of a railroad extending from Abidjan to Cotonou. Such a rail line would provide not only a transport link for four West African countries, but also pass through manganese deposits in northern Burkina which Sankara wished to develop. Between 1985 and 1987, sixty-two kilometres of rail were laid, by students, by civil servants and by foreign dignitaries who were invited out to the project to see what the Burkinabe were doing by themselves, and in some cases, to help heave a concrete block into place, in the blazing sun and blowing dust.

Sankara said that the World Bank had offered to build a road from Ouagadougou to the northeast of the country, but that the Bank, foreign donors and investors could not be convinced that the mineral deposits — and the completion of the Abidjan–Cotonou railroad — warranted the 40 billion CFA needed to build it. So, Sankara decided the Burkinabe would do it themselves. As far as I know, those sixty-two kilometres of rail line were laid without any foreign funding, and the only foreign assistance came from Canada, which contributed some rails and cars made at plants in Nova Scotia.

But volunteer work, such as laying of rails, was not the dream of most school graduates, and it didn't help keep a family fed. Development agencies were a remote career possibility for young graduates. Ouagadougou hosted about two hundred aand eighty different development agencies and organizations and was awash in development expertise and stickered four-wheel drive vehicles.

There was also the army, a water bottling plant, moped and bicycle assembly plants, a firm which produced sugar, one mechanized gold mine and two breweries.

Outside the major towns and cities traditional farmers still comprised over ninety per cent of the population. But farm land was becoming scarce. Over-use and misuse had rendered much of it infertile and harvests were dropping. Young people flocked to the city, illiterate and unskilled, to find there was no hope of work. In 1987 there were officially four million Burkinabe, close to one quarter of Burkina Faso's population, living and working in neighbouring countries, primarily the Côte d'Ivoire where the Burkinabe manned the cocoa plantations. The money they sent back to family in Burkina Faso constituted almost a third of the country's revenue.

The most easily accessible work for people in Ouagadougou was in the "informal sector" — the official name given to any unofficial way of making a living, or at least making ends meet. This included everything from roadside car and moped repair, to roadside hair-dressing and peddling.

In 1987 Sankara passed some laws to try to bring the informal sector to order. There were rules detailing hygiene laws for roadside cooks, specifying the number of tables, even the number of flower pots to be put up beside any establishment serving food on the edge of the road. He wanted roadside mechanics to register themselves and to build decent and attractive sheds. He wanted sellers of second-hand clothing from Europe and North America to start "producing and selling Burkinabe" instead. This second-hand clothing, cast off from the developed world, was piled in heaps in "Bend and Pick Boutiques." These clothes were called "Dead White Man" because Africans could not believe that any living person would part with such clothing. They were collected by charitable agencies in Europe and North America, which saw that the clothes were not the best form of assistance they could offer the developing world, and were then sold to finance their programmes. These clothes were bought by international merchants, some of whom then became very rich importing them by the container-load to Africa. The second-hand clothing may have been cheap and durable, but it did nothing to help tailors and struggling textile industries in Burkina Faso.

Sankara wanted to reduce the importation of such cast-offs, that cost Burkina so much of its foreign exchange and brought nothing except a few pennies to the peddlers. He wanted to formalize, and to tax, the informal sector. He wanted the impossible.

Hawkers and roadside repairmen were as much a part of Africa as the hot pepper on the kebabs grilled over coals on the sides of the road. The informal sector kept people alive. It was what made African streets such a dizzying delight of colours, sounds and smells, and also such a mess.

In Ouagadougou, official statistics said that one quarter of the population made some kind of living from trading and hawking; in reality it was probably double or triple that. These people had little or no overhead and rarely built anything more than a haphazard stall of thatch mats, cardboard or bits of scrap metal, where space was available on the side of a road, all too often directly over open sewers. Many couldn't even afford to invest in a kiosk, but traipsed instead through the city with their wares displayed in boxes or bowls carried on their heads. For some, especially the tiny girls sent out to peddle peanuts or oranges or kola nuts, the net was mere pennies a day. It was inconceivable that they should register themselves and come up with the 200 CFA francs to pay for a peddlars' permit.

Unfortunately, the most common wares were the easiest things to sell: plastic trinkets, "activating" cremes for hair, outrageously expensive fake hair to be woven into fantastic hairdos, cheap but spectacular and short-lived "disco" watches that were almost guaranteed to stop a few hours after purchase, jaunty mirrored sunglasses, lacy nylon underwear and other irresistible consumer goods, which people craved and bought at the expense of their family budgets and diets. Many of these came from the Far East or the Iron Block countries and were of appallingly poor quality, but they were bright, modern and to the people of Ouagadougou, they signified the good life they dreamed of and watched on video.

Sankara's government tried to organize all of this with a decree. Sankara wanted to take the people back to the beginning; he wanted them to give up the newly acquired suits and ties for traditional hand-woven cotton smocks.

What I remember most clearly about those heady days of revolution in Burkina were the governmental decrees or "kitis." Almost every decree hit exactly at the heart of a serious problem and offered a radical solution to it, were it possible to change a people overnight with just rules. Decrees, like development funds, were not solutions. But the decrees were usually a start, a step in the right direction.

They covered everything. Firewood collectors and sellers, those who made their living chopping down the sparse trees on the fragile Sahelian plains, had to be licenced. Vehicles transporting firewood — from donkey carts to trucks — were identified and legalized with huge white and green stripes. They paid taxes and they were limited to specified areas. Their taxes went back into afforestation projects. Sankara dismissed his government each year during the rainy season and sent them out to plant trees on these forestry plots. Alas, following advice of foreign experts, the trees they were planting, usually eucalyptus, consumed vast amounts of underground water and nutrients for their rapid growth, and contributed to the desertification process they were intended to combat.

Then there were decrees on marriage. Couples were obliged to plant at least two trees to qualify for a marriage certificate. Wedding costumes were to be made of the home-grown, home-spun and home-woven cloth called "Faso Dan Fani," which was also the obligatory dress for all civil servants. This would help local cotton production, increase local consumption and increase income opportunities for rural women who produced the traditional cloth.

There was nothing wrong with these decrees. They were quite pointedly and brilliantly drawn up to wipe out Burkina's problems — overnight. And that was, of course, impossible.

Still, the kitis continued to fall like cleavers. Almost every week there was a new one. The BBC could not get enough reports from Ouagadougou, where Thomas Sankara at least provided a bit of refreshing and intriguing news from an otherwise morbidly depressing continent that filled newscasts with stories of wars, famine and political stagnation.

One of Sankara's most spectacular decrees had to do with the social ills of prostitution and begging — two more job possibilities in Burkina Faso. Both were to be wiped out with a slash of the pen — and a few words of encouragement from the president himself.

The decree specifying the law on begging in the country coincided with the establishment of social centres set up in major towns and cities, where beggars should go and train as artisans. Donations from the public would be accepted to feed the beggars who moved to these social centres.

Beggars had always bothered me, aroused conflicting emotions of guilt, pity, revulsion and anger. They tended to position themselves in front of passers-by, especially foreigners, and hold out a hand, which often did not have its full quota of fingers. Leprosy was common. Confronted with that pathetic sight, I used to give to every beggar. But there was no end to the numbers of beggars, and when I avoided giving to one, there was no end to the amount of guilt I felt. Beggars seemed to have an extra and highly developed sense, one that sniffs out guilt. If I walked past pretending not to see the outstretched hand, they might extend a leg, often one with no foot on the end, and practically trip me. I had catalogued the sequence of thoughts that ran through my head every time I met a beggar and it went like this:

"I was lucky to be born where I was, how I was."

"Did I deserve this luck?"

"By the grace of God that's him/her, not me."

"Should I give something?"

"What are a few coins to me? I won't even miss them."

"Then I'll have to reach into my purse or money-belt, and open it and there are lots of thieves waiting for me to do that."

"I could do it quickly, just reach in and grab."

"How shall I give it to him? I don't want to touch his stump because even though I know that leprosy isn't highly contagious his stump makes me cringe. On the other hand, I can't toss it on the ground, that would look like tossing a dog a bone. He's human."

"He doesn't look human."

"I think I'll keep walking. Let some of the rich local people in the Mercedes take care of their brothers. He's probably one of those millionaire beggars I've heard about."

"Phew, I'm past."

"That wasn't nice."

"I wonder if he's going to eat tonight."

"It wouldn't have hurt to give him something small."

"I'll have to go back...wait, here's another one."

I would then be so relieved at this second chance to assuage my guilt, that the next beggar would receive a whole handful of money. Sometimes I even placed it directly on their stumps, making hand contact to prove to myself that I was a kind and just benefactor, which of course I wasn't. I gave to assuage guilt.

Shortly after Sankara's government banned begging, I met with the Minister who had drawn up the kiti and conceived the social centres. She explained to me that the real goal of the decree was to curtail the rapid increase in the number of beggars from Koran schools, the boys known as Garibous, who went out with tin cans to collect money for their schools and their Marabouts, or teachers. She said that disabled persons and women with twins would still be permitted to beg, but only on Fridays and only in front of the mosques.

"But you know," I ventured, "there are some people in front of the post office, young boys for example, who are always asking me for something. They are ragged and very sad. What am I supposed to say to them? I can afford to give them something."

She looked at me long and hard. She was an impressive woman, an ethnologist who commanded both respect and admiration among rural and urban people I knew. "You whites are too soft. That's our problem. We wouldn't have all these able-bodied young people out begging if you had not created them. You are turning our country into a country of beggars."

"But..."

"You are free to take donations to the social shelters where the beggars are to be housed and trained in crafts. The real beggars will go there, the people with handicaps. Never give money to anyone who is not handicapped. Whites are too soft."

I visited a social centre the next day, and found that it was indeed functioning. I donated some money on that visit, but never made it back to donate more. When I went back to Ouagadougou, after Sankara's revolution had finished and that Minister had gone into a self-imposed exile, the social centres were empty and the beggars were back on the roads.

It was not just the beggars who were proliferating because of the large expatriate community in Ouagadougou. It was also the prostitutes. There were bars and nightclubs frequented almost exclusively by African women from Burkina, Ghana, Togo and the Côte d'Ivoire and by expatriate men. It was from these men, and in these locales, that the women could make the most money. The next strata of prostitutes sat on stools in particular sections of town, wearing only flimsy nightgowns gleaned from the second-hand clothing market. Perched on stools in worn lingerie, looking for clients, these young women and girls presented a sorry picture.

A third class of prostitutes, the very very young or the prematurely aged, were relegated to take up positions on the sides of the road, flagging down passing vehicles.

When the announcement came that prostitution was to be forbidden, Sankara followed it up with a conference for prostitutes one Friday evening in the Officers' Mess in the centre of Ouagadougou. Five hundred women turned up to hear him speak. He told them they were victims of "social injustice," and advised them to take up more "honourable professions such as hair-dressing, tailoring or restaurant work." State-owned restaurants were to employ them immediately — alas, the prostitutes-turned-waitresses merely changed their venues for finding clients.

Indeed many of the prostitutes in Ouagadougou in 1987 were not, in the strict sense of the word, prostitutes. Many were young Ghanaian school-leavers who had fled their economically depressed country with its plunging cedi, to find work in Ouagadougou where they could earn CFA francs, stabilized by the French franc. Rose, twenty-two, told me she had come to Ouagadougou to earn money to send back to her family. She had found a waitress job in the Moulin Rouge Bar, a grimy drinking establishment where the only attractions were Christmas lights strung overhead and very loud music.

"When I came here, the owner say me he pay me 12,000 CFA (about $44 U.S.) a month. I serve drinks, you know. I rent a room with some of my sisters from Ghana. It costs 8,000. Some of these men come and drink and leave without paying me. At the end of the month the owner give me only 3,000 francs. He say that the rest I owe because of all the people who don't pay for their drinks. What am I to do?"

"What do you do?" I asked.

"Well, it's this way. One night a man say to me he like to see me after work. He wait for me and take me in his car. He say he pay me a thousand. How can I say no? I can't pay the rent. So that's how we do it. We go with them."

She narrowed her eyes and grabbed my arm. "But sister, I tell you something. I sell my body for that, but I don't sell myself. Inside here..." She beat a fist on her chest. "Inside here, I'm still Rose. I'm a good girl."

"What do you think of Sankara's idea?"

"The man is good. I like the man. But what can I do?"

Over the years I have often heard it said that people in Africa do not "get ahead" because they have no desire to "better themselves" and "they are always after money." I wonder, sometimes, when I hear these comments if there shouldn't be a mandatory exchange programme for development people who come to work in Africa, in which they spend a week in the shoes of an African worker, and the African worker spends a week with the expatriate's privileges and salary.

By the end of the week the expatriate would undoubtedly have alienated the entire family with whom he or she is staying by refusing, on the basis of self-interest and lack of money, to share with them. The African would probably already have built a thriving business for him- or herself with the capital of just one week of the white man's salary. The average African is missing capital; the average European is without the burden of the extended family. In Burkina Faso anyone who found work would suddenly discover the extent of his extended family, as distant cousins and sons of distant cousins converged on the "working man" to beg for money to help foot his bills — for weddings, for funerals, for naming ceremonies, for hospitals, for food, for medicine, for schools, for almost anything. It was impossible to say no to the family. The family was the only welfare apparatus around.

Once someone has, however, got over the initial obstacle of obtaining capital, there may be no stopping them. The market women and multi-millionaire contractors and entrepreneurs not only in Burkina Faso, but throughout West Africa, were good examples of that. Opportunities for "getting ahead" simply lay in different areas than they did in western industrialized countries. Fast money could be made by breaking rules, trading imports or scarce food supplies, by greasing palms and contracting (usually to government and foreign-funded construction projects) and by currency exchange.

The currency traders were a study of roadside genius, if not morality. Maybe my brain had been dulled by so many years of soft-core liberal education with a focus on the humanities, but I found currency trading almost incomprehensible. I was constantly impressed by the rapidity and accuracy with which money deals were handled in dark corners or markets or near border crossings, with no calculators or digital up-to-the-minute exchange rates flashing across a screen. Big-time money changing was often done by foreigners or Lebanese merchants in West Africa, but many Africans were also involved, particularly in dealing smaller amounts. They were more often than not illiterate, had never been out of their own country and could quote a rate on a Dutch guilder or Italian lira faster than a computer, and certainly faster than some clerks I've dealt with in Canadian banks when asked to change anything other than one kind of dollar into another.

Another major part of the "informal sector" in Burkina Faso was the informal banking system. The banks were "tontines" and they functioned on trust much like a credit union or even a revolving lottery. In our neighbourhood, all watchmen, baby-sitters and domestiques belonged to one.

Banks in Burkina Faso were enormous palatial structures that intimidated the ordinary citizens, and invoked a strong feeling of mistrust. People didn't want to put their money into banks; they had legitimate doubts about where the banks got all the money to build such fabulous buildings, a couple of which had elevators in which the director could levitate his Mercedes to an upper floor where he worked.

Nor did they feel that banks were intended for ordinary people like themselves. Nor was it wise to keep any amount of money on their person. A brother or cousin or elder might demand a share, and there was too much temptation to spend an entire month's salary on one much-desired item. It was too easy for such small incomes to be whittled away in a few minutes.

Tontines were the ideal arrangement. A group of ten or twenty work colleagues or close friends formed a group and on pay day would pay an agreed-upon sum to one person, the beneficiary that month. Each member waited his or her turn, waiting their turn to receive the lump sum so that they could invest in a major purchase such as a gas cooker, or television or moped, making do on a reduced income during all those months of waiting. The tontines were found throughout West Africa.

In recent years, as traditional networks of trust and honour break down, Burkinabe friends of mine have lost out when a tontine member absconded after taking the whole purse. But these same friends remained within the tontines. Their mistrust of each other was far less than their mistrust of Big Men in Big Financial Institutions, banks with pan-African names and inevitably the word "Development" in their titles, linked to global financing institutions like the IMF and World Bank which operated in a sphere as foreign to them as a snowy mountain.

Institutions of almost any sort were daunting to the ordinary rural farmers who comprised the vast majority of Burkinabe society. Not only did the banks, hospitals and government offices seem to belong to another world, the domain of a class of people who, before Thomas Sankara came, had taken no notice of them, but the ordinary Burkinabe citizen steered clear of such institutions because they feared they would be asked to pay for something they could not afford.

Sankara understood the silence of the "popular masses," a silence built up over the centuries of domination by traditional kings and chiefs and heavy obligations to them, by foreigners there to exploit and by the new elite who took over after independence. He understood the silence, and their fears — and he set out to combat it.

"The limits of the human being are infinite," he told me. "Mediocrity and laziness are not human. The human being is the most powerful machine there is."

For the most part Sankara, unlike many of his followers, refused to get bogged down in weighty Marxist documents and bureaucracy. However, he did use a lot of lofty slogans. "Fatherland or death," Sankara said at the end of every speech to his people. "We shall overcome." Would they? For a while, I thought — wanted to believe — they would.

*Chapter 18*

# Another world of dreams

The squatting figure painted on the signboard had squiggly white things emerging from his anus. Next to him was a crude-ly-drawn woman who was clutching her gut. Large tears splashed from her eyes and blood poured from her vagina. I had paused to examine the graphic sign, propped up against two large stones, on the shoulder of the road. There were twelve such drawings on the board. Under each was written, in shaky white lettering, the lay name for the disease or ailment it portrayed — menstrual cramps, haemorrhoids, worms, diarrhoea.

In front of the sign was a fantastic array of medicines, some in recycled injectable penicillin bottles, other large pills were piled into colourful mounds on the plastic mat that served as the shelves of this roadside pharmacy. There were also bundles of different barks and leaves and lumps of stone.

The young pharmacist/doctor/healer was across the road, shouting in Mooré through a megaphone at passing motorists and pedestrians. I assumed he was calling on the sick to come and be healed.

He saw me and sprinted across the road.

"You really have medicines for all these ailments?" I asked.

"Yes, everything."

I squinted at the individual piles of brightly coloured tablets. I bent down and picked up a bottle of injectable penicillin, that held a clear liquid.

"Is this really penicillin?" I asked.

He nodded.

"But it's expired. Three years ago."

"You need some?" he asked.

I continued to peruse his display of medications, and that fascinating signboard.

"You have menstrual cramps?" he asked, pointing at the haemorrhaging figure on his sign. "Or constipation? You have constipation?" He gazed closely at my face. "You have constipation," he announced, leaping into the middle of his makeshift pharmacy and retrieving a bottle of large yellow pills.

"You have terrible cramps, yes? Cannot sleep, yes? You take these. Two in the morning. You wait. Ten minutes, twenty minutes. Then, you *feel free!*" He hardly needed a megaphone.

I put a finger to my lips. "Ssshhh," I said. A large crowd had gathered around us. Most were bug-eyed children; some were adults who watched with bemused expressions.

"I don't have constipation," I said. "I was just curious about what you have to sell, what all this is for."

"But you must have something. Everyone has something. Worms? Malaria? You have malaria?"

"I don't have anything," I said.

"Oh, thank you. Then you come back to me when you have something. I can cure anything."

Roadside healers were everywhere in West Africa. They moved from one country to another, setting up their wares anywhere they could find a patch of free ground, or boarding long-haul buses and bush taxis and haranguing the passengers for the duration of the journey. They were for the most part quacks, who had fallen through the enormous gap between modern medicine as practised in hospitals and clinics, and the genuine traditional healers and gri-gri men who worked their cures with medicinal herbs and a few spells, in villages and city alleys.

I tried to get Karl to come and see what was involved in the "miraculous five-minute cure for impotency," not because he suffered from that problem, but because I was curious and I needed a male guinea pig to try the cure. "You can always say you're doing it for a friend who's too embarrassed to come himself," I said. Karl refused. His excuse was that he wanted to avoid getting mixed up in African juju, gri-gri or fetishes, which was probably quite valid. That world of spirits and demons and witches and curses and poison and medicines was one unto itself, one I could no longer disregard as I had when I first came to Africa with my "rational" western theories about the world around me. I no longer dared to dismiss necromancy as I had; I had had too many brushes with its powers.

"I had a visitor last night," Raymond, our cook, told me one morning as he poured a generous amount of murky peanut oil into a saucepan for a yam stew.

"Oh yes?" I replied, concerned more about the oil slick in the pot than any visitor he may have had. He often recounted real-life midnight horror stories, from his own neighbourhood, about thieves beaten to death, or the victims they murdered and robbed.

"It was an old man," he said.

"An old man. Did you know him?"

"No, I don't know him. My grandfather sent him. He was carrying a fish."

"In the middle of the night?"

"Yes, he knocked on the door and when I opened it he was standing there with a fish in his arms. He said it was for me, a message from my grandfather."

"That seems, well, a bit odd. So you have fish to eat today?"

He eyed me, and stirred the meat which was drowning in oil. "Of course not. The fish wasn't a real fish. It was a message from my grandfather."

"What an odd message to bring. Are you sure it wasn't a dream?"

"No, it wasn't a dream. It was a message from my grandfather in the village. He can't come himself."

"What was the message, I mean, why would he send it that way?"

"There's an old man in my village who turns himself into a 'silmande' whenever something is not right in the village, and he goes about informing all of us who aren't in the village. A silmande moves very fast."

"Silmande?" I asked. The word was familiar to me only because it was the name of Ouagadougou's International Pullman Hotel, a luxurious edifice perched on the edge of the city's largest dam and catchment area, a place where development consultants, diplomats, dignitaries and arms dealers stayed while in the city.

"A silmande is a dust devil, like you see blowing across the road. When you see one, you know an elder is moving about," he explained.

"So this old man, your visitor, was really a dust devil..."

"No, the dust devil was really the old man, who was sent by my grandfather to inform me that something was wrong with him. He had to have his foot cut off last week. The operation must be finished, and he sent me the messenger. Otherwise he would have sent the other old man to inform me something was wrong."

Something was inherently faulty with his logic, or my own, but I couldn't pinpoint it.

"But your village is a long way from here. You mean this old man who came to see you could also turn himself into a silmande?"

"Yes," he said, with a sigh.

"Then you will go to the village to see your grandfather?"

"No, because he sent the man and the fish to tell me everything is okay now. The operation went well."

I paused, wanting to get to the bottom of this, but not wanting to pull at threads in a fabric with warps and wefts I could not possibly — and probably should not try to — unravel.

"Well," I said brightly, "that's good news isn't it?" And I left him to finish the yam stew in peace.

The world of African spirits, that other dream world from which foreigners were truly excluded, was something I had read and heard a lot about. Years before, in Niger, I had disregarded the whole complex matter of shamans and healers and fetishes; I was still naive and ignorant enough to believe that what I could not see or what could not be documented with tangible evidence so that I could understand it, did not exist. I took an academic approach, a hangover from my years studying anthropology, and looked at all of these mystic men as intriguing human and anthropological phenomena, accepting that they were important figures playing important social and spiritual roles, much like any religious figures anywhere.

Later, in Cameroon, I became more fascinated by the world of African spirits and spells, but only in an idle and patronizing way. I liked to hear about other peoples' experiences, and then cast my own doubts on them.

There was the case of Sophie, an African-American Peace Corps volunteer from Philadelphia, who had just arrived in Africa and a few weeks later was robbed. This, and the fact that her mother had just died of alcoholism back in a Philadelphia ghetto, plunged Sophie into depression bordering on total breakdown.

"We just got running water and electricity at home," she told us tearfully one night, after robbers emptied her house for the second time. "I came over here to help the poor Africans. And I get invited by rich Africans to banquets with seating and champagne for three thousand people. I'm here to help poor people. It's not right. And now thieves come and rob me. Why don't they rob the rich people?"

I said that the rich people barricaded themselves behind impenetrable security, and that intruders on their large grounds were shot on sight. She told us that her colleagues in the Community Development Department had taken her to a traditional gri-gri man to find out the identity of the thieves.

"It was really bizarre," she said. "I gave him a chicken, and then they took me to this dark room and there was a radio playing outside. And the old man was sitting on the floor and he took two sticks and waved them and he was chanting and moaning. He didn't tell me who the thieves were, but he told the people who took me there."

I was highly sceptical, back then. If he really had uncovered the thieves' identities, then I was sure he was behind the theft, or perhaps he knew the townspeople so well that the sticks and the chanting were just frills, for show.

Sophie didn't get her things back, and when she left, she was completely disenchanted with Africa and with development work.

By the time I arrived in Ouagadougou, I was to the point of accepting that traditional medicine men were capable of working cures and curses with empirical causes and substances. Certainly, it was documented that many of their herbal cures were effective, and I was ready to believe that many of the sudden deaths blamed on witches or spells were probably caused by deliberate poisoning, which was common throughout West Africa. In some households wives were expected to sample the food they placed before their husbands before the men would touch it. And friends had told me that when I served bottled drinks to guests in my home, I was expected to open the bottles in front of them, to ensure no substances had been administered beforehand. African friends with whom we went out in the evenings always emptied their glasses before going to the dance-floor, ensuring that no one dropped some poison in while they were away from the table.

I had begun to realize that for every occasion when an African had done something I did not understand or appreciate, I had probably committed ten graver social crimes — such as neglecting to greet someone, offering opened bottles of beer or soft drinks to guests or pooh-poohing beliefs in witches and spirits.

I also began to realize that most Africans saw, heard and felt things to which I was still, in large part, oblivious. It was at this point that I visited a traditional healer in a market in Ouagadougou. The day was October 15, 1987. That bright and hot morning I was wandering through one of Ouagadougou's small markets, searching for a famous healer I had been told about. He was the head of the Traditional Practitioners' Association in Burkina Faso, and his name was Soulemane Sinaré.

I finally spotted the signboard in front of a dusty little hut fashioned from mats and rickety poles. It claimed in hand-painted letters that there would be "Health for All by the Year 2000" — one of Sankara's and the World Health Organization's most optimistic slogans.

Sinaré was sitting on a bench, in a shaded antechamber. He was staring at the blue sky. I paused, inspecting the selection of medicinal products laid out on the sand in front of the hut: dried monkey heads, baboon skulls, lizards, tortoise shells, leaves, barks. On the signboard Sinaré's credentials and awards from the various medical groups were listed very neatly.

I had observed similar and to me equally gruesome displays of medicinal wares in markets from the northern tip of Cameroon to the southern tip of Togo. Why I had never paid any attention before, I don't know. I had been meaning to do some stories on traditional medicine for over a year. That hot morning there was tension in the air. Perhaps it was the lull before the storm which would break later in the day, bringing the rainy season and an end to an era in Ouagadougou.

Sinaré grinned at me. I introduced myself and he invited me into the shade cast by mats laid over a small porch area in front of the hut.

"You have an interesting display of healing agents," I began.

"Yes, I have many more inside. Would you like to see?"

I nodded, and rose to follow him inside the dark and surprisingly cool hut.

"This," he said, pulling a great lump of something that looked like charcoal from where it hung on a flimsy pillar supporting the centre of the thatch roof, "is elephant skin. It is for curing measles."

"Really?"

"Yes, I can treat almost any disease that you know of with my herbs and medicines. It is only the new diseases, the white man's diseases like AIDS and cancer, which I cannot cure. Not yet, anyway." He chuckled.

This was a rational man. There was nothing mystical about him or his market clinic, I concluded, a little too quickly. Nothing here that wasn't tangible and testable in the right laboratory with the right expertise.

"You use herbs and skins and things to treat all your patients?" This was something I could cope with, something solid that my brain could wrap itself around.

"Yes," he said, eyeing me.

"I find it so interesting," I said. "I hope that people like you are going to share some of your wealth of knowledge with western science so that modern medicine can adopt some of your tried and true cures. Many of our own medicines come from tropical flora. It would be nice if you got some credit for your medicinal knowledge."

He nodded.

"But I've been told that traditional medicine men shroud much of their work in secrecy and mystery, don't want to divulge secrets." Health workers had said that they struggled to obtain herbal cures from the traditional practitioners, who guarded their health secrets, handed down from one generation to another. So far they had already proven the effectiveness of seven traditional medicines and were marketing them in Ouagadougou. But they knew there were many more.

Sinaré was smiling at me, non-committal. A man carrying the inert form of a boy entered the hut. The boy's face was almost grey, and his breath came in quick, small puffs. I could see his heart palpitating too fast underneath his prominent ribs, pulsing double-speed in his neck. The boy's father greeted Soulemane Sinaré, and said the boy had been suffering from fever and faintness for three days.

Sinaré moved to a bench, gathering his long white robe around him. He placed the boy before him on the sand, holding him upright between his knees. He clasped the boy's head in his large and strong hands, and rubbed gently on the back of his skull. He whispered words I could not hear. He spat twice on the boy's forehead, while rubbing his hands over his head. The boy's eyes opened very wide and he said clearly, "I want to sleep."

Sinaré laid him out gently on the wooden bench and the boy slept. His breathing had steadied, as had his pulse.

"Is he better?" I asked eventually, breaking the eerie silence.

"Not yet. I haven't finished. But he will be."

"You gave him no medicine," I said.

"He doesn't need any yet."

"What does he have, malaria?" I asked.

"Yes, but not just malaria."

"I don't understand. I thought that you used herbs for malaria."

"Madame," he said very softly and slowly, "I use whatever I need to heal. It is much more than you think."

He leaned back in a sloping chair made of thousands of sticks lashed neatly together and secured with strips of hide. He stared at me speculatively, and I felt like a student being scrutinized by a professor who's judging the extent of her intellect.

The boy's colour was returning. Sweat had broken out on his face, which moments before had the same texture and sheen as the dried elephant hide used to cure measles.

"What do you mean?" I asked. It seemed suddenly very quiet in the market. In the heat, I had begun to shiver.

"I can do more than just heal people. I could, if I wanted to, also make them sick. I can heal many diseases that you don't even know about, because you do not have them. The ones caused by invoking spirits."

Perhaps my incredulity showed on my face. His gaze intensified. I rubbed my arms.

"Look at that tree," he said, pointing to a brave little neem tree which had sprung up in the sand just beyond his hut.

"I see it."

"I could, if I willed it, make you fall dead when you leave here and walk underneath it." He paused. "Do you believe me?"

I glanced at the tree, back at his eyes which in the gloom of the porch were like pinpoints of light focused on me and my stubborn western dogma that denied the existence of the supernatural, or forces not yet harnessed by scientists and physicists. Up to that moment in my life, I had enjoyed the shade of the twentieth century scientific paradigms under which I had been sitting like they were a large umbrella that warded off unwanted questions. I did not want my shelter yanked away by this old man in this forgotten market in this obscure country. But I didn't want to challenge him. Not under that stare.

I nodded. "Yes, I believe you." And I did.

"Good. This is very good. You do not need to believe but it would be very bad if you said you did not believe."

The boy began to stir on the bench. Then he sat up and rubbed his eyes, as though he had slept an entire night and didn't know where he had woken up. He looked at his father, who had been watching him closely, then at Sinaré.

He stood, stretched and followed his father out of the hut. Sinaré smiled at me. "Tomorrow I will give him medicine to combat the malaria. Now that what was ailing his spirit has been removed." I thanked Sinaré for taking the time to talk to me. As I left I was careful to avoid walking underneath the tree.

Although I thought I had taken down careful notes during and after our conversation, for some reason every time I re-read the notes, most of which are reproduced here, I felt I had missed out on something Sinaré had said to me. Perhaps he sent me messages that morning without using the spoken word? He opened my mind to an entirely new world; he changed me. I finally acknowledged that our western world, the rational world I lived in, was in general too quick to dismiss too much as hocus pocus. Perhaps there was more to man, the mind and the soul, than science or even some churches dealt with. Perhaps that is what Sinaré managed to convey to me. An illusion or an ethereal message like Raymond's night visitor with the fish? I will never know.

My next encounter with the metaphysical world of the psyche, and African magic, was with a friend who worked at an embassy in Ouagadougou. She told me she was going crazy. Nervous conditions and breakdowns were common among expatriates. I knew of many women, usually wives of prominent diplomats or international representatives, who could not deal with the constant strain of their roles as diplomatic spouses. They were usually dissatisfied with their life of protocol and small-talk, bored by their role as hostess. But any such breakdowns I had seen had been in people who detested Africa and who tended to sequester themselves away in houses behind large walls, where boredom and isolation eventually overcame them.

Juliana was different. She loved Burkina Faso; she was out and about discovering it and perhaps she discovered things she should never have touched.

I had been out of the country for some time, to have a second baby. On our return, she met us at the airport. The first thing that struck me about her was her eyes, which were green and devoid of any expression I knew. I had read in popular literature about people with "haunted eyes," which had, to then, always seemed to me like literary hyperbole. But Juliana's eyes were haunted. They did not seem to belong to her face, which was longer than I remembered it, as though a great weight had been attached to her chin. Her nails were gnawed and bleeding. She said she had decided to leave Ouagadougou, and now, too late, she had changed her mind and didn't want to leave. She was already contracted for a post in an embassy in the Caribbean.

"I'm going crazy," she repeated.

"Turning down a post in the Caribbean would be crazy," I countered, trying to cheer her up with flippancy. I knew she had led a charmed life in Ouagadougou, which may not be the city of everyone's dreams, but which still offered a smattering of the exotic life of evening cocktails and diplomatic leisure that lured people to the tropics. She had only a few hours left before receiving her pilot's licence, played tennis and rode at the equestrian club. She said she had fallen in love with the hot, dusty city. Still, a post in the Caribbean! Ocean breezes and waves on the doorstep — there were many moments in the peak of the scorching days of the dry season when those images floated like sirens just behind my eyes and in front of the raging sun-induced headache.

"You'll be okay," I assured her as we sat on her veranda that first evening, the children tucked up asleep in her guest room. "Just take it easy."

"You don't understand," she said. "I'm really crazy."

I laughed, jumping to the conclusion that life and the people living it are essentially normal, and any excesses can be dealt with by platitudes. "You're not crazy. It's the stress of leaving. I have that every time I leave Africa, even for a holiday."

"I need a psychiatrist," she said.

"No, you don't."

"I do."

Our verbal ping-pong continued until she finally turned her haunted stare on me. Shivers crawled up my neck, just as they had done under Sinaré's gaze. I scratched, thinking about a huge, stinging millipede I had just seen cross the tiled floor of her patio.

"Come on, Juliana, I'm beat. You're probably just tired." I stood up and tried on a smile which didn't fit.

She allowed me to lead her to her room, where she flopped onto her bed on her back.

She seemed to have fallen asleep. I really was exhausted. It had been a long flight; Karl and the children had been asleep for hours on the floor of the room across the hall. I crawled in among them and turned out the light.

I don't know what woke me. I do know that I woke with my stomach in a knot of terror, and I was trembling. Juliana was standing in the doorway, a dark shape outlined by a lone light in the corridor. The full-length mirror near the door caught her shadowy image and doubled my fear. I jumped for the light.

"You scared me!" I said, merrily as I could, but still shaking all over.

She walked into the room and sat down on a couch along the wall. Then she rolled off that and onto the floor where, still hugging her knees, she began to roll about like a favourite wobbly toy belonging to my five-month-old son.

I pulled her to her feet, then gently moved her onto the couch, where I tried to coax her into a position of repose. I asked her to tell me about the last movie she had seen. She said she had seen *The Fly* a few weeks earlier at the American Recreation Centre and started describing creatures crawling out of stomachs and mouths and horrors that I didn't want to hear about and she didn't need to recall, not then.

I waved my hands in front of her. "No! No! Tell me about what you've eaten today."

"Nothing," she said, her voice flat her eyes glazed. "I went to see a gri-gri man, you know. I was so unhappy about leaving Ouagadougou, I thought he could help me make the right decision. I told him I never wanted to leave Ouagadougou. He told me to put a big pot of water beside my bed, and to chant some things each night. He said I would feel better."

"But Juliana..."

She continued, as though she could not hear anything. "He knew I had a boyfriend, and that I was sorry not just to be leaving Ouagadougou but also to leave my boyfriend. He just *knew* it. I didn't say anything about it. He told me to put the water beside my bed and to say..."

"Well, did you do it?"

"Yes!" She jack-knifed to a sitting position and glared at me. "But I didn't mean it. I did it but I didn't believe it. So he cursed me, put me under a spell. Next morning when I woke up my face felt as though it was being pulled down by something. And I couldn't eat. It's getting worse."

"Wait a minute. Try and calm down." I glanced at the two sleeping children, hoping they would not wake up. Or hoping they would. There is nothing like a crying child to bring one back down to earth and reality, as I know it.

"No one put a spell on you. He wanted to help you, not hurt you."

"I didn't believe in what I was doing."

"Then if you don't believe, it can't hurt you. It's all psychological. If you believe something can hurt you, then it can. If you don't believe, then it can't." I looked at my watch. It was 3 in the morning.

"But you see, I didn't believe so now he's proving to me that he can do anything he wants."

"Okay, okay. Now that you do believe, let's go and see the psychiatrist tomorrow, to get you to stop believing again. I know him. I've interviewed him. He's very nice."

She was seized by a fit of trembling and once again I caught sight of the double image in the mirror. The hair rose on my neck and I stood up. I began to sympathize with condescending nurses with difficult patients. "Let's just get you back to bed now.

It will all look different in the morning." I'm surprised I didn't offer her a cup of tea, I was working so hard on returning to the mundane.

In the morning, it didn't look different. It looked much worse. She refused to go to the psychiatrist and went instead to work. We contacted another friend, who was able to convince Juliana to take some tranquilizers, which didn't solve anything but which allowed her to sleep the next night. In the morning I told her I had accepted an invitation from some other friends to move myself and the children into their house for a few days, and we left while she was at work. This was not a very valiant or kind move, but my children were afraid of her, and frankly, so was I.

The diplomat for whom she worked was, at that point, preoccupied with a Burkinabe mistress he had had moved into his residence, while his wife and four children moved into the servants' quarters out back. He remained oblivious to Julian's state of mind and body until the next day. Then he moved her into his residence, where things were getting a little crowded.

Five days later the embassy, in consultation with the one psychiatrist in Ouagadougou, arranged to have Juliana flown out in the company of a medical doctor. She called me to come and see her a few hours before the flight, which she was still fighting tooth and bleeding nail.

We rehashed all the events leading up to the "spell" over and over. She clung to me, crying, and exacted a promise that I would go and see a certain driver at the embassy, who would take me to the gri-gri man, whom I was supposed to tell to lift the curse. To placate her, I promised.

I extricated myself from her cloying embrace, and she wailed, as I walked out the door, "I can't leave Ouagadougou. I will come back here. I will. I will. I will."

She was admitted to a clinic in Germany, where she spent six months. She has now recovered fully. I did not go to the gri-gri man. I never tried to decide whether I did or didn't believe that he had put her under a spell; but I was no longer ready to dismiss the possibility, as I once might have done.

*Soulemane Sinaré, head of the National Association of Tradition-al Practitioners in Burkina Faso, in his practice in an Ouagadougou market. This photograph was taken on the morn-ing of October 15, 1987, six hours before the coup.*

*Chapter 19*

# Graveyard for dreamers

Thomas Sankara, from a devoutly Catholic family, was himself a steadfast believer in the human brain and in the essential goodness of man. "He wasn't a revolutionary or a politician," said one of his ministers to me one day in 1988. "He was a preacher, a missionary." He paused then and searched the night sky as if searching the stars for an explanation, for words. He sighed. "Maybe he was a kind of Messiah. He was not down here with us. His inspiration came from above — somewhere beyond you or me." Sankara was in fact a mystic only in the sense that he said, and seemed to believe, that whatever the human mind could conceive, it could also attain.

Whatever he was, he was neither orthodox nor always reasonable, in the strict sense of that word. He angered liberals with his dogmatic adherence to what looked, to them, like hardline Marxism; his revolutionary "comrades" said he swerved from the true line of Marxist doctrine and revolution and invented his own. He annoyed ordinary citizens with his Committees for the Defence of the Revolution or CDRs, a concept and revolutionary cadre imported from Cuba, and made up primarily — according to the critics — of "former shoeshine boys and petty thieves." After two years, Sankara disarmed the CDRs, noticing that they were no longer serving the people and were serving themselves more than anything else. After that, the CDRs began to turn against him.

His regime was also stained with blood — five people had died in the coup which brought him to power, and there had been summary executions in 1984 of seven coup plotters. Sankara's opponents said he was responsible. Others said it was the hardliners around him who ordered the executions. Sankara tried to dispel international press suggestions that he was following the path towards despotism. He met with almost every journalist who asked to see him and continued to appear in public at every opportunity. There were many who detested him; there were the others who loved him. No one was indifferent.

He didn't hold publicly with the traditional African world of spirits, and the fear they invoked. His method of combatting ancient rules which were shrouded in legend and mysticism was by example. That was why he moved into the presidential palace in Ouagadougou, a two-storey building dating back to independence, which resembled a rusted ship more than a palace. People in Burkina Faso said that the palace, in which former presidents had lived, was haunted by bad spirits and that Sankara should not challenge them. They said it would bring him bad luck. He ignored them.

In fact, he ignored almost all the advice he was given. When I interviewed him in April 1987, I asked him about the speed with which he was trying to change his country. It was a criticism I had heard from even his most devoted followers. "Don't you think you're moving too fast?" I asked.

"No," he said, wringing his hands and meeting my question and my eyes head on. "Look around you. You see the children. All the children. Hungry, malnourished, illiterate. You see the desert moving in on us. If this were twenty or thirty years ago, we could afford to move slowly." He paused and his shining eyes settled on me. "We have no time left," he said.

And so, he continued to break almost every unwritten rule in the Burkinabe book of etiquette and tradition. He trod on almost everyone's toes, or feet, even those of the Mogho Naaba, the King of the Mossi people. The Mossi were Burkina Faso's largest and most powerful ethnic group — a veritable dynasty of larger-than-life chiefs and princes and elders. The Mogho Naaba had been living in his palace in Ouagadougou for many years at the expense of the state. In addition to the tithes the Mogho Naaba received from his own people, as tradition demanded, his palace was manned with servants whose salaries were paid by the state; it was lit by the national electricity company but no bills were ever paid. His car was a gift from the state, and his driver's salary was also handled by the government.

Such traditional rulers straddled the ancient world of kingdoms, conquests and undisputed power over their subjects, and the modern world of laws and notions of equality. They appeared to think and to rule as they always did, but their wisdom and integrity were often corrupted by their desire for modern amenities. Some picked what they liked from the twentieth century — cars, technologies — and discarded those aspects, human equality for example, which did not suit them. And yet, they were still revered and still commanded as much respect as, or more than, the official government. They had an important role to play in keeping peace among their people, but their roles needed to be redefined; they would have to make some concessions to the reality that times had changed and their subjects' needs had increased and altered. At least that was how Thomas Sankara looked at the situation.

So, the Mogho Naaba's power was cut off, and his chauffeur, cook and secretary removed. If he could not pay for these amenities, with all the traditional gifts and taxes he was receiving, then it was felt — at least in revolutionary quarters — that he should go without.

Only one man — Thomas Sankara — would have dared to take such drastic and unthinkable measures against a king who, for many people, embodied their gods and their entire ancestry. It did not make him popular with the royal figures of the Mossi kingdom. He was one-quarter "Peul," or Fulani, an ethnic group whom the Mossi traditionally looked on as inferior human beings, or even as their former slaves, and the impenetrable and powerful Mossi chieftaincy could not abide his attempts — subtle as they may have been — to humble them. Blaise Compaore, his closest friend and the man who had orchestrated the coup in 1983 which brought Thomas Sankara to power, was a Mossi prince. The Mogho Naaba had warned Compaore from the beginning that he was denigrating his own tribe when he walked behind, in the shadow of Thomas Sankara, who was according to the Mossi kingdom "little better than a slave."

Sankara's attacks on the traditional superstructure of chiefs, princes and kings were part of his overall attack on the myth of the African "Big Man" — those men whose wealth and traditional connections or education entitled them to every privilege, legitimate or illicit, they wanted. Average people accepted this status quo, that theirs was the lot of loyal subject and their role was one of subservience, whether they liked it or not. Sankara wanted this to end.

His Popular Revolutionary Tribunals, in 1986, had already tried and found guilty three men from the West African Community's largest bank union. They were men who had held top positions in the bank; they were regarded throughout West Africa as untouchable. They had also embezzled millions of dollars. So Thomas Sankara acted. When the men visited Ouagadougou for a meeting of the West African Community Bank, they were charged, and were found guilty. All three were imprisoned in Ouagadougou. I went to visit the prison when, in another typical Sankara move, the prison doors were thrown open one day for visitors. Two of the men had adapted well to their life in prison, and had opened a mosque and were coaching a football team. The third, the biggest man of all, from the Côte d'Ivoire, had refused to join in the prison life and stayed in his cell. I entered, with a prison guard. He had his own "houseboy" in a white jacket with him, and was drinking bottled French water which he had sent to him. He promptly dismissed me and my microphone with a look of scorn and hatred that frightened me. I remember thinking that Sankara, and his government, had earned themselves a mortal enemy in that man, who commanded enormous power in neighbouring Côte d'Ivoire.

Then in the middle of 1987, the government launched an Anti-Corruption Committee, to vet members of the regime and to assess their wealth and assets after almost four years in power. Sankara was the first to appear before the committee.

It was, once again, the kind of exercise which, when related in international press reports, sounded like pure propaganda and mere public relations, part of a great show of revolution which made cynics laugh derisively. But from a back bench in the "Palace of Justice," where I sat to watch Sankara, no one was laughing and no one was derisive.

He stood with his red cap clutched in his hands that were joined behind his back, and met the stony-faced committee, which admittedly were all men close to his regime. He listed off his assets — two guitars which were cracked from the dryness, two bicycles, three radios, one deep freezer which did not work, a refrigerator which did, a small house which he and his wife had not yet paid for, a monthly income smaller than his wife's, a

1978 Mitsubishi car (which I knew often needed to be pushed to get it going), and gifts from visiting dignitaries totalling millions of dollars that had been donated to the State Treasury. It would have been easy to laugh this all off, as many people did. Broadcast live as it was on national radio, some people in the villages were shocked at how wealthy Sankara was, so naive were they about how the wealthy — those who did not have to toil for mere survival — really lived. In Ouagadougou, several people said it was all a hoax; he could take whatever he wanted from the state whenever he wanted.

But Sankara's intention was not lost on the vast majority of people in the country — his point was that you could be a Big Man, you could be a president, you could be an honourable and patriotic Burkinabe, you could be somebody without being wealthy.

And secondly, Sankara was not accumulating wealth, or handing out favours and riches to his family or his father. It was hard for me to imagine how important it was for a son to share any wealth he had with his father and family. Building a house for your father brought more gratification, honour and prestige than building one for yourself. If Sankara had been pilfering from state monies, the results would have been visible in the lives of his parents. His mother, however, still peddled spices in the market and his father, desperately in need of medical attention for old war wounds, was getting assistance from Blaise Compaore, number two man in the regime. Sankara refused to give even his father or his wife "anything that any Burkinabe could not have." Later, people would say this was where he had gone wrong. They said he should have looked out for his father, his family, himself. That they would have understood. As it was, they understood nothing. Not at first.

Was he right, or wrong? Should he have moved more slowly, should he have made the compromises he needed to make to appease enemies and to please his detractors both inside and outside Burkina Faso? Should he have taken more care to avoid what was coming?

It was inevitable that such radical policies, which inspired chuckling and sarcasm among condescending foreign powers and deep seething anger in high places within the country, would bring a backlash. It was sure too that the pace of development and change could not continue. Several western powers had drastically cut assistance to Burkina Faso when Sankara came to power — including the United States and France. Sankara knew he had rankled many foreign powers.

Canada had closed its embassy in reaction to the use of Canadian aid vehicles during the 1983 coup. The Canadian ambassador, who in 1987 was based in Abidjan, told me that Sankara had once asked him why Canada kept its embassy closed in Burkina Faso. He wanted to know why Canada wouldn't do more to support a country that was trying to develop itself from within. The Canadian ambassador told him that there had been cutbacks — many foreign missions had been closed. "One of your cocktail parties in your Washington embassy would keep an embassy in Ouagadougou going for a year," Sankara retorted, laughing. "And your building here, still manned by the same number of staff, costs the same as the embassy did. The closure is symbolic." The ambassador didn't dispute it. But while he found Sankara amusing and interesting, my over-riding impression was that he also didn't take Sankara and his revolution very seriously. I've had the impression over the years that few ambassadors take obscure African postings or countries very seriously.

Sankara had not only insulted and angered the French and the Americans, whose power politics in that part of the world were still blatant and/or insidious, he had also turned on former friends — Khaddafi in Libya for example, and belittled the so-called "Dean" of African Heads of State, Houphouët-Boigny, in the Côte d'Ivoire.[*] He had also refused to join the "Brotherhood," the Croix Rose sect to which French President Mitterand and many of the presidents in francophone Africa were reported to belong.

In the end, I suppose what happened was inevitable — the bubble had to burst, reality had to be restored to the dream world in which we were living, where hope was springing eternal and self-confidence was flowering. Had it not, Sankara might well have become like his friend to the south, Flight Lieutenant Jerry Rawlings in Ghana, who was forced to surround himself with sycophants and make so many compromises in order to survive

*     Felix Houphouët-Boigny died in 1993.

and retain power that his "revolution" seemed to go flat. Sankara had made it clear to me when I spoke to him — there would be no recoiling from reality and problems and the difficult solutions. He was not a man of compromise.

Still, when it happened in Burkina Faso, none of us were prepared. On October 11, 1987, the outgoing German ambassador, who was a great fan of Thomas Sankara, said to me that "All is well now. It seems any differences there may have been between Sankara and Compaore have been patched up. I think that things are going to go well. Sankara himself said in his last speech that two steps without the people are not as good as one step with the people. He said change would have to slow down. I am very optimistic." Weren't we all?

October 15, 1987 was the Thursday I had spent with Soulemane Sinaré, the traditional medicine man in Ouagadougou. Thursdays were sport days, and in the afternoon civil servants headed back to work on their mopeds dressed in sweat suits ready for sports at 5. We were getting into our car at 5, heading to the lake for a daily jog, when a breathless neighbour approached.

"Don't go out," he said. "There's shooting in town."

"What do you mean?"

"Shooting. A coup. It's a coup."

We raced back into the house and turned on the radio, which had gone off the air and didn't resume broadcasting until the fateful announcement came shortly before 6. Sankara was called a traitor, and listeners were told that the Popular Front, headed by Captain Blaise Compaore, had taken over to launch a "rectified revolution."

A curfew had been imposed. Violators would be shot. We spent the evening and the night behind closed doors and windows. Fleeing soldiers faithful to Sankara's regime were passing through our compound and shots were being fired all around us. An American journalist, Marco Werman, who had just arrived in Ouagadougou to report for an American press agency, took refuge in our house for the night. My telephone was out of order, and I was unable to contact the BBC or Reuters, for whom I should have been reporting. There was no way to reach the telex office until dawn brought an end to the night's curfew, and some illumination on what had actually happened. I was sure Thomas Sankara was in prison somewhere, and that the people would mobilize and have him released. It had happened before.

In May 1983, shortly after Sankara had been appointed Prime Minister by a weak military president who was on a very short leash from Paris, he was arrested. His arrest came during an unofficial visit to Ouagadougou by Mitterand's advisor on African affairs, Guy Penne. In his short term as Prime Minister, Sankara had been very outspoken about the continued French domination of Burkinabe politics and French policies in all of her former colonies. That, apparently, was not to be tolerated. Penne had been in Ouagadougou, covertly, for a few hours when Sankara and two of his closest political allies were put under house arrest. On that occasion, massive demonstrations, some funded by Sankara's then political allies in Libya, by students and trade union leaders, resulted in his being freed. Sankara's appeal was not something that could be kept behind bars. His liberation was led by Blaise Compaore, who had evaded arrest and was able to bring military support from the south of the country. It was also Compaore who led the coup in August 1983, which put Sankara in power. Compaore knew only too well that he could never hold onto power if Thomas Sankara were allowed to live.

The dawn brought a "journée feriée," or a holiday to Burkina Faso. The Popular Front, that nebulous entity issuing periodic radio messages about the "rectified revolution" and closure of the airport, called ceaselessly for "nation-wide marches of support" — for itself. The messages were signed, but not read by Blaise Compaore, Sankara's so-called best friend and "right-hand man." By mid-morning we were all still in the dark about what had happened. Where was Compaore? Where was Thomas Sankara?

I had already been to the morgue at the hospital and inter-viewed some children in the emergency ward who had suffered bullet wounds in the indiscriminate shooting that had taken place the evening before around the university, the radio station and the "Conseil d'Entente" — a high-security conglomeration of buildings where West African leaders were supposed to meet from time to time to solidify relations and policies.

I was in the telex office, reporting on casualties, when a Burkinabe reporter arrived, his face dusted pale brown. "He's dead," he said.

"Who's dead?"

"Sankara."

The site of the burial was easy to locate. I had only to follow the processions. They came — the multitudes — from all corners of the city, mile after mile of people on foot, moving slowly and almost fearfully towards the tomb of their fallen president. It was my first inkling of what that amorphous entity that Sankara had called the "Masses Populaires" and Orwell had called the "Great Public" looked like.

The processions raised clouds of brown dust that cast shadows along the roads and paths leading to the burials. The peoples' faces were covered with the fine brown powder that stuck like make-up to sweat-dampened skin. It was easy to tell who was crying. Tracks of tears were etched into the dust on many faces, mostly those of young men and older women.

For the most part, the people were silent. Shock had silenced the city. It was an eerie and immensely moving kind of vacuum; an emotional concussion in a pall of dust.

The grave site was in a forgotten slum on the outskirts of the city, in an area called Dagnoen. To get there, we moved through row upon row of baked mud dwellings, a labyrinth of heat and poverty. I left my moped in the hands of some enterprising young men who had already established a parking lot for mopeds and bicycles. I made my way on foot through the crowd. It required a lot of indecorous pushing and then apologizing to make it to the front of the mob, to the side of the graves. The people, confronted by those burials, were immobile, frozen with disbelief. I was shaking. I did not believe myself, that he was really dead.

The graveyard had been cordoned off by armed commandos who were standing guard around the thirteen mounds.

"Murderers! Assassins!" Young men fell to their knees in front of the commandos and howled accusations. The soldiers, in fatigues and heavily armed, gave the impression they were deaf, or in communion with something just over our heads. Many people suggested to me that the commandos were heavily drugged, when they were on active duty and required total self-control.

"Ce n'est pas possible," whispered a woman beside me. She repeated this refrain "It's not possible" as a requiem, rocking back and forth as though trying to lull a baby, or herself, back to sleep.

Most people, however, were as silent as I was. They shook their heads and stared. It was difficult to do anything else. It seemed far too unreal, impossible. The stuff of delirium. The fine dust clogged my nose, mouth and lungs. My eyes had begun to water, at last.

The thirteen bodies were just barely covered with sand. Some people said they could see Sankara's foot; others that they could see dark rivulets in the sand where blood had trickled out and baked under the oppressive and unrelenting sun. I don't recall now if I saw those horrors. I saw thirteen mounds of brown earth strewn with flowers and messages hastily scribbled on notepaper, and illegible names on scraps of paper which had been impaled on small twigs stuck into each mound.

"We will never forget you, Toma," was the message on a piece of loose-leaf, and signed "The Youth of Burkina."

"For us, you cannot die, Captain," read the epitaph scribbled on another paper by an anonymous class of "Students."

I had known, if only briefly and superficially, three of the men underneath those mounds. There was Sankara, a young press man named Babou Paulin Bamouni and Patrice Zagré, an energetic advisor to the president who had helped organize an anti-apartheid conference in Ouagadougou the week before — at which I had my last look at Thomas Sankara, alive.

The twelve men who had been killed with him happened to be at the meeting with him at 4 o'clock on the afternoon of October 15, when the commando forces came and opened fire at the Conseil d'Entente — just a stone's throw away from the market where Sinaré had schooled me in the invisible forces of African mysticism.

I still don't know how those thousands of people at the grave that day knew which mound housed the bullet-ridden corpse of their former president. Once again, I was overwhelmed by the way Africans were able to transmit and absorb knowledge, as though by osmosis, without any official source. It is one of the great paradoxes that people who do not have free press frequently develop such a healthy sense of scepticism and independent thought. There was a collective common sense with superbly developed powers of observation, that, in the developed world with its information overload and glitz and time pressure, seems sometimes to elude us.

The processions continued, increased, swelling to fill that whole squalid quarter of town with Burkinabe, with those who came to see for themselves the graveyard of their president and his dreams. Their own news service never did make an official announcement that Sankara was dead, and indeed the news was only unofficially alluded to four days later, when Blaise Compaore, the new president, went on national television and explained to the nation that his "comrade in arms" had "gone astray."

Sankara had been buried, people told me, in his red track suit which he had put on for Thursday evening sports, scheduled for after his meeting in the Conseil d'Entente. One young man, who lived in a hut near the graves, told me that an unmarked and unlicenced Peugeot pick-up had come to the site at 3:30 in the morning, in the stillness of the curfew, stacked high with cadavers. He had seen men, prisoners he thought, with shaved heads and colourless overalls, pitch the lifeless forms of the thirteen men into hastily dug graves hardly deep enough to contain them. Then they had sped away.

I returned to the telex office to file my report. I still could not believe that what I was writing was true. He had been so full of humour and the joy of leading the revolution, that it had been too easy to forget how much he was hated in crucial circles — trade union leaders said he ignored them in favour of the peasants (true), foreign dignitarites said he criticized their countries too much (true) and local powers that be had always given the appearance that they were hiding their wealth and biding their time, waiting for Sankara to go.

Sankara was dead, his revolution was over, and the new man at the helm, the man who had orchestrated the coup and killing, was his "best friend," his "comrade in arms," his "brother." Of course, Compaore's version of the truth was yet to come out. And when it did, it would fool some people in the outside world — but few people in Africa and certainly not the people of Burkina Faso. But they were no longer to be masters of their own country or destiny — that little dream was over and buried in that miserable plot of earth on the outskirts of Ouagadougou.

*A young woman defies authorities who forbade visits to the grave and mourns over Thomas Sankara's burial mound in Ouagadougou, October 1987*

## Chapter 20

# The Tears of Mariam

There were no marches of support for the Popular Front. I did see six drunken youths — members of the Committees for the Defence of the Revolution — weaving through town shouting insults at Sankara, who could no longer hear them. The country, for days, was strangely silent.

The Popular Front began trying to fill the silence with proclamations, their version of the truth. They alleged that Sankara had put together a special, private security team that had been planning to eliminate Compaore the night of October 15. They said that no one had wanted to harm Sankara, but that he had been shot trying to escape arrest. "Lies," people said. "What can you expect from murderers, the truth?"

Sankara had been with Compaore long into the night of the 14. Sankara's widow, Mariam, told me she had heard them laughing like the former schoolmates they were at 3 A.M. She said Thomas had shown no signs that anything was amiss on October 15. After his late night with Compaore, he had taken a nap in the afternoon, risen, showered, dressed in his track suit for Thursday sport and gone off to his meeting. She said she had been talking to him by telephone moments before the coup,

"If he had been planning to eliminate anyone, which he wouldn't have done anyway, he would not have left me and his two sons here undefended and unprovided for," she said.

Meanwhile, Compaore's wife, an extremely wealthy and opulent woman with close relations to the president of the Côte d'Ivoire, Félix Houphouët-Boigny, had flown to Paris and as the coup occurred was having cocktails with the Burkinabe ambassador there.

A friend, Jacob, who worked at the presidential press office, recalled Sankara being very upset on the morning of October 15, because of an article which had just appeared in a West African publication partly owned and heavily influenced by Houphouët-Boigny, depicting him as a man who was on the path to total despotism, and likening him to Guinea's former president Sekou Toure, who had tortured or exiled as many as three million of his countrymen. Sankara had called Jacob in, and talked about inviting the authors of the article to come and visit Burkina Faso to dispel the horrific tale they had concocted. Sankara had asked Jacob to fly to Senegal on October 16, to meet with the men behind the cover story and ask them who had prompted them to write it. But on October 16 Jacob was out of a job and in deep shock and mourning, and keeping a very low profile in his home. Eventually, after his home had been searched and most of his books and private papers confiscated, he would be moved to a menial job on the state daily, *Sidwaya*, where he still works as a copywriter today.

One lone surviving witness to the actual events in the Conseil d'Entente, who had jumped over the walls to safety, reported later from exile — before he lost his sanity — what he had seen. He described the arrival of the commandos, Compaore's men he said, in their fleet of military vehicles. First they pulled Sankara's driver from the seat of his Peugeot, and shot him. On hearing the shots, Sankara ordered the men in the meeting to lie on the floor. "It's me they want," he shouted. Then all the men raced from the room to meet the attackers. The eye witness said Sankara was shot seven times, although the young press man Babou Paulin Bamouni threw himself in front of the president, in a vain effort to shield him.

After my immediate emotional reaction to the violence and the gruesome graveyard, I tried to look at the coup objectively. Sankara had come to power by the gun, had carried a gun, and was fated to go out the same way he came in, through a coup. He was by no means on the same blood-stained path Guinea's Sekou Toure had followed, but he had refused to talk about returning the country to constitutional rule. Sankara's biggest failure, I concluded, was not that he had "derailed the revolution" as the Popular Front maintained, but that he had insisted on continuing it without the mandate of his own people. As puritanical as he was, as sincere as he appeared to be, as much as he believed in his revolution — his was an old story. The revolution had devoured its own prodigious son. Politics of any kind spawn intrigue, but military dictatorships — and his was a military dictatorship — give rise to intrigues so complex and intricate and explosive, that violence is inevitable.

I knew, intellectually, that all of this was true. But I could not help feeling that Africa and the world had lost a great man on that hot October afternoon.

On October 17, the world's stock markets crashed, erasing that unfamiliar name, Burkina Faso, from the world's headlines. In Burkina, people were still asking how Compaore could have orchestrated a coup against his own regime, against the man he called his own "brother." But no one on the outside seemed to be listening to them. When the outgoing West German ambassador requested, at a diplomatic New Year's ceremony, a moment of silence for the man who was not there, he was lambasted in the Burkinabe press and ridiculed by other more "protocolic" diplomats.

On the inside, Compaore and his henchmen began the long process of eliminating Sankara's name from the national vocabulary. The first item on the agenda was to turn him from fallen hero into villain. It did not seem to bother any of these self-titled "avant-garde révolutionaires," that by criticizing everything Sankara and his government had done over four years, they were slandering their own new leader, who had been number two man throughout. Indeed, many of these young visionaries who attacked and derided Sankara's National Revolutionary Council had been, until the afternoon of his death, members of the same Council.

It was fascinating, if depressing, to watch history being re-written overnight. It would have been more depressing if I had believed anyone was being fooled. But the "popular masses" were not nearly so gullible as their leaders liked to believe.

The people were much, much more subtle than the propagan-da-makers, and were highly sophisticated in communicating their views to their new president. Shortly after the coup a new cloth appeared in the markets throughout West Africa. Brightly printed cloth was one of the ways a woman had of indicating her status in the region. Those with money wrapped themselves up in outfits made from the expensive wax prints from Holland or England, made exclusively for the African marketplace. Everyday and cheaper pagnes were the ones produced by local textile firms. Each cloth had a name, and sometimes a meaning. They were constantly changing. Every few months new and dazzling patterns were introduced, which would sweep the fashion market for a few months, then slowly fade from view. Only a few cloth designs would become classics and be reprinted year after for year.

The new cloth that appeared in the markets of West Africa after the coup in Burkina Faso was covered with tiny red and black flecks shaped like hot peppers, on a brilliant gold background. It was called "Sankara cloth," or "The Tears of Mariam." Mariam Sankara was mother of two small boys, aged five and seven at the time. Within weeks this new cloth became the biggest fashion rage in Burkina Faso and was produced in a myriad of different colour combinations. Entire families decked themselves out in the cloth. The "Tears of Mariam" were coursing through the country, and there was nothing the Popular Front could do about it. This kind of political statement, people said, was called "passive resistance." It was the Africans' greatest — and only — defence against repressive regimes and gross injustice.

Not everyone was shedding tears for Mariam Sankara. In late October, at an afternoon birthday party for the daughter of western diplomats, expatriate wives sat about drinking coffee from porcelain cups, and talk turned to the coup. A German woman was lamenting the lack of butter in Ouagadougou. The airport had been closed since the coup d'etat, and imports from France were thus curtailed. Another woman, vaguely curious about Sankara's death, wondered aloud whether he had a family.

"Yes, he left a wife and two small sons," she was told.

There was a polite moment of silence. "Well," said another diplomatic wife who claimed to be well-briefed on the country and its people, "you know they don't have the same kind of feelings for their husbands as we do." They had not heard of the "Tears of Mariam."

While people continued to digest the events in their country, there were small incidents that propped up my faith in that wry African sense of humour, that "passive resistance." One evening we were watching a re-run on television of a national bicycle race. The camera moved in on dancers, and then panned to the dignitaries on the presidential marquee. There was Thomas Sankara, sitting beside his "brother" Blaise Compaore. They were laughing and chatting like the best friends they were reputed to have been. The close-up shot of the man the people were now supposed to hate, or to have forgotten, lasted about five seconds. Then the screen went blank, and it took technicians at Broadcasting House ten minutes to round up a television hostess to take up where the broadcast had been cut off. She offered a sheepish grin to viewers and offered a list of the evening's programmes. The showing of that clip may have been accidental; it may also have been on purpose. Intentional or not, it made its mark on viewers. The next day people were chuckling about it everywhere I went. Minds did not go blank as the government information brokers, who controlled the media in the country, seemed to believe.

Nevertheless, in the months that followed, people began to speak less and less about Sankara, and certainly not openly. The new security director had hired three thousand young men to inform on would-be subversives, or "Sankaristes" as they were known.

Ali was a friend who worked in the telecommunications office, who had done much for me in ensuring that my telexes went out even when the office was officially closed after the coup. I asked him if he felt safe. "It's okay," he said, smiling. "I know how to do these things. I never speak to anyone here at work any more. I go straight home after work, and only open my mouth around my own family. Then I know that no one can put any words in my mouth. You know when the 'other' one was here, we used to criticize everything. Some people thought that meant we didn't like him. We liked him. That's why we criticized him. Not this guy. With him," he said, jerking his thumb in the direction of the Conseil d'Entente, where Compaore had holed himself up since the coup, "we won't open our mouths. But it doesn't mean our brains are not working."

Immediately after his first television address, Compaore's press attaché agreed to grant me an interview with the new Head of State. The new president was living and working in the Conseil d'Entente, in a building adjacent to the one where Sankara had been gunned down. This high-walled security zone illustrated the lunacy of security zones anywhere in the world. As in Cameroon in 1984, the president's biggest threat was not from the people, who were subdued and silenced by their own fear and their need to survive, but from within. High-ranking officers and close political allies were the only ones with the power and means to stir up political violence. Security zones offered entry only to the very people who were always the leaders' most lethal enemies.

The security zone had done nothing to protect Sankara. I wondered, as I entered the zone, what Sankara had thought on that fateful afternoon. Friends of the late president said he knew that his life was in danger, and that he chose, rather than to start killing his enemies to save his life and his position of power, to die, a martyr to his many causes. Others said he was so caught up with his causes, that he forgot to look about him; such was his trust in his closest friend.

It was clear from the beginning that Compaore was taking no chances. For almost a month after the coup d'etat, he did not leave the Conseil d'Entente. To reach that complex, I had to pass through three new military checkpoints, manned by heavy artillery and slit-eyed commandos. In addition, that entire part of town, which encompassed almost ten square kilometres behind the presidency, was slowly being enclosed by massive concrete walls. Residents of the area were given short notice; dozens of expatriates who occupied the exclusive housing area moved out overnight. The premises of the American Cultural Centre, where hundreds of thousands of dollars had just been spent on a new security system, had to be vacated. Compaore's new right hand man, a shadowy and menacing young lieutenant who had led the commandoes who killed Sankara, moved into the posh cultural building, a move which coincided with his promotion to Captain.

Later, when Compaore finally ventured forth from his fortress to deliver his first public speech in January, it was in a bullet-proof Alpha-Romeo which had come as a gift from the Libyan leader, in a Libyan plane on the night of the coup.

Compaore was far too clever to fall the way he had had his friend felled. He protected himself on all sides. Not only had he had lengthy consultations with a host of leaders — French, Ivorien, Chinese, Togolese, Libyan, before the coup to ensure their support for him as Head of State, after the coup he did much fancy footwork to assure everyone that he was a reasonable man and an unwilling Head of State.

When I met him a few days after the coup, he was still establishing himself in his new role. There were rumours of counter-attacks from military officers in remote camps, who were faithful to the ex-president. Would-be rebels in the town of Koudougou were burned to death and the town was bombarded by battalions under Compaore's orders. Ouagadougou was still suffering from the jitters.

Three tanks were parked across the road from the entrance to the Conseil. I was frightened, passing each checkpoint, alone on my red moped. This was no man's land. Most of the international journalists who came to Ouagadougou to mop up the blood-soaked story of Burkina's sixth coup in twenty-six years of independence wisely moved in large and secure groups. I felt very lonely in the silent labyrinth of walls, surrounded by machine guns and nervous soldiers.

Inside the walls, I was grilled by soldiers outfitted for jungle warfare, at a desk set up under a tree. My press card was examined, and there were loud comments made about journalists — such as Sankariste Sennen Adriamirado of *Jeune Afrique* who, they said, would be shot down from the sky if he tried to land again in Burkina Faso. I was eventually ushered to a metal chair under another large tree to wait to see Compaore.

I sat down, folded my hands on my lap, and looked around me. Heavily armed soldiers were flaked out on camp beds around the building. The grounds were beautiful; mango seedlings dotted the lawns and tree trunks and curbs had been whitewashed. I was reminded of Sankara's whimsical Opération Ville Blanche and fanatical tree-planting exercises, and something caught in my throat. It was not the first nor the last time that I shed tears over the death of the man and his idealism.

Then it occurred to me that the white-washing was very fresh, probably done after the coup to obliterate the blood that must have covered the place.

A pimply-faced soldier plopped himself down in a chair beside me.

I smiled.

"Ça va?" he asked.

"Oui, ça va," I replied. Then, because he was regarding me speculatively, "Et vous? Ça va?"

"Oui, ça va," he said. "Journaliste?"

"Yes."

He looked me up and down. Then he unrolled a magazine, one with photographs and balloon captions, and began to read the photo-romance and the tale of love and betrayal related on its pages.

I looked furtively around me to the "Upper Volta" pavilion where Sankara was supposed to have been killed. Workmen were installing new light fixtures on the outside, and two more men were applying a fresh coat of whitewash.

The man next to me was watching me. "Looks like we've had our last rain for the year," I said, pleasantly.

"Yes, it does." He returned his attention to his paper soap opera. I pulled out a notebook and began revising questions I had prepared for Compaore.

A half dozen soldiers were pushing a large motorcycle up and down the circular driveway, while its rider kicked in vain at the starter. It suddenly roared to life, emitting as it did, a loud explosion, much like a gunshot.

The soldier beside me leapt to his feet, gun skyward, searching for a target, for the enemy. The commandos in the garden were already on their bellies, guns pointed. The motorcyclist braked and grinned.

*"Don't do that here! This is not the time for that!"* boomed the man beside me. "Mon Dieu," he said, sinking into his seat and wiping his forehead with a sleeve. "We're all a little edgy these days," he said.

After an hour, a sliding glass door in the central pavilion opened and a tall figure in fatigues leapt out sideways. "Venez!" he shouted, beckoning for me to come.

I followed him inside, taking a place beside him on the black leather sofa. Unlike Sankara, Compaore had always kept his distance from journalists. I had seen him on several occasions at press conferences, but he was just the silent, tall, handsome figure towering over Sankara, in the shadows.

I was very nervous and, while preparing to take his photograph, dropped my flash unit on the floor. Compaore joined me in the search. Seeing him like that, on his hands on knees on the floor, it was hard suddenly to believe that I was in the presence of a man who was being accused from all quarters of having master-minded the death of his best friend. I was beset with doubts about my judgement. Maybe I was all wrong about the man? Maybe, as he contended, he really had had nothing to do with the coup. Maybe he really had been "asleep and ill" when it happened; maybe he had really "run outside in his underwear with his own gun" thinking that the shooting meant someone was trying to kill him. There were so many truths — no truths at all.

I may have been nervous, but in that first interview he behaved like a frightened little boy. He repeated stories he had already told other journalists, that his men had enacted the coup to protect him — that he was not even aware of it.

I recorded it, because I could not write when I was studying his face and eyes so intently. I decided I had never met anyone who lied as well as he. Or perhaps he wasn't lying? He said he had never wanted to be president, that he only cared about helping the "masses populaires." He looked like a juvenile and bounced up and down on the sofa as he spoke. It was clear he thought I believed his story. Maybe he had begun to believe it too.

Then he began to tell me about the massive support shown for the Popular Front. He spoke of the "mass demonstrations" for him which had taken place on the day after the coup. I questioned this, saying I had searched Ouagadougou and seen not even one demonstration in his support. He seemed confused. "Oh, but then you missed them. I've been told there were many massive demonstrations all over the city, everywhere in the country. The people are behind us."

I suggested this wasn't the case, that he had not been out to see for himself.

"Well," he said, wrinkling his high and smooth brow, "you know the Burkinabe people. They do not like violence. They are not used to bloodshed. Some people may have stayed home because they were so shocked. As I was myself."

He said he had been in such a deep depression and shock that he had been unable to meet even the foreign diplomats who had been called to meet with the Popular Front on the day after the coup. And it was true — during that first interview he acted like a man in shock, like someone who had just lost his best friend.

Two months later, however, he was no longer in shock. He admitted me officiously into his new office in the Conseil, sent all his commandos out and closed the door before taking my hand like a long-lost lover and saying, "Oh, it's been such a long time." He held my hand longer than was necessary. His was dry and warm, like a snake's skin. I was reminded of the name he had been given by the Burkinabe: "A Snake in the Grass."

He made it clear from the outset of the interview that the time for asking about his dead "comrade in arms" was over. He wanted to talk about the Popular Front's "rectified revolution," how the revolution was continuing on the path that it should have followed four years earlier. He spoke about the importance of loans from the World Bank for keeping the revolution going, and a structural adjustment programme which was being launched — he didn't mention that Sankara had already been negotiating with the World Bank before his death.

He praised himself and his government and their reconciliation with trade unions and workers whom Sankara had alienated. There was no sign that this was the man who had not wanted to be president. In the intervening months, he had travelled to several other African countries where, despite hostile reactions from the press and the populace, he seemed quite at ease dining at wonderful banquets with former "enemies" — in Togo for example. He seemed to like the limelight; it must have been refreshing after all those years in Sankara's shadow.

And yet, nothing of what he said could possibly be true, and this was obvious if you walked for even five minutes on the streets of Ouagadougou or drove a few kilometres in the rural areas. The energy was gone; people said they had been foolish to believe they could do it themselves, to develop their country. Murder had been committed, they said, and there was nothing they could do about it. The best thing to do was keep low, say nothing, and hope no one could read your subversive mind. The "revolution" was as dead as Thomas Sankara.

The new regime, with its groupies running about waving pistols and threats, dressed like young second-rate executives in ill-fitting suits and ties, did not seem sure of what the rectified revolution was all about. First they held a national conference to evaluate the four years of revolution. This "open and fair" conference was held in January. Marco Werman and I, the only foreign journalists present, were escorted out of the building before we could even take a seat.

Everywhere we went there were contradictions. Compaore's newest and closest ally on the continent became General Gnassingbe Eyadema of Togo, a man he had two years earlier tried to depose by training commandos for the foiled operation, one in which Ghana was also allegedly involved. Colonel Khadaffi also hosted almost continuous delegations of top people from Compaore's new regime. France seemed to embrace Compaore and his new government which, after all, knew how to behave as leader of a former French colony — with decorum and opulence. Compaore fit in well with the "old boys" in their other former African colonies. He knew the rules, abided by them, and didn't hurl insults. Burkina Faso began to vote with France again at the United Nations, on issues such as the independence of the French island, New Caledonia.

The one thing the Popular Front did seem clear on was its right to be in power. There were spates of arrests, mostly ministers and former ambassadors, who were taken in for questioning, and months later still in detention until their cause was taken up by Amnesty International and foreign diplomats who represented aid donors, some of whom began to increase aid to Burkina Faso despite the renewed corruption.

In May 1988, university students and high school students took to the streets of Ouagadougou to demand that the Popular Front resurrect the image, and the ideals, of Thomas Sankara. They were chanting "Four minus one equals zero," referring to the elimination of Sankara from the core group of the defunct National Revolutionary Council, which had comprised the former president, Compaore, Henri Zongo and Jean-Baptiste Lingani, and had been known affectionately as the "Gang of Four." Zongo and Lingani were very quiet in the months after the coup, and the students could not have come with a more poisonous insult for Compaore.

It took only moments for the army to arrive, truck after truck loaded with armed soldiers who dispersed the chanting young people and rounded up the ring-leaders.

Most of the fifty students arrested were released after questioning. A handful, however, were kept locked up and out of sight. A midnight informant gave me some of the names, and stories of brutal beatings, one of which left a young medical student blind and almost paralysed. I went to interview the Director of National Security, to ask about the students. He didn't bother to deny it.

"The police are not angels," he replied after I had given names and eyewitness accounts of the beatings. "You must understand that these people were threatening the security of the country and the peace. If on occasion some of them get beaten, it's not surprising."

The report, with the quote, went out over the BBC. Moments later my telephone rang. The security director invited me over for a chat. I was told that this kind of reporting "would not do." If I hadn't been a woman, and six months pregnant, as I was again, he said he would have taken more stringent measures. Other journalists, Marco Werman of American Press, had recently spent a night in detention at the gendarmerie for his investigative reporting; Stephen Smith of Reuters and Radio France International at the time was barred from the country.

About a month after the coup d'etat I went to visit Sankara's parents, who lived, and still live, in a typical cramped and hot compound just a stone's throw from the Conseil d'Entente. His illiterate mother headed off to market each day with a heavy load of herbs and vegetables to peddle. His father was a pensioner who had fought for the French during World War II. He was a devout Catholic, and after the death of his son, he spent much of his day in the cathedral, praying. Attempts to organize a mass for Sankara were thwarted by the Popular Front.

Apart from his wife and parents, Sankara was also survived by several brothers and sisters. One of these brothers, Valentin, resembled his deceased brother in many ways — he was lean and athletic and he shared Sankara's prominent ears and his wide, contagious smile. He was a farmer, and while he was pleasant, unassuming and very sincere, he shared none of Sankara's genius, ambition and creative wit. I wondered, not for the first time, what went into making a man like Sankara, what had inspired him, where his genius and belief that he could change something had come from. He came from parents who were docile, good citizens who did not question the powers that be, have been, will always be.

The family greeted me very solemnly, and rushed to provide us with bent metal chairs. We sat in a circle, under the night sky, in a very black compound, in silence for many minutes. The family was still in deep mourning. Finally, I asked them how they felt about the coup, and about Compaore's new status. Valentin took me inside one of the small square mud houses. He told me he was the son in charge of the family, now that Sankara was dead. But he said he had been for some time, because Sankara never had time enough for his family.

He wanted to show me some photographs. He pulled them off the shelves where they had been placed since the coup. Before that they had covered the wall, and had left their marks. Compaore was in all of them, standing with his arm around one of Sankara's sisters, or his mother, smiling happily at the camera or at the family into which he had been accepted as a son. "Compaore was marked by the death of his own father when he was small," someone told me. "He was more of a son here in this family than was Toma. He came and spent time with us. He gave my father money to buy a moped. Toma refused to help us at all. He said no one could receive favours not available to everyone in the country."

"But Blaise hasn't come to see us since the coup," one of the sisters said. "Mother is still waiting for him to come. To explain to us what happened, how he could do this to his own family. He was part of our family."

I've since been back many times to visit that family, usually at night, in that same humble compound in the heart of Ouagadougou. Every time it is the same. They say they have never heard from Compaore; they have never been permitted to hold a mass for their departed son. The sense of loss in that small, hidden house is so great that each time I visit, I feel again the same sense of hopelessness I felt as I stood and looked at those brown mounds of sand the day after the coup. It's the permanence and finality of it all, as though a door to Africa's future, a brighter one, had been closed and locked.

Joseph Sankara, the father, said few people felt comfortable coming to visit them. "We know that the people have not forgotten him here. They must not forget him. The world must not forget him."

Twice he asked me to send a message to Jerry Rawlings, Ghana's Head of State who was said to have been a great friend and ally of Sankara. He too had been a frequent visitor in the Sankara family house, before the coup. "But we have never heard from him. Not even a message. Please tell him we are all okay, and that we hope he has not forgotten his friend Toma."

In 1991 I passed this message on to Jerry Rawlings. He wrote a note for himself, a reminder to make contact with the Sankaras in Ouagadougou, but when I visited the family six months later they had still heard nothing.

Mariam Sankara was left without even the most basic household appliances when her husband was killed. She moved into the bungalow, two blocks from my house, on which she and her husband had still been making payments. Friends provided her with a refrigerator and furniture.

And yet, rather than take this as proof that Thomas Sankara had been true to his word when he declared his assets before the Anti-Corruption Committee, many people in Burkina Faso said he had erred terribly. He gave his life to his country, yet he neglected to give to his family — which should have been his first priority.

In April 1988, Mariam Sankara and the rest of the family began to pool their CFA francs to make a proper burial for the thirteen men who fell on October 15. Valentin Sankara told me that when the rains came, the sand covering the bones would be eroded, and the remains would be exposed. Each time I visited the graveyard in that barren area of Dagnoen, I was harassed by security men, who demanded papers and reasons for the visit. The family underwent even worse treatment. Nevertheless, they went ahead with their project. They piled earth on top of each grave, and surrounded it with rows of bricks. Reports about this work went out on BBC and other international radio programmes. International pressure was exerted on Compaore to make amends for the "dog's burial" he had given his fallen comrade.

Finally, just days before Compaore was scheduled to depart for the Organization of African Unity summit in Addis Ababa, where he would be grilled on events in his own country, the military arrived at the graveyard and set to work. They poured thirteen slabs of concrete, dug neat ditches and prepared to mount name plates on each grave.

"Why are you doing this now?" I asked.

The military man looked up at me. "We do what we're told," he said, "even if it's too late. Who are we to ask questions?"

I took photographs as the black plate bearing Sankara's name was neatly placed on the new, white-washed concrete tomb, and slowly, with heavy thuds of the hammer, nailed into place. Today, photographs of the grave are forbidden.

Mariam Sankara and her children, after being terrorized by the authorities, or young unidentified men acting under their orders, were finally allowed to leave Burkina Faso. Her two sons, Auguste and Philippe, who knew Compaore as "Uncle Blaise," attended a small, over-crowded school near a large military camp. She had told them their father was "in heaven." She said she had never been able to tell them who had killed their father, and why. But the other children in the school did, and taunted them without mercy. The youngest boy closely resembled his father. Mariam said she was afraid Compaore's men would try to eliminate him, to prevent a resurrection in twenty years time of Toma and his ideas, through his own son.

President Omar Bongo of Gabon finally sent an airplane for Mariam and her two children. The Sankara family went to see them off, all dressed in the gold "Tears of Mariam," which flowed freely in the final minutes before take-off. Mariam Sankara stayed two years in Gabon before finally seeking refuge in France where she was, last I heard, studying for a doctorate and keeping a very low profile.

In January 1988, Mariam Sankara was finally issued the death certificate she had been requesting for three months. It was an official military document, and it certified that "Comrade Sankara, Thomas Isidre Noel, born December 1, 1949, at Yako in Burkina Faso, had died on October 15, 1987 at 1630 hours, in Ouagadougou, of natural causes."

Each year on October 15, Burkinabe still throng to the graveyard where Sankara is buried, to lay notes that still promise "We will not forget you. You will live forever." The last taxi driver who took me to the graveyard in 1993 was still speaking about "Toma" in the present tense, as though he had never died. "He opens our eyes," he said. "We cannot close them again. That is why today we are so sad. We cannot forget."

The man may be buried, but his dreams will survive a long time.

*Captain Blaise Compaore (left) with Henri Zongo (centre) and Jean-Baptiste Lingani (right), January 1988. They and Sankara were the core of Sankara's revolutionary council before the 1987 coup. When Compaore took power, he kept Lingani and Zongo in his government. In October 1989, they were secretly tried and executed for allegedly plotting against Compaore.*

*Chapter 21*

# No Dark Continent

After Burkina Faso we intended to stay in Canada for at least a year, or maybe even find work and stay for good. But the longing for the sights, sounds, tastes — the feel — of Africa grew stronger by the week. On sunny summer days in the paradise of rural Nova Scotia I would find my mind drifting back to the people who had become part of our lives and our family in Burkina Faso. I would get out my photographs and study faces, writing in my head the fantastically difficult life stories of the people behind the indefatigable smiles.

There was one snapshot of a ten-year-old boy who worked in the gold fields of Yako with his seventy-two-year-old grandfather, Boukary Sawadogo. Yako, about an hour's drive from the capital, was an epicentre of a new gold rush in Burkina Faso. The excavations covered thousands and thousands of hectares and stretched across the northern half of the country. Even a few years earlier that land had been used for cultivating the country's two staple crops, millet and sorghum. But drought, desertification and locusts had made even subsistence agriculture almost impossible. And there was gold under that dust and rock.

Villagers from all over Burkina Faso and from as far away as Ghana and Togo had laid down their digging sticks and traditional hoes and taken up shovels and picks to dig, and dig, and dig. They dug holes so deep that the man at the bottom, working the shovel to fill another bucket of rubble and rock, was visible only when shafts of sunlight caught the sweat gleaming on his dark back.

Each bucketful of rock was hoisted out by ropes and blistered hands by family members on the surface. They pounded chunks of rock into fine dust by banging one lump of stone against the other. The sound of wooden pestles in wooden mortars, the heartbeat of Africa, had been replaced by the sound of stone crushing stone in that golden wasteland.

Holes grew into yawning ravines, and dust filled the air. They had created a moonscape of crevices and canyons that stretched as far as the eye could see. Theirs was a search for gold, fuelled more by desperate need rather than greed, although the people who could afford the large claims offered by Compaore's government in 1988 tended to be men who held high office in Ouagadougou. Those people made small fortunes by sub-leasing plots, metre by metre, to poor village people who flocked to the sites with nothing apart from a shovel and bucket and the rags on their backs.

Young Sawadogo had been digging there with his grandfather and his brothers for two months. They said they bought their water from sellers who brought it by donkey cart in barrels from distant and murky pools. A day's find of gold could hardly pay for a bucket of water. Priorities in that warped and unearthly place were such that water was used to wash the gold powder from the dust before it was drunk.

I had snapped photographs of grandfather and son, smiling, as they showed me their total find, holding up a white enamelled bowl. The particles of gold were so small that I had difficulty seeing anything of worth. The old man pointed to them with a finger as hard and weathered as elephant hide.

Dust devils whipped across the parched craters where thousands of people were pinning their survival on enormous hopes, and the minuscule chance of unearthing a large nugget of gold. They lived under scraps of cloth that flapped in the hot wind, suspended haphazardly on rickety sticks. They lived off almost nothing but hope. Children died of malnutrition and disease and adults died of illness brought on by exhaustion or they plunged to their deaths in the very pits they had excavated.

There was no way to describe the horror of that place, no way to account for the smiles on the faces of Sawadogo and Boukary in those hellholes near Yako, Burkina Faso.

Sometimes, as I sat and pored over these photographs and stories in my home in Nova Scotia, it frightened me to think how much we in the developed world had cushioned ourselves from the harsh realities of nature and mere survival. I was still deeply awed by the vast powers of people to show signs of thriving when they were really just barely surviving. And if they didn't survive, that was also something they could cope with. The family and village would mourn, and fete that spirit as he or she returned to the world of ancestors. Neither the ancestors, nor death, were ever far away.

Yako, I decided, was the real graveyard for dreamers; it was also the birthplace of Thomas Sankara. But in that part of the world, death was only a step on the path to re-birth. There was no beginning, no end, just days and lives stretching in all directions, as far as the mind could go.

I would lose myself in those African paradoxes as I sorted through the photographs in Nova Scotia in 1988; it was impossible to put worlds together which simply did not fit.

The photographs evoked memories and made me miss friends like Mary, the Ghanaian woman who had been like a second mother to my daughter, teaching her how to pound "fufu" out of boiled yams or dancing about our living room with her, showing her how to make her "bottoms" gyrate to hi-life music. Mary had taught me a lot, not just about patience and spontaneity, but also about Ghanaian warmth and the pressures on her, as a young African woman who had left her family, her village and her country in the search for an income, before meeting and marrying a German in Ouagadougou.

I now had a son, and I felt sorry that he would miss out on so much of the fun Mary, and so many other African men and women I had met, knew how to make with children. There was a name for my nostalgia and longing. It was homesickness, but I was embarrassed to say so, because I knew Africa was not my home.

When the telephone rang one December morning in 1988 and Mary's husband, Andreas, a German development consultant and anthropologist, said he had work for us in northern Ghana, it took us ten minutes to decide that we would go. In early 1989 we moved back to the continent which had once depressed me, a place I had once thought too chaotic, unstable, and yes, unlovely.

When we passed through Ouagadougou, en route to our new posting in northern Ghana, I felt as though I had come home. We settled in the northern Ghanaian town of Tamale, about 300 kilometres down the road from Ouagadougou and about 650 kilometres north of the capital, Accra, on the beautiful shoreline the British had once called the Gold Coast. In Tamale we started the whole process of adapting and learning all over again.

We stayed in Tamale for four happy years. There were periods of frustration. There were shortages of water and power. There was no shortage of illness and infection. There were, at first, no schools with a teacher-student class ratio of more than 1 to 100. There were arguments with politicians and their lackeys when I reported on events in northern Ghana for the BBC African Service. There were Ghanaians who were wonderful people and friends; there were expatriates who were the same. There were arrogant, opulent and ignorant expatriate development experts and co-operants; there were arrogant, opulent and ignorant Ghanaians. Mostly, there was life and learning.

There were local tragedies. The water corporation was in the habit of shutting off water taps in Tamale. Sometimes this was because residents had failed to pay water bills, occasionally it was because of technical problems and often it was simply because it gave the personnel of the water corporation, who owned or operated water tankers, the chance to sell water to desperate people and make some fast money. When people talked about this it was always with dry wit and understated disgust, and shrugs. There was nothing they could do.

There were local journalists who helped me get to the root of the many Tamale "mysteries," stories which involved juju and fetishes; there were others in town who informed on me to the national security network. There was no room for generalizations, not about Tamale, not about the Northern Region, not about the country — how could I ever have listened to, and worse, believed, generalizations about an entire continent? Tamale alone was a puzzle, the pieces of which I tried over four years to put together. The mosaic of religions, ethnic affiliations, alliances, hostilities and larger-than-life individual personalities was so fascinating, so absorbing, that I felt I could spend the rest of my life trying to analyse it.

I tried, in vain, to express solid, rational reasons for the love I felt for that hot, economically depressed part of Ghana. The town had few attractions; that is, it had few obvious attractions. It was filthy, squalid, crumbling, desperately poor and it was seething with rivalries and conflicts that stemmed from regional, ethnic and religious differences which exploded from time to time in violent riots that consumed the town. Ethnic slaughters had become almost annual events in that northern savannah.

Despite the lack of amenities, the dearth of public toilets and public sanitation, the sorry state of the hospital and the schools, Tamale had its own charms. First, it was bursting with life, and people who always took the time to stop and talk, with people who would not think of passing without offering a greeting. Although a quarter of a million people lived there, it was like a small town. Everyone knew everything about everyone. It was rife with intrigue.

It was also full of individuals who were working to make life better. I met and got to know more people who seemed but were not too good to be true in that one town than I had in a lifetime. Despite all the injustice, the hardship and what looked to me like a desperate future, the Ghanaian people were full of humour, talent, wisdom, hope and tolerance.

There were twenty-five different tribes living in Ghana's Northern Region, meaning there were also that many different languages. The lingua franca was Hausa, which had spread from northern Nigeria throughout West Africa over several centuries. In Tamale there was a Hausa saying which friends used to quote when I tried and failed to explain my affection for Tamale. "Tamale baa gudu, nkaa gudu, kaa koomo," they would say. "No one can run away from Tamale, if you run away, you will return."

I wanted to believe that I would come back because we felt that we had put down roots in that town. Tamale and the people of the region had taught us more than we had learned in all our previous postings put together. The friends my children made there, the people we met there, the people who schooled us, the children with whom my children were educated, were the best friends I made in ten years in Africa.

I don't know what had happened, maybe I had at last become colour blind. I stopped looking around me through a filter of guilt. It had been foolish to believe that all Africans would be virtuous because they had been the victims of so much injustice at the hands of Europeans, Arabs and Asians. I now saw African oppression and exploitation of fellow Africans in the same light as I already saw oppression of Africans by foreigners. Wrong was wrong. Europeans — and others — had wrought terrible and unforgivable crimes in Africa and were still doing so; the same could be said of Africans themselves.

In Tamale I knew one of the direct descendants of one of Ghana's biggest slave-traders; he was a progressive citizen and entrepreneur in Tamale, and when we were trying to build a community school, he donated generously of his construction equipment. The only person I knew of who had reproached him for his forefather's role in selling off African slaves was an African-American he met at university in Accra.

I had stopped generalizing about continental problems, which were like global problems and too daunting, tragic and big to contemplate, let alone to solve. Ghanaian friends, and non-Ghanaian friends who had made their permanent homes in Tamale, taught me to narrow my focus, concentrate on small problems, on smaller tragedies and on smaller causes for joy. They helped me put things, African politics for example, in some kind of perspective.

Africa had not achieved the unity which it has dreamed about for so many years, the pan-Africanism which Ghana's first Head of State, Dr. Kwame Nkrumah, envisioned when he led the country to independence in 1957. But maybe that, too, was a false dream, a goal so lofty and impossible that instead of hope, it invoked and caused only disappointment because it was doomed to fail. How, after all, could a continent divided into tiny, often unsustainable nation states ruled by despots with bank accounts larger than their nations GNPs, with artificial borders dividing families and ethnic groups, with hundreds upon hundreds of languages and cultures, be regarded and function as one unit? Could and should the colour of one's skin unite a continent?

That implied, to me at least, that African identity and identities were still a negative image — that of being one colour and not another. Furthermore, some of the most rabid ethnic prejudice I saw was between neighbouring tribes. And what separates ethnicity or tribalism from racism? Sometimes I was confounded by highly intelligent and worldly Ghanaians with high-profile positions in government, when they launched into tirades condemning people of a traditionally "enemy" tribe, calling them "sub-human." These were prejudices that went back hundreds of years, and pre-dated the first Europeans on the continent. They were also prejudices that greatly helped the Europeans take control of not just Ghana, but most of Africa.

Paradoxically, I also felt that an African Identity was not a myth — Africans had more things in common, more common problems, cultures, traditions and dreams, than they did differences that could separate them. Unfortunately, few Africans had the resources, opportunities or the will to travel to other parts of Africa. The traffic was much heavier between Africa and Europe or America. It was only through music, dance and film festivals that I ever had an inkling of that African unity that was so elusive on the political and economic front.

We left Burkina Faso because we could not live with the shattered dreams. In Ghana we realized Sankara was not unique; there were many Africans with dreams, working on solutions for the problems in their country. Each of those people had stories which could fill books; each of them was too busy struggling to survive, trying, often unsuccessfully, to provide their children with a decent education, a roof over their heads and basic amenities such as clean drinking water, struggling at their work, usually in development or health or education, to write the books that need to be written before the rest of the world would understand what has been troubling the continent. Those people were busy developing their region and their country, for a reward that was not monetary.

There was the doctor who treated us when we were ill, any time of day or night and who refused to charge his fellow Ghanaians for treatment. His younger sister charmed children and parents alike at a daycare centre opened by his wife. Apart from the daycare centre, she also headed up a Canadian project to help rural women get much-needed credit for farming, or processing of sheanut butter. And her sister ran a small community-owned school, sharing her humour and insights with students.

Doctor David Abdulai was another who had shunned a career, and the salary to go with it, in Britain. After his medical studies he returned to Tamale to realize a dream formed during his difficult childhood. He said he was the son of a leper and had grown up dirt poor. He remembered scavenging as a child for discarded scraps of fruit in town gutters. An American Catholic sister recognized his need and potential and assisted him through school. In 1991 he resigned from his post with the government health service and got the land to start the Shekhinah, or Glory of God, Clinic. In 1989 he performed his first operation, removing a tumour from a village woman's neck, under a mango tree. By 1993 the Shekhinah Clinic was treating hundreds of patients — the poorest of the poor. Villagers from throughout the region had come and erected their own waiting and recovery huts of mud and thatch. Dr. Abdulai, his wife who was a nurse, and the volunteer staff made do with donations from well-wishers, and when those were scarce, with ingenuity and with faith that God was with them. They also fed the fifty "lunatics" who inhabited the roadsides and gutters in Tamale, and on Christmas Day, invited those outcasts to their home for a feast. Dr. Abdulai also provided rooms and counselling for AIDS victims who were cast out of their family homes, and for whom there was no room or care in government health centres. Some people in town, particularly the rich and powerful who were not welcome in the clinic unless they took their place in long lines, called him crazy. Dr. Abdulai merely laughed.

I also spent some time in the remote village of Kukuo, a community which housed a famous fetish shrine, which was used for "de-witching." In Kukuo there were five hundred old women who had been driven, many violently, from their villages after a death in their community was blamed on them, on their alleged witchcraft. They were usually past child-bearing age, generally no longer able to perform the hard tasks assigned to women, and not coincidentally, many had occupied a hut in their villages that a nephew or male relative decided he wanted.

In Kukuo, Rabiatu Damba had been elected as District Assemblywoman and she single-handedly took on the enormous tasks of developing her village and caring for the hundreds of old women who sought refuge in Kukuo to undergo "de-witching." Rabiatu Damba was seriously deformed by a childhood illness, her bent frame too tiny for all the goodwill, energy and hope she exuded and wore about her like an aura. Months after I left Ghana, she was still writing to say she had new hopes that Kukuo would get a well or a dam "soon."

Journalists struggled by on monthly salaries of less than $100, had no typewriters or transport, and almost every week were subjected to verbal, and occasionally physical, abuse for writing what came close to the truth about corruption in government and other high places.

All of these people weathered it, stayed on, held there by their belief that things could only get better, when they seemed to be steadily getting worse.

Some of the people who made the greatest impressions on me, the women in villages whose lives were one long arduous labour — of suffering, love and humour — couldn't read or write. Some of the wisest and most worldly and godly people I'd ever met, I met in Tamale; and they had not progressed past primary school, or had never been to school at all.

When we moved to Ghana it was not this wealth of human resources and friends we set out or even expected to find. Initially, we decided to go to Ghana because both Karl and I looked forward to being in a country ruled by someone we believed to be a kindred spirit to Thomas Sankara. Ghana's Head of State, Flight Lieutenant (retired) Jerry John Rawlings, had been a friend to Sankara, and on the morning after the coup in 1987, had sent troops to the northern border of his country, prepared to invade Burkina Faso to free Sankara, had he still been alive. Sankara was already past saving but Rawlings had distanced himself from Compaore's regime, and named a traffic circle in Accra after his fallen friend.

Rawlings had seized power twice in Ghana. In 1979 he was pulled from a prison cell by coup makers and made Chairman of the Armed Forces Revolutionary Council which ruled Ghana for three months. The AFRC took over a country where nothing worked except the black market and, as part of Rawlings' "house-cleaning" measures, secretly tried and then executed three former Heads of State. Elections were held in October that year and Rawlings handed over constitutional rule to democratically-elected President Hilla Limann. Eighteen months later he led another coup and ousted Limann, set himself up as Chairman of the Provisional National Defence Council and launched his revolution. Like Sankara he spoke out vehemently against social injustice and traditions which no longer fit, such as female circumcision, bushfires and unplanned families.

When Rawlings began his revolution, two decades of corruption along with unbridled and unwise spending had taken their toll and Ghana's economy had bottomed out. People recalled lining up for hours to purchase a tea bag, a loaf of bread or a cube of sugar. The PNDC's heavy-handed policies to eliminate corruption and get people back to the land to produce food were relatively successful and popular in the early years of the revolution.

But when we arrived in Ghana, Rawlings and his revolution had been around for a decade, and there was little left of his original plan to promote the "small man" and work with the "grassroots," except his occasional frenetic speeches where he still harped on what was wrong with the people, the country, the "old" politicians, although he had enticed many of those into his revolutionary regime. He railed against the west and capitalism and the economic order dividing north and south, separating exploiter and exploited; at the same time he and his government embraced economic and domestic policies drawn up by western banks. Visiting journalists whose itinerary while in Ghana was often limited to a few interviews with western diplomats, World Bank officials and perhaps an intriguing evening of off-the-record conversation with Rawlings himself at the "Castle" in Accra, sent off rave reviews such as the one which appeared in *Newsweek* in 1992, entitled "Africa's Test Case," headed by the bold words "By moving towards a free-market economy, Ghana has won praise in the west — and could become a new role model for a continent in despair." The price of cocoa, the mainstay of Ghana's economy, was dropping steadily. Increased logging and gold mining, which helped pay Ghana's debts, or at least the interest on them, were devastating non-renewable resources, the tropical forests and the environment. Foresters estimated that odum, Ghana's prime hardwood for export, would be gone within five years.

Behind the scenes, members of Rawlings' government were doing what they could to maintain total power. They were wooing powerful traditional rulers and chiefs with gifts in exchange for their allegiance, silencing opponents and misusing state monies as any other government that is not checked by an independent judiciary and a free press.

The World Bank and the IMF called Ghana their success story on the African continent. Ten years of heavy-handed rule had provided them the opportunity to push through a Structural Adjustment Programme — optimistically or euphemistically known as Economic Recovery. This meant that by 1992 the GNP was growing by about three per cent, but decent education and health care were beyond the reach of anyone who was not wealthy. To become wealthy it helped to be an outspoken supporter of Rawlings' government.

Rawlings and his men still rode on their reputation of "accountability and probity" which they had proclaimed for themselves at the start of their revolution. Ghanaian journalists shook their heads and asked "What accountability?"

In late 1991 I met with Rawlings in Tamale. The interview I had requested turned out to be what he called a "chat" and "off the record." I was taken with his apparent sincerity, but unnerved by the sudden swings in his mood, which went from openly hostile to almost seductive and charming. I left confounded by the man. I concluded that he meant well, that he had integrity, but that he was handicapped by his ego and his certainty that only he could run Ghana. The same conviction which had led Sankara to his grave seemed to have led Rawlings down the road to compromise of his principles and beliefs for the sake of his own survival and his power. He appeared to have surrounded himself with sycophants who kept him in the dark about what was really happening in the country and he seemed to have blinded himself to the corruption and lies which had mounted around him. Or had he? Perhaps he had merely taken the only realistic road there was, and done his best. I could not decide, and was in no position to judge.

In his desire to explain his revolution to me, he referred repeatedly to the great moment in Ghanaian history when he had taken power in 1979, to the thunderous applause of the people, who had called him "Junior Jesus." Thirteen years later he was no longer the lean and novel hero he had been then, and the people were not calling him Junior Jesus any more. He seemed to waver between wishing and then believing they still did.

Ghanaians fell into two categories: those who hated and those who admired the man known as "J.J." Was he a human being with great vision running a difficult country, or a human being with a thirst for power, or was he a bit of both? One thing was sure. He had opened Ghanaians' eyes, schooled them in their rights, and in 1979, had dared to voice the question of how some people had grown fat while others around them starved. This question had come back to haunt him; by 1990 he himself had grown much thicker around the middle and his critics asked why and how. Demonstrating students from the Tamale Polytechnic wrote it on walls in chalk — "J.J. why are you fat?" Moments later frantic security men from the "Special Branch" were there to rub it out, begging me to give them names of the students I had interviewed, who had dared to voice those forbidden words about their leader, their emperor. While I lied and said I had no names, I was really wondering if that was Rawlings' problem — no one dared to let him hear the truth about what was going on below him, or about himself.

Members of the Provisional National Defense Council under Rawlings were indeed a new generation of leaders — they were brilliant administrators and often highly competent technocrats. They were also wise and tasteful enough to keep the corruption and consumption that existed well hidden. No palaces were constructed, government Mercedes gave way to four-wheel drive vehicles from Japan, and Rawlings still appeared in public in simple garb shouting what sounded like sincere words of revolutionary advice for his people. Significantly, the outside world hailed him as Africa's "golden boy," not because his Scottish father had bequeathed him fair skin, but because — and here is the real crux of his success and stability in power — he ruled a country that looked stable and also paid its debts. What bothered so many people in Ghana was that the debts were incurred over a decade of revolutionary rule, when they had no say in what was being done with the money that they now owed to international lending agencies. In Tamale, for example, at least a million dollars of it had gone to build a lavish clubhouse, tennis court and swimming pool for the electricity corporation, the Volta River Authority. And this in a town where thousands of people had no clean water to drink and where there was no running water in the regional hospital.

During our stay in Ghana, the Berlin Wall collapsed, the Cold War fizzled out and western (and eastern) donors who had earlier supported dictators on the basis of their friendship with the west (or the east) started clamouring for democracy in Africa.

For a while, it looked very encouraging. In Benin, President Kerekou was ousted in an election. So was Kenneth Kaunda in Zambia.

But then things began to change. Perhaps dictators began to learn from the mistakes of these ex-presidents who had permitted themselves to be voted out. Perhaps some of the opposition parties frightened foreign investors. Election rigging became the order of the day. Blaise Compaore was elected as constitutional president in Burkina Faso in an election which the opposition parties boycotted on the grounds of the huge bribes being handed out to bring voters onto his side. A Canadian election observer interviewed on BBC defended the poll as "free and fair." In Cameroon even the foreign observers could not call Paul Biya's rigged election free and fair, but Biya was still in power, the country still receiving assistance from the same donors who had called for democracy.

In Togo, Eyadema clung to power although a national conference on democracy had nominally stripped him of that power in 1991 when a Prime Minister was appointed. In early 1993 the country came to a complete standstill as the southern opposition called national strikes and the military — Eyadema's men — came out shooting. Development projects were closed. The killing and unrest continued.

In 1991 Rawlings announced that he did not think that multiparty politics was an appropriate form of democracy in Ghana. But the pressure from within and outside his country eventually forced him to acquiesce and announce a calendar for elections and a return to constitutional government although the ban remained on political parties. That ban was lifted just four months before the Presidential elections, but by then Rawlings' party, the National Democratic Congress which had emerged from the PNDC, had had a head start of almost ten years. Rawlings apparently changed his mind about party politics and let his party nominate him as its presidential candidate.

In November 1992, he won the presidential elections, and two months later he handed over constitutional power to himself after eleven years of "revolutionary" power. The opposition called foul, with substantial evidence of serious problems in the presidential election. I had taken photographs of children voting, but what was I to do with them? The Commonwealth Observers had already declared that election "free and fair" before counting was finished. They inadvertently — or studiously — ignored the preparations for the elections, which Rawlings' PNDC government had been carefully orchestrating for three years, to ensure victory. Revolutionary cadres, Rawlings' wife's "Thirty-first of December Women's Movement" and Rawlings' appointed officials throughout the country had all the bases covered, and their finances were not open to scrutiny. But even in Tamale, it was obvious state money was flowing and influence peddling was the order of the day.

I was dismayed by members of the Commonwealth Observer team who were responsible for monitoring the polling in the north of the country. They arrived on the eve of the elections, complained bitterly during their two-day stay about the heat and the dirt and the poor accommodation in the best hotels and guesthouses in the north. One man said he would not come back for a second round of elections because there was no accomodation comfortable enough for him in Tamale and he defended his right as a Commonwealth Observer to fly first class.

I asked him how they could have made the verdict of "free and fair" in the face of so many blatant cases of irregularities. "Look," he said, "this is Africa. What do you expect?" He was from Tanzania, where elections had not been held since independence.

Canadian observers, sent independently to monitor the elections, told me that Canada had refused to join the Commonwealth team. But the Canadian report on the elections was for internal purposes only, and of little help to the hundreds of thousands of Ghanaians who expected more of foreign observers. When they saw that they were in for four more years of Rawlings because of the "free and fair" elections, they took to making light of it; if a market price were too high, it became a "free and fair" price, and eventually, we would hear people passing on the road shout to each other in code, "F and F."

In Niger, elections were postponed and marred by the rebellion of the nomadic, desert-dwelling Tuaregs who were tired of being ruled and taxed by a centralized government which claimed the vast sandy lands, and the minerals underneath, as its own. In fact, war was breaking out all over in Africa, as the superpowers began to back away from iron-fisted dictators they had supported when it served their interests during the Cold War. Decades worth of suppression of opposition and stifling of ethnic tensions under totalitarian governments had had the same effect as they had in former Yugoslavia — the pressure cooker was simply exploding after simmering away for so many years.

From Tamale I watched and listened to all of these horror stories — from Liberia, Somalia, Cameroon, Angola, Rwanda, Togo. It had all been inevitable. The rest of the world, which shouldered a good part of the blame for the mess, had closed its eyes and buried its head in the sand. Democratic governments had been playing dirty games in Africa — our bilateral development agencies which tended to plough large amounts of money into government departments, and thus into the hands of the African powers that were, had inadvertently helped keep dictatorships afloat, and only a handful of people who paid taxes to pay for this aid even knew what was happening. How could they know? Media attention was generally on South Africa, if it wasn't temporarily diverted by famine in Ethiopia or more recently by the tragedy of Somalia, Burundi and Rwanda.

During a visit to Toronto in 1991 I complained to a prominent media man about the lack of coverage in Canada of the ongoing slaughter in Liberia. He said Canadians wouldn't be interested, then continued, "Let's face it. South Africa is between whites and blacks. When the whites are no longer involved, we won't be interested in South Africa any more, either."

Even if I fretted about his lack of vision, I admired his honesty. He was probably right. One American journalist who came to Ouagadougou after the coup, and who stayed for only two days, answered my question about the lack of interest among editors back home about everyday Africa with the quip, "Africa is off the map, these days. It's no longer interesting." The continent where traditional and modern worlds were meeting, exploding, trying to mesh, where music, art and humankind were born, not interesting? That made me feel a despair I had almost stopped feeling about Africa itself.

In Tamale I could hardly remember the alienation, the depression and despair I felt when I first arrived in Africa. I had been blind to the role our countries and those behind the Iron Curtain had played in propping up corrupted African governments and cementing Africa's ills into place. It hurt to acknowledge that we weren't the nice guys I had thought we were, to admit that hypocrisy was not unique to communist regimes and military dictatorships.

Sometimes we met up with former friends from previous postings who filled us in on people and places we knew back then. I realized how fast the decade had passed, how far we had travelled since those early days when Karl and I were trying to find some common footing on African ground. We had grown back together in Burkina Faso and Ghana. We were also afraid to leave behind the life we had built together in West Africa.

Yes, Africa was still troubled. Around us, the political, environmental and health problems mounted. AIDS and population pressure competed for priority in the countless conferences and seminars on African development. The desert was still growing, bushfires and slash-and-burn agriculture were taking their toll on the soils and the harvests. Dictators, disguised as constitutionally-elected presidents, were still "chopping" national revenue and growing fat while they preached to their people to "tighten their belts." How many Africans did I know who had belts to tighten?

People were leaving the continent in droves, if not legally, then illegally. The political and war refugees usually wound up in neighbouring countries, because they did not have the funds to travel abroad to greener pastures. But, African hospitality being what it is, they usually found relatives or tribesmen who would squeeze them into their huts and offer them a share of their already meagre family meals. The majority of those who made it to Europe and America were economic refugees, fleeing the injustice of their homeland where social mobility was almost non-existent.

But for all that, life continued. In Tamale I watched the people juggling their tiny incomes to make ends meet, laughing about their hardships, cursing their leaders, marrying, bringing forth new life, and pursuing their dreams that one day, for their family at least, things would get better — if not in this life, then in the next.

By the end of our third year in Ghana, Iddrissu, a twenty-two-year old Ghanaian drummer had moved in with us after his father drove him from home. His father did not want his son in school; Iddrissu wanted an education. Iddrissu had grandiose dreams — of acquiring knowledge and an understanding of the world around him and the world beyond his own, of sharing his talent and expertise as a traditional drummer with people from all over the world. His dreams filled our house; they were big enough for all of us, too big for him — we thought.

At first we tried to bring him around to our kind of reasoning, thinking to prevent him from future disappointment by pedantically explaining to him that he had few chances of doing much beyond selling a few drums to foreigners and perhaps finishing school with a diploma and an education so miserable that it would take him nowhere.

His father wanted him to quit school, and spend the rest of his life farming and drumming for him because he himself had recently been "enskinned" as drummer chief in his village. Iddrissu had refused and his father handed him unceremoniously over to us, saying he no longer bore any responsibility for "that troublesome boy" who asked questions and wanted to learn. In his native village his age-mates and relatives resented his ambition and his quest for understanding of questions that traditionally were not asked; they ridiculed and insulted him mercilessly. But Iddrissu had no intention of giving up on his goals, or his dreams of turning the ancient art of drumming into a modern profession.

In time, Iddrissu changed us too. We stopped lecturing him on shaping down his dreams and started, instead to try to find ways to help him realize them.

He was just one of dozens of young people I met who, despite the odds and the reality around them, seemed unacquainted with despair. The despair exists, as it does everywhere. But there are millions and millions of Africans who are unscathed by hopelessness, with which so much of the world has painted them. If there is despair about Africa, then indeed it must be despair about the whole planet that allows and in some cases perpetuates the poverty on that continent.

The Africa I got to know is a continent, maybe the only one, where strangers are welcomed with open arms — whether we deserve to be or not. The paradox is that their tolerance of strangers does not always extend to their neighbouring tribe.

*Hand-dug pits and gold miners at Yako, Burkina Faso, April 1988.*

## Chapter 22

# Three-day war

When we left Tamale in May 1993 it was, on the outside at least, a peaceful and happy town — in the enchanting way of any impoverished, out-of-the-way community where one can't be quite sure when the twentieth century arrived or what it's all supposed to mean.

The days passed quickly, marked by the rising and setting of the sun, and the heat. Before dawn the night insects ceased their screeching and the cocks began crowing. There was animated chatter of the girls and women passing on their daily search for water as the sun rose red over the acacia trees on the horizon.

Iddrissu headed off for school each morning at 6:30 on his bicycle. Back he came late each afternoon, often having had no classes at all. His teachers, or "masters" as they were called, didn't show up. Or his class hadn't been assigned a teacher for a subject. In six months he had two classes in agricultural science; on his timetable it was scheduled for once a week. He muddled through homework and West African examinations intended for a student doing O-levels in Britain; he was supposed to understand atomic isotopes and laboratory procedures. He had no idea what an atom was and he had never seen a laboratory. In his senior secondary school, one of the best in Tamale, students who had no money to pay for a desk might lie on the concrete floor to take notes, if they had a pencil to write with and a notebook to write in. Textbooks were seldom available and teachers were often without chalk to write notes on blackboards. Some teachers didn't bother to teach during regular hours but charged enormous fees for "outside classes." Occasionally I went to complain. The teachers complained right back, saying the students in the high school could barely write their own names and didn't make any efforts to learn. Iddrissu, they told me, was doing very well. He was eager and attentive. And off he went each morning, as though it was the first day of school, if not a first world education.

The markets in Tamale were a study in hospitality, humour and haggling, all done under the broiling sun to the scent of rotting produce and public toilets. The roads were really just paths to be trod to get from one place to another; people complained about the potholes and muddy quagmires, but only in passing, much the way we discussed the weather in Canada, as a given, and part of the challenge of life. However, trees were being felled to make way for a new thoroughfare being driven right through the heart of Tamale, a recipe for disaster in a town where pedestrians, livestock and bicycles had always had the right of way.

Most people did their dancing to drums, at weddings or funerals or "outdoorings" where new babies received gifts and names. The Saturday "Old Timers" dance was a meeting place for uptown young and old who could scrape together the 40 cedis (50¢) to enter and dance. In their second-hand clothes they outshone those of us in first world jeans. In the sauna that was the dancehall in the "Catering Resthouse" they celebrated, with their bodies and their souls, the joyous sounds of hi-life, the eternally optimistic sounds of Reggae and the frenetic bone-melting rhythms of "Kwasa Kwasa" from Zaire.

Despite its one traffic light and the quarter of a million inhabitants, Tamale was not a town; it was magical village where one century overlapped another and people mattered more than speed and success. Words of greeting were worth more than a thousand photographs. A local drummer or "gong-gong beater" could summon a crowd faster than it took to place a telephone call. Suffering was a way of life and faith, tolerance and humour the essence of life. Tamale had charmed us, spoiled us, bewitched us. We did not want to leave.

The sadness I felt driving through and out of Tamale for the last time felt like death. Mother became child; my son reached for my hand and offered condolence. It was okay, we would come back.

We may well go back, but nothing will be the same again in that part of Ghana, not for a long, long time. There are no dances at the Catering Resthouse; instead there's a curfew and a state of emergency. The market, and the town, are off bounds to anyone who is Konkomba. Konkombas are killed in Tamale. Some of our closest friends, neighbours, were Konkombas. But that is now history and they have fled or are dead.

Long before we left, it was clear that the peace and happiness I sensed in the region were very fragile. In 1992, a year before our departure, there had been ethnic fighting — the "three-day war" between the Gonjas on one side, Konkombas and Nawuris on the other. The year before that it had been fighting between the Nawuris and Nchumurros on one side, the Gonjas on the other.

In 1991 it began as a dispute between the small Nawuri tribe in the eastern corner of the region and the overlord Gonja state. In 1992 it was a bloodbath that consumed the East Gonja District. But when did it really begin? Hundreds of years ago when the centralized ethnic states with their superior weapons were conquering and seizing land from the smaller groups who were without royal leaders and warriors on horses? Or perhaps it started a century ago when the British and Germans were carving up their territories that comprise the modern states of Ghana and Togo and splitting ethnic groups with their lines drawn on maps in Berlin? Or was it seventy years ago when the British were setting up four overlord states — the Gonjas, Dagombas, Nanumbas and Mamprusi — to rule indirectly for them and keep the other subordinate, landless groups under control in the Northern Territories of what was then their Gold Coast?

Not to forget that in 1978 the Alhassan Committee — comprising mostly men from those four overlord states — recommended that all the land in the Northern Region be handed back to their own Paramount Chiefs, assuming that what their forefathers had conquered still belonged to them. And the government of the time did just that, even though those conquests were mired in the vague and subjective oral histories of the four dominant tribes.

Or did it begin when Ghana's Head of State, Jerry Rawlings, came to Tamale and announced that if he could, he would arm the "minority" tribes to take over the land from the dominant groups?

In fact, the clashes I had seen in 1991 and 1992 were not the *beginning* of anything. They were resumptions of wars over land and recognition of traditional rulers — or chiefs — that had begun centuries earlier and never really ended. Colonialism had been a hiatus of inter-tribal wars over land and the power that goes with it. The British had vested the land in the region in the hands of the state and it had stayed there for the first two decades of independence. Giving the land back to four Paramount Chiefs, and to no others, was a blueprint for trouble. In the fifteen years since its enactment there have been six serious outbreaks of ethnic fighting in the region — all over land and recognition of traditional rulers.

Much had changed since the British set up their policy of indirect rule and carved the region up among four Paramount Chiefs. Subordinate, landless tribes no longer agreed that land ownership in Ghana should be based on ancient conquest. One of those so-called minority tribes, the Konkombas, now outnumbered all but the Dagombas in the region.

The problem, at its simplest, was that four overlord tribes owned all the land in the region. But there were twenty-five tribes living in the Northern Region, twenty-one of them without land and no official recognition of their headmen, or chiefs. Without land and chiefs they had no power and no representation in the House of Chiefs that still wields enormous power, parallel to that of the modern state. Members of these groups spoke of the "Northern Equation," saying, "If you are not a Dagomba, Gonja, Nanumba or Mamprusi you will not get a directorship in any government office."

The Konkomba–Gonja conflict in 1992 was such a complicated mess of ethnological and historical tangles, it was not the stuff for short news dispatches in world headlines. News reports needed statistics — body counts — and short, snappy explanations. Trouble was, counting fatalities was almost impossible in that forgotten niche of Ghana in May 1992, just a few months before the first elections in a decade. The last thing the government wanted was bad international press that indicated the country was not as stable or "democratic" as it would have the outside world believe. Regional authorities, ever fearful of letting bad news leak from their region lest the leaders in Accra ask them questions, were busy trying to play the whole thing down.

On the Monday following the three-day-war, I asked the Northern Regional PNDC Secretary, and Head of the Northern Region Security Council, how many had died. "Why do you people always want to know these petty, petty details?" he retorted. He went on to tell me that this clash was not the business of the BBC and to lecture me on what I should be focusing my attention on — the troubles between Ireland and England, the genocide in the former Yugoslavia. That didn't make very useful copy for the reports the BBC was requesting from Tamale.

I had spoken to refugees in Tamale, who had poured into town on Saturday and Sunday during the fighting. They had escaped with their lives and their stories, and nothing else. They came loaded like sacks of grain in trucks on which the words "Goods Only" were painted beside the proverbs — "Good Brothers" or "The Evil that Men Do." They came on bent and broken bicycles; they came on foot through the bush. There were men with wounds to attest to their scrapes with warriors brandishing machetes, mothers hugging naked and dazed children.

They described in great detail how small boys were slaughtered because boys grow up to be men, potential warriors. The women spoke of the rush to pierce the earlobes of baby boys to disguise them as girls in the final moments before the attackers reached villages. They told how pregnant women were bashed against trees or cut down as they fled, because they might be carrying a male child in their wombs.

But these were stories from the homeless survivors camped out in the Community Development complex in Tamale and I found it difficult to believe them, let alone write them down in reports. The next day I set out with Iliasu Adam, a friend and journalist with the Ghana News Agency, to go to the war zone and separate fact from hyperbole. We thought we could do this dispassionately. We had not reckoned with reality. Tamale had lulled me into believing that the peoples' tolerance of inequity and poverty was infinite.

We drove to Salaga, a dusty little town that was once one of the largest slave markets in West Africa — a town that I knew only from the Ghana tourist brochures that invited visitors to view the ancient iron rings where slaves were once chained in the Salaga market.

We began with a visit to the Gonja divisional chief, the Kpembewura. He received us in a small, dark room at the end of a maze of mud dwellings. His face was very long and drawn, under the blue and white hand-woven cap of the Gonja traditional state. It was adorned with small leather packages that contained fetishes — his powers. He sat cross-legged on a leather pillow in a corner of the room, his carved wooden staff propped up against the blue wall beside him. His linguist and elders kneeled around him on the floor. (Chiefs in the region are never addressed directly. To communicate with a chief one has to speak through a linguist, who kneels on the floor, just to the side of the chief.)

This was not his palace. The room was a temporary refuge in Salaga, capital of the district over which he ruled and in which he controlled all the land. The aged man before us embodied Gonja history and the past of glorious conquests over other tribes, that had won him and his people the land. Even in his temporary refuge he inspired respect and awe.

Chiefs are all-powerful among their people, respected more than the head of the modern state. Although selection of chiefs, always from royal families, has been corrupted in recent years by commercial and political interests and influence-peddling, for the most part the chiefs must still respect all the laws and fulfil the role demanded by the office, or they can be "deskinned", losing their chieftaincy. Paramount Chiefs, at the top of an intricate hierarchy of divisional chiefs, village chiefs and elders, have an almost mystical hold over their subjects.

The Gonja Paramount Chief, or Yagbunwura, owns more than half of the region or about one-sixth of Ghana. The Kpembewura, one of four Gonja divisional chiefs, was the supreme caretaker in the East Gonja District. But his palace in the nearby village of Kpembe had been burned and gutted; he had fled his palace in Kpembe and gone into hiding in Salaga. The Gonjas and their Chief had fled, lost the three-day war with the Konkombas.

Hundreds were still thronging the roads of Salaga, trying to get to Tamale and out of the district that Konkomba warriors had seized. Their villages were burned; they were terrified of the Konkomba warriors who, they said, were still hiding in the bush with their bows and poisoned arrows, their machetes and their guns. Even the police and soldiers sent to Salaga to end the fighting told us they didn't dare hunt down the Konkombas. "They know the bush," said one excitable policeman. "You see them, then they're gone. They're like guinea fowl. You can't catch them. And they're not afraid of our guns. You shoot one, they don't mind. They're in their numbers and they'll fire back." In any event, the soldiers at the District Administration who were sent to ambush remaining Konkomba warriors in the bush were having a problem organizing any assault on anyone; when we left them they were still bickering over the few remaining litres of fuel for their vehicles. They were, however, enjoying the spoils of the battle and freely slaughtering and roasting the cows they found grazing in the bush, abandoned by their rightful owners.

Still looking for some hard and cruel facts that would fit into a three-minute news report, I asked the Kpembewura how many people had died. He shook his head. "Too many to count," he replied. "Before I became Kpembewura, I was chief in the village of Sabon Guida. I left family there, twenty-five children. I have no word from any of them." I later learned that fourteen of his sons had been killed in that one village.

The Kpembewura told us the fighting he had just witnessed was the worst he had seen in his lifetime — and he was an old, old man. He told us to go and look at the destruction of Gonja villages, to see for ourselves.

From Salaga we drove eastward, on a red muddy road leading to villages where the battle had begun. We passed a family of refugees heading out of the war zone. The man was on a bicycle and the handlebars were covered with bunches of leaves, the flag of truce in the bush. His wife and children walked behind, their few possessions wrapped in bright prints and balanced on their heads.

The first village we came to was Kitoe. A blue armoured vehicle of a special army unit sent north from Accra to stop the fighting and to clean up after it was parked at the entrance to the village. A grassy path led towards the collection of mud huts, vulnerable and gaping where the grass roofs had been burned. Vultures circled overhead.

In ten years I had never been in an African village where there was silence; villages exude life — children running to stare at visitors, chickens, goats, the sounds of pestles in mortars and voices. There are always voices and laughter. In Kitoe, though, there was silence interspersed only with the occasional grunts and shouts of the soldiers down in the village, who had the grisly task of burying the dead.

The two men on the armoured vehicle waved to us, grimly. They wore white masks over their mouths and noses. We started off slowly down the path towards the village, where we could see soldiers stacking corpses, and stopped short when we came upon the first body. It had been a boy, maybe seven years old, wearing a school uniform with brown shorts and a yellow shirt. The path was strewn with more body parts. The smell was powerful enough to make us retch. The two soldiers standing atop the armoured vehicle shouted that it got much worse inside the village, where their colleagues were working.

I turned back, heading out to the main road to escape the stench of death. I stared off across the savannah, newly green and luxuriant after the year's first rains, at "flamboyant" trees in full, fiery bloom, and at the cows concentrating on their cud, blessedly oblivious.

Life was a terrible struggle in northern Ghana, even at the best of times. So why, I kept asking myself. Why? Because it was such a struggle, because there were too many people fighting for land and its scanty resources? Or because of the social inequities in the region, where four tribes owned all the land because they had conquered it centuries ago? Or because land went hand-in-hand with power of traditional rulers, and subordinate landless groups were no longer content to allow their overlords to represent them in the House of Chiefs? But an election was coming; the numbers of the Konkombas would ensure them seats in the modern parliament — was traditional power still supreme here? Why did that young boy in the school uniform have to be hacked to death? Would that right the wrongs? Settle the score? My head churned out questions, but no answers.

In the months that followed I interviewed everyone I could, trying to get at those elusive answers, collecting masses of paper and points of view that all pointed to further trouble.

The Konkombas were what anthropologists called acephalous, or without a centralized and hierarchical state. Over the past century they have slowly spilled westwards across the Northern Region, from their original territory straddling the Togolese border. Highly traditional, they lived in the bush, clearing and farming the land they were permitted to use, by one of the dominant, land-owning tribes. Wherever they settled, a chief from one of the dominant groups would be sent to govern them, and to collect hefty tithes from them.

Konkomba males, between the ages of ten and their "first time with a woman" formed a class of "holy warriors" schooled in the art of bush warfare with bows, arrows, machetes and more recently, guns. "We can be mobilized in ten minutes," a young Konkomba man told me. "We live in the bush, so the battlefield is our home."

Until the 1970s, they had been largely ignored by government and colonial administrators who were trying to encourage education in the region, and illiteracy among Konkombas was extremely high. They were in no position to question their subordinate position to their overlords. But missionaries had been working with them intensively during the previous two decades, and a new generation of educated Konkombas had emerged. The Konkomba Youth Association was formed. It was to combat traditional betrothal of girls before they were even born, something that discouraged parents from sending daughters to school. The Youth Association wanted to bring the Konkombas into the modern state of Ghana and to make their demands known to government and to the Paramount tribes, their overlords. If government didn't listen, they were prepared to go to war, as they did for the first time in 1981 against the Nanumbas and then against the Gonjas in 1991 and 1992.

The Gonjas and other centralized states regarded the demands of the Konkombas and other acephalous tribes as ridiculous. They viewed them as tenants or guests on their land; "guests who come to eat and then want to take over our house" was how one Gonja man put it.

The Konkombas countered that in a modern state, land ownership could not be decided by conquest, especially conquests made centuries earlier. If the government didn't amend the situation, they said, then they were prepared to conquer the land, now, from the dominant tribes. To make matters worse, the four Paramount states were predominantly Muslim; the acephalous "subordinate" groups had been influenced heavily by Christian missionaries, adding religious differences to the social, political and ethnic grievances they harboured against each other.

What could be done, once the blood had been shed, to restore peace? And who was to blame for the slaughter I saw that afternoon in Kitoe? Warriors had done the killing, but responsibility for the war was shared by many people far from the scene. Some blame could be laid at the feet of the PNDC government which had commissioned a lengthy and costly commission of inquiry into the causes of the clashes between the Gonjas and Nawuris in 1991; then failed to publish or act on the report. The dominant states had never forgiven Rawlings for the speech he had made about arming the "minority" tribes to fight for land.

And in May 1992 the elections were in the offing. Political parties were busy wooing chiefs and elders of all the groups, making promises in exchange for their votes. Rawlings' NDC Party won; Konkombas and others expected the elected government to fulfil promises made in the heat of the campaign.

But Rawlings was just the last of many who had been petitioned by the smaller groups to make changes in the status quo in the region. Several of the acephalous groups — including the Nawuris and Nchumurros who had fought the Gonjas in 1991 — had taken their case to the United Nations in the 1950s. They had demanded recognition of their chiefs, something the British had denied. The British, who had always relied on the four dominant ethnic states to carry out their indirect rule, were in no mood to accede to the wishes of the smaller tribes who were demanding a share of traditional power and the land that went with it. The Nawuris and Nchumurros had lost their case in the 1950s. The case they had made in 1991 in the lengthy Ampiah Commission of Inquiry into the problem had led only to government silence on the matter.

And so, the three-hundred-year-old problem had erupted in the three-day-war. In the months that followed each side licked its wounds while freely insulting "enemy" tribes and stockpiling arms in preparation for war. The government in Accra seemed to have closed its eyes and ears. Development projects in the region were often and not coincidentally steered towards the four districts where the four Paramount Chiefs sat, but donors were largely oblivious to the deep tribal divisions and jealousies they were reinforcing.

The official figure for the fatalities in the three-day-war remained sixty-three; the authorities said that hundreds had been left homeless. In the village of Kitoe alone the soldiers buried seventy-nine bodies. And there were a dozen villages that had been destroyed in the same way. It is more likely that hundreds died and thousands were left homeless.

But who, besides the journalists looking for "petty, petty details," was counting? The war was over, elections were coming and Ghana was, according to many observers, an African success story. The north was, in any case, not considered economically important and was poorly understood by people in southern

Ghana who often referred to the Northern Region as "hot, backwards and primitive," although they had never been there to sample its charms and unravel its mysteries.

In Tamale there was unease. The government silence on land and traditional power in the region was ominous. The Konkombas had voted heavily in favour of Rawlings' NDC Party, looking to him to grant their traditional rulers the status of chiefs, and thus, the right to a portion of Ghana they could call their own.

In the months before we left, people from all sides of the dispute whispered to me that war was brewing. Influential Gonjas and Dagombas told me they were prepared to wipe out the Konkombas, who they said were arming themselves for the greatest battle the country had ever seen. The Konkombas told me they were not arming to start a war, but that the Paramount Chiefs were preparing for war and they had to be ready. They said that if they were provoked they were ready to fight. "I am going to tell you something," a Konkomba youth said to me. "We are prepared to fight them all. And with our numbers we can fight until there are only ten Konkombas left, and we will just rebuild our tribe."

When I left Tamale, the army was still in the district, keeping the "peace" while rumours of war swept the region. On my last visit to the Kpembewura, in his new palace, I asked him if peace had been restored to the area. "There is no peace here," he said, "only soldiers."

What will bring peace, I wanted to know. "There is only one solution," he said, as he sat on his chief's podium, surrounded by the regalia of his position while beside him his youngest, his four-year-old, son stared down at me. "The government has to expel every Konkomba man, woman and child from Gonjaland. Or else there will be battles much bigger and worse than this one you have seen."

It was impossible to discount those words from that aged man whose power — and land — had been handed down to him by his forefathers and the legendary conqueror who founded the Gonja state, Jakpa of the Spear.

I left Tamale with a sense of profound loss — and foreboding.

# Epilogue

It happened as he said. In February 1994, the Northern Region of Ghana dissolved into war. This time it was not a three-day war and the dead could be counted in thousands, not hundreds. The displaced persons number in the hundreds of thousands.

The story made the international news, briefly. Iliasu Adam broke the news blackout that was imposed on the region and reported it on BBC. The international press got wind of it; the story went out on the wires, trivialized as the guinea-fowl war because it was sparked off by a dispute between a Konkomba and Nanumba man in a market in Nakpayili, over the price of a guinea fowl. Of course it had nothing to do with guinea fowl, or prices in the market. It was a war waiting to happen, and no one did anything to forestall it. The private press published warnings that it was imminent; once again the government closed its eyes to the arms shipments, the rumours and the tension. The Bureau of National Investigation, or "Special Branch" in Ghana had the time and resources to tail ordinary citizens and to keep files on anyone they construed as a potential threat — even me — so it's hard to imagine the government was unaware of what was going on in the Northern Region.

The story didn't stay in the news long because even bigger and bloodier stories were breaking in East Africa. In March the presidents of Burundi and Rwanda were killed when their jet went down over Kigali Airport and Rwanda turned into the worst killing field Africa has ever known. The butchery in Rwanda made the destruction and slaughter in northern Ghana look only mildly tragic.

But tragedy is always relative. The tragedy in Ghana is still too awful to grasp, whether it's reported or not. Iliasu says that the slaughter we saw in Kitoe in 1992, was "nothing" compared to what he saw when he drove through the Nanumba District, where the 1994 war began. He writes of roads strewn with bodies, dismembered men, women and children, and of toddlers with arrows sticking out of them — days after the fighting — staggering about among the bodies.

Friends write me devastating letters, saying that attacks continue in the bush. About two hundred villages in the Nanumba District where Karl worked for more than four years were destroyed and their inhabitants killed. Only the health post his project helped to fund in the district is still standing.

In the bush that they know so well, the Konkombas continue to ambush Dagomba, Nanumba and Gonja villages. Dagombas say they are still terrified of attacks and allege that security forces sent to keep the peace are unable, or unwilling, to disarm the Konkombas.

In Tamale, Konkombas — no matter what age— are massacred. Hundreds were holed up for months for their own protection in the military barracks a stone's throw from our former house in Tamale. My daughter's friend, Diana, who shared our house and our lives for three years, is a Konkomba. We have finally got word that she escaped with her mother and brothers and taken refuge in the south of the country — somewhere. Her father is still in hiding. Dagomba friends say that no Konkomba will be allowed in Tamale for the next century, or maybe longer — only Allah knows.

One of the private newspapers has reminded the nation of an ancient pact between the Dagombas and the Ashantes to the south, that could, theoretically, bring the Ashantes into the dispute. Friends write that landless tribes throughout Ghana are being chased off the land by the land-owning tribes, afraid that similar demands on their territory will be made by these tenants.

The government missed many chances in the past decade to make land reform or re-distribute land and traditional power. No move they make now can please all sides. Someone is bound to take up arms. Too much blood has been shed; ethnic hatred is at a fever pitch.

We finally received reassurance that Rabiatu Damba, the Assemblywoman who was trying so hard to improve the life of the people, including five hundred old, "dewitched" women in Kukuo, is alive and that the village was not destroyed. Maybe the fetish shrine there frightened off attackers, protected Kukuo from the madness.

From thousands of kilometres away in Nairobi, I think every day about the ongoing tragedy in the region which inspired me with hope, for Ghana and for Africa. And I wonder, not for the first time, how the government of Ghana and the governments that support Ghana's development and run development projects in the Northern Region of the country could have been so blind to what was so obvious to all the people there — that war was coming.

As I drive the roads of Nairobi, where the twentieth century has definitely arrived and urban squalor means street children hounding — or robbing — passers-by for coins to purchase more glue for sniffing, I try to block it all out by recalling Tamale as it was, as I remember it best. One night comes back clearly; nostalgia for what was and could have been consumes me. We were at a friend's house for a party and stayed well into the early morning hours. The air was still sultry, the night alive with bats, insects and the stars. Orion the Hunter was almost directly overhead. We were at a table under a tree and the men — Dagomba, Konkomba and Gonja — were sharing jokes about each other, and laughing about their differences and rivalries. There was a lot of talk of who had taken more women from whom. There was laughter and humour and comraderie there. That will not happen again, not in their lifetimes.

Ethnicity in Africa, like ethnicity elsewhere in the world, should not lead to war. The tribe is an extension of the extended family, a social unit — a welfare net — that ensures no one is without help in times of hardship and trouble. Ethnic differences in language, culture and physique should be something to celebrate and not synonymous with hatred.

Of course the poverty and competition for scarce resources and land aggravate rivalries. But would these rivalries result in ethnic slaughters if governments were truly accountable to the people they govern, if governments themselves didn't toy with ethnic differences in their play for absolute power? I doubt it. And one has to ask where all the arms come from, and why some donor countries in the business of "aiding" African countries in their development efforts are also in the business of selling arms and supporting corrupt and repressive governments. Such questions, asked of those in a position to anser, generally earn the one naive enough to voice them a look of contempt or patronizing answers. These countries aren't ready for democracy; it's not in in their tradition. There is, you must know, a geopolitic. We have to support "stable regimes." There are investments to be protected and debts to be paid back. There was once a Cold War and each side needed allies in Africa. Many who have given me answers like this over the years think that I cannot possibly understand these things — their lofty reality. It's not that. I simply cannot accept them, nor can anyone who has watched their devastating effects on the poorest of the poor in Africa.

Thomas Sankara had other answers. He called it neocolonialism; he dared to demand fair prices for Burkina's commodities and if those weren't forthcoming, he said the Burkinabe would consume the products themselves and pull themselves up by their bootstraps. He made sure development money wasn't wasted; the Americans and French reduced the aid. Canada closed its embassy in Ouagadougou, ostensibly because of general cutbacks. He spoke out, loudly, particularly against American and French policies in countries where leaders refused to toe the line, enjoy the champagne and play the game of international diplomacy and platitudes. He spoke out too loudly and gave his life for the cause of an economically and thus truly independent Burkina Faso, without corruption abetted from abroad. He gave his life for dreams of a prosperous and independent Africa. He and how many millions of others?

In Ghana, as in most places in Africa where war is breaking out, it's not easy or productive to lay blame because there are so many involved — despots, their sycophants, corrupted armies and militias, traditional rulers with a lust for new power, former colonial and the neocolonial powers and of course, the men and women of any ethnic group who allow themselves to be manipulated into hating and fighting.

The innocent can be hard to find. Many have been killed or silenced by fear. Others are unknown or just too busy helping out and working to do much talking. There are the journalists, writers and thinkers who have been imprisoned, exiled or killed for daring to speak the truth in the face of government lies. There are the countless hidden saints — doctors, teachers, farmers and development workers on miserable salaries or even none — who struggle against all odds to make life better for their people.

And, of course, among the blameless are the children, whose only battle is one for survival. Dare they hope that eventually *that* will be the battle — for survival and a life of opportunities rather than obstacles and tragedies — that consumes Africa?

Dreams may be buried, but they never die.

Nairobi
June 1994

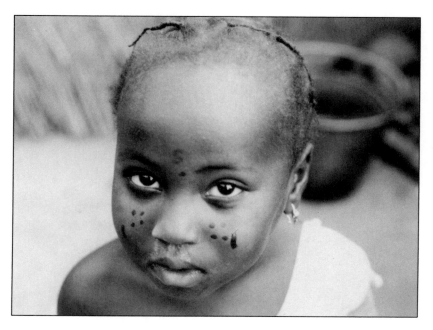

*A small girl, with decorative paint, in Kukuo, northern Ghana, 1993.*